The new Georgia

Changing Eastern Europe

Editors:
David M. Smith
Queen Mary & Westfield College
University of London
R. Antony French
University College London

1 *Regional development: the USSR and after*   Oksana Dmitrieva

2 *Plans, pragmatism and people*   R. Antony French

3 *The new Georgia: space society and politics*   Revaz Gachechiladze

4 *Contemporary Poland*   Gregorz Węcławowicz

The new Georgia
Space, society, politics

Revaz Gachechiladze
Professor and Head, Department of Human Geography
Tbilisi State University, Republic of Georgia

With editorial assistance from R. Antony French

UCL PRESS

© Revaz Gachechiladze, 1995
This book is copyright under the Berne Convention.
No reproduction without permission.
All rights reserved.

First published in 1995 by UCL Press.

UCL Press Limited
University College London
Gower Street
London WC1E 6BT

The name of University College London (UCL) is a registered
trade mark used by UCL Press with the consent of the owner.

ISBNs: 1-85728-417-8 HB
1-85728-418-6 PB

British Library Cataloguing in Publication Data
A catalogue record for this book is available from the British Library.

Cover photograph by David M. Smith.

Typeset in Times New Roman.
Printed and bound by
Biddles Ltd, Guildford and King's Lynn, England.

CONTENTS

Preface   ix
Acknowledgements   x
Introduction   xi

PART I

1 Location, territory, resources, regions   1
  The geopolitical situation   1
  Administrative–territorial division   5
  Space for economic and social life   8
  Natural resources for economic development and their use   12
  Social regions   14

2 The historical–geographical background   17
  Language and the identification of the nation   17
  Ancient and medieval Georgia   18
  The Russian domination   26
  The First Republic   31
  Communist Georgia (the Second Republic)   33
  The restoration of independence and after (the Third Republic)   38

3 Population   45
  Population dynamics   45
  Geographical distribution of population and urbanization   47
  Trends in fertility, mortality and natural growth   49
  Sex and age structure   52
  Family, marriage, divorce   53
  Education   56
  Employment and unemployment   57
  Social stratification and class structure   63
  Migrations   67
  Way of life and types of dwelling   68

4 Ethnicity and religion 73
Ethnic dynamics and structure 73
Georgians 75
Location of the non-Georgian population 79
Abkhaz 81
Ossetians 86
Armenians 89
Slavic peoples 90
Azeris 92
Greeks 93
Jews 94
Kurds 94
Geography of religions 95
Inter-ethnic relations: sociolinguistic patterns 98

PART II SPECIFIC ISSUES

5 The changing problems of society 106
Problems of transition to a market economy 106
Social problems as perceived by public opinion 111

6 Regional differences in welfare 117
Changing trends of welfare 117
Spatial patterns of welfare in the late 1980s 119
Criteria for analysis 120
Evaluation by individual indicators 121
Summary rankings 130
Public opinion of the welfare of social regions 133

7 Spatial aspects of deviance 137
General trends 137
Changes in the dynamics and structure of crime and conviction 138
Spatial patterns of crime and conviction 143
Spatial aspects of drug abuse 148

8 Tbilisi and its metropolitan region: social problems in space 153
Tbilisi Metropolitan Region against the background of Georgia 153
Development of the TMR under socialism 156
Social problems of the TMR in late 1980s 160
New trends in the social problems of the TMR 163

Contents

9 Ethnic tensions in geographical context   169
  Background for ethnic tensions   169
  A geographical approach to ethnic tensions in Georgia   173
  The geopolitical context of the conflict in Abkhazia   175
  Conflict in Tskhinvali region, formerly South Ossetia   181
  The problem of the return of the Meskhetian Muslims   183

10 Conclusion   185

  References   187
  Index   197

PREFACE

This book was written mainly between August 1993 and March 1994, although most of the data were collected earlier and there were also some later additions. The precise dates are necessary to explain certain influences in selecting the aspects of a social geography of Georgia, written by a Georgian. However one tries to be as fair and objective as possible, one cannot avoid at least some subjective attitudes in a book dedicated to the geographical background of social processes and social problems in one's native country. This will probably be the more explicable if the exact dates of writing the book are specified.

The recent period, especially since September 1993, has not been the best in the turbulent history of Georgia – civil wars, military disasters, hundreds of thousands of hungry and angry internally displaced persons, expelled from their homes in Abkhazia, stormy political debates in Parliament over the future of this Newly Independent State (NIS), supposed by some politicians and political observers to be on the brink of losing that very independence. Above all, there has been total economic crisis, mass unemployment, poverty and frustration of the people. All these formed the broad social–political background while the book was being written. Purely social issues also surely influenced the writing – and not all the factors should interpeted as negative. Part of the manuscript was written by the light of a candle, using the short bright intervals, when rationed electricity was available to enter the text into the computer. Shortage of fuel also meant the absence of central heating in our high-rise homes. Meanwhile, daylight was utilized for more earthly needs – in long queues for bread (very useful experiences for acquiring more information on social problems) and in walking daily up to 12 miles to the university and back (very useful for personal health), avoiding an overcrowded trolley bus, and an unreliable underground, which sometimes became a trap because of the sudden electricity cuts. The crime rate was very easy to monitor; one felt the shooting during the night stretched or exceeded the limits of a normal background.

All these factors made writing the book a very romantic affair, and perhaps any biases, if detected, will be understandable.

ACKNOWLEDGMENTS

I am very grateful to Professor David M. Smith and Dr Tony French, who first suggested preparation of the book, and to Mr Roger Jones who supported the idea. This gave me an opportunity not to spend a long winter in Tbilisi in idleness. It began with the first heavy snowfall on 12 November 1993 – I remember the date as it was my daughter's birthday, and it was the first time in her life when her friends could not reach our house; usually we have snow in January and February. I am grateful to my students at the Tbilisi State University, who attended my lectures in the cold building and with their attentive listening and wise questions compelled me to formulate clearly some ideas that previously had been fluttering rather vaguely in my brain (and especially to Ia, Margo, Shorena, Natia, Keti and Guranda, who helped me compile the index).

Acknowledgments are due to my colleagues Professor Vakhtang Jaoshvili, Professor Rismag Gordesiani, Professor Zaza Gachechiladze, Dr Vazha Gujabidze, Dr Alexander Rondeli, Mr Paul Mecklenberg, Ms Dodo Karaulashvili, Dr Anzor Totadze, Mr Michael Gogatishvili, Mr Gela Charkviani, Dr Tedo Japaridze, Dr Zaza Kandelaki, Dr Levan Mikeladze, Dr David Sumbadze, Professor Avtandil Menteshashvili, Professor Levan Toidze. All of them either examined some drafts of the manuscript or supplied me with some data. Dr Zurab Davitashvili, Mr Brian O'Halloran and Professor Steven Jones read all the manuscript. I benefited greatly from their suggestions and comments, which encouraged me to proceed in my work. Dr Joseph Salukvadze co-operated closely with me in preparing Chapter 8, notably by supplying three original maps of Tbilisi. I would like to thank Ms Makvala Loladze and Mr Teimuraz Gogishvili of the Committee of Social–Economic Information of the Republic of Georgia for supplying me with statistical information. Ms Galina Mdzeluri has turned my rough drafts into handsome maps and diagrams.

I would like to acknowledge the Russia, Ukraine and Commonwealth Branch, USIA Office of Research, notably Mr Steven Grant, and the Institute of Demography and Sociological Studies, Georgian Academy of Sciences, for permission to use the data of their sociological surveys.

My special gratitude is due to the British Academy, which sponsored my visit to England, a visit that proved to be extremely useful in preparing the text.

INTRODUCTION

After the dramatic collapse of the socialist system (often called "communism" in the West) on the brink of the 1990s, up to two dozen new, previously almost unknown, countries appeared on the world stage. In some respects, this event resembled the emergence of the New Africa some 30 years earlier. But those countries, which were known at least to their former colonial masters, were given independence for the most part in a civilized manner, although their internal peace did not last long. Most of those countries did not have to undergo a fundamental economic transformation, as they were already on the way to capitalism while still colonies of the west European powers. Moreover, their former masters very soon lost strategic interest in the majority of the countries, because, among other reasons, they were quite far away and settled by alien peoples.

In contrast, the new "post-socialist" States are being born in torment; the Caucasus and Tajikistan are already on fire, to say nothing of Yugoslavia. They have to undergo the inevitable but rather painful change from a less effective socialist system to a market economy and this must be done speedily. It took several centuries for western Europe to overcome the residues of feudalism, and even the Third World had more time for the change. The former Metropolis of the post-Soviet countries is itself in heavy economic crisis; it is in doubt about what to do with its former subjects, but is strong enough either to become their patron again or to be an equal partner with them. In addition, Russia borders the majority of the Newly Independent States, which have large Russian-speaking minorities, which can be used as an excuse for a new "Monroe Doctrine".

What does the average Westerner know about the geography of the post-Soviet world? Almost nothing. However, geographical ignorance has no boundaries: my compatriots always confuse Austria with Australia, are frankly astonished to find out that Sweden and Switzerland are not the same thing, and are absolutely sure that the Scottish, the Irish or the Welsh (whom they obviously have heard of, as they watch football on TV) are "some other sort of English". This honest statement will, no doubt, outrage the Glaswegians and Dubliners, but I too, alas, was once similarly made indignant. Some 20 years ago, Professor Derek Diamond introduced me to his colleagues from LSE as "a young Russian with a sense of humour". At that moment I felt that only the first word from this phrase was true – I was relatively young in those days – but I did not immediately dispute the second word so as not to put in question the rest! I strongly suspect that the British people in those times (and probably even now) considered that the Ukrainians, Uzbeks, Chechens, Georgians, Yakuts and others were "some other sort of Russians".

Introduction

Derek needed to explain to his highly educated colleagues what the term "Georgian" meant in his opinion, I thought.

And I doubt if, for the average British person, the word "Georgian" meant anything until the beginning of the 1990s, when this word appeared on TV screens and became associated with permanent wars. An older British person, however, may associate this word with the name Stalin. It is not a very pleasant association, I admit, but as the late Professor David Lang, a leading specialist on Caucasus, told me once on this issue, "*iz pesni slova ne vykinesh!*" (you can't drop a word from a song!). To great football fans the word "Georgia" may recall the team "Dynamo" from Tbilisi, once the European Cupholders Cup winner. And a Western man with geographical knowledge slightly above average might argue that this is a former Soviet province where people speak a dialect of Slavic (or maybe Turkic?) language. I hasten to assure you at once that neither of these is true.

Even for the majority of Russians, in spite of their co-existence within the same State for almost two centuries, Georgians were associated with changing stereotypes that had rather distant resemblances to reality. In the Stalin era, however, when "unorganized" mobility of the population was restricted, the rare Georgians, who outside of their own republic were seen predominantly as folk-dancers on the stage, were considered almost as romantic heroes from the native country of the Great Leader. Later the romance faded as the contacts became more tense, especially in the *kolkhoz* bazaars of the northern cities, where all non-Slavic, dark Caucasians were considered to be *gruziny* (Georgians). To the average Russian, Georgia was known as the producer of good dry wines and not-so-good tea (although there was no real alternative on the Soviet market) and of the famous mineral water *Borjomi*, as the country of tangerines, seaside resorts and determined moustached young men on the beaches (the latter were better known to Russian women). The intelligentsia of Moscow and Leningrad (now once again St Petersburg) knew and liked Georgia for its more sophisticated aspects: the Caucasus had been "the Parnassus of Russian poetry" since the early nineteenth century. Old Georgian poetry was translated by the best Russian poets. Many of the best Soviet films were shot and many of the best Soviet plays were staged in Tbilisi (the capital city of Georgia). Many Georgian scholars were well known in many branches of the Soviet science. But nowadays Georgia has become a foreign country to Russia. "Dynamo" plays in a national league and without difficulty become champions every year. The dark southerners in the bazaars are no longer *gruziny* (they just have nothing to sell at all). Muscovites may watch American films. And, as for the young moustached Georgians on the beaches (now bearded as well), in the early 1990s the Russian volunteer or mercenary soldiers fighting on the side of the Abkhaz insurgents looked at them through the sights of their Kalashnikov submachine guns.

The modern Russian philosopher, A. P. Butenko, called the system built in the Soviet Union by the end of 1930s "State-administrative socialism", with supremacy of the Party–State bureaucracy, absence of open information, mass reprisals and human fear – the system that corresponded to the canonical Marxist image of "barrack socialism" (Butenko 1988: 558). It can be added that such a system could have come into existence only in a certain sociogeographical environment, in an underdeveloped society with many residues of feudalism. With great respect to the talent of George Orwell, it is difficult to imagine *1984* in modern England. But in the vast spaces of Eurasia, the system of *1984* became possible. Moreover, it was well grounded theoretically by the great Marxist, Lenin, who started to build it, and was brought to perfection by the great Leninist, Stalin. The inertia of fear inspired in 1930s rolled forwards for half a century, but when new generations of leaders who did not remember the Great Terror came to power, they attempted to alter the system in a new manner.

However, it was impossible to alter (*perestroyka* means "restructuring") the system. It had to be either demolished or left alone. It was demolished. The logic of history and historical justice were victorious and the last empire has been destroyed. The world could have a breath of relief after decades of fear. Yet remnants of the system appeared to be viable, to say nothing about the nuclear weapons still able to destroy the world. Hardly any of the 15 new States that came into existence after the break-up of the USSR can consider themselves nation-States. Their economies were so interwoven that it is impossible to speak about the economic independence even of such a giant (from the European point of view) as the Ukraine. Even more important from the point of view of social development is that the majority of the former "Soviet nations" are not ready psychologically, or economically, or in legal terms, to build in a short time a free market system (i.e. capitalism), whether "liberal" or "socially orientated".

No-one expected a velvet-smooth transition from totalitarianism to democracy in the post-Soviet world, but even those who most "rocked the boat" (the expression beloved by Gorbachev) probably did not expect the depth and heaviness of the disintegration in every case. In this country we have to live in the ruins of an empire, which is very picturesque for a temporary visitor, but very inconvenient for a permanent dweller in those ruins. The rupture of economic ties between the Union republics, ties that were artificially interwoven over decades to make impossible that very rupture, the downfall of a totally ineffective planned economy, could not lead automatically to the establishment of free market relations and to the total welfare of the population (which had been the unfulfilled promise of the Communist Party). On the contrary, they put almost all post-Soviet States on the brink of economic catastrophe. Some, among them Georgia, have already gone over that brink. "Quasi-market" relations have been established where free competition is limited by residues of the command economy. Those best adapted to such a situation appear to be small groups of energetic, but mostly dishonest, people (groups called "mafia" or "kleptocracy" by different observers), some connected in the past with the management of that very command economy, who enrich themselves while the majority stay below the poverty line.

Of course, one may explain to people that this is the first stage of capital accumulation, a stage that Britain, continental Europe and North America passed through in the sixteenth to nineteenth centuries, and that, in those countries too, capital first accumulated mostly in the hands of pirates, slave-traders, "nabobs" (who made fortunes grabbing India), bootleggers, and the like, people whose descendants became respectable lords and honest bankers. Many people here understand that in the post-Soviet world a social change is taking place, the transition from something like social-feudalism (hypocritically called "real socialism") to something like capitalism. Moreover, this is an uneven process and its success in different geographical areas will be strongly influenced by the initial economic or social position of each of the new States at the moment of starting the change. But knowledge of basic Marxist political economy by quite a few in this country by no means helps, in the absence of daily bread. Moreover, the capital accumulated through robbing the people of Georgia does not stay in this country, but tends to migrate to safer lands.

Social problems, that might lead even to social explosions, were inevitable – rising prices, growth in crime and growing unemployment became the leading concerns of the public. The widespread possession of firearms was also becoming a leading problem – one more result of the chaotic break-up of the supermilitarized State, full of former Soviet (now Russian) Army officers, who are sometimes not paid their salaries for months and who are ready to sell everything.

Political life is in full swing. However, in this sphere also, the majority of the new countries with more or less liberal regimes are full of quasi-parties, dilettantes, demagogues and populists. It was simply impossible to have well prepared politicians under a one-party dictatorship that lasted for decades. As one author noted, "for most of the former Soviet Union a democratic heritage is a far distant shadow."

Worst of all for the post-Soviet States, the ethnic problems of minorities, previously swept under the carpet, now moved to the foreground, and by their importance in many cases overshadowed purely economic or social problems. If earlier the Union republics produced headaches for Moscow by their "national problems", now these headaches have moved to Tallinn, Kiev, Tbilisi, Dushanbe, Kishinev, Baku, and the other new capitals (with the most active "help" of the very same Moscow, naturally). The USSR, like the Russian Empire, was an artificial conglomerate of ethnic groups with different cultural backgrounds, which could never have been unified into a nation. In the 1970s, there was an unsuccessful attempt to declare "the emergence of the Soviet people", a concept that never existed in reality. Perhaps the only logic of the co-existence of these peoples in one State, apart from the will of Russia's rulers, was their geographical closeness. The Bolsheviks created an artificial hierarchy of peoples and gave it a legislative basis (Tishkov 1992). But when the hierarchical ties in the USSR in the stage of decay were deliberately loosened, ethnic conflicts immediately became the major social problem, and have continued to be so in the new States.

All these unusual complications give rise to nostalgia among the common people of the post-Soviet world for the "law and order that was present under the communists", whom the people had disliked when they were in full power. Although not many dream of the restoration of the USSR (different polls have revealed that among Georgians they account for less than 15 per cent, mostly elderly), one can frequently hear complaints such as "the government should not allow the private shops to sell goods for such high prices", "the government must pay us more" (while we do not work at all!).

Neither liberty, nor property, nor new social groups are created in an instant. Under Soviet power, private property and really free enterprise were absent. The stage of classic capitalism has not been undergone by the majority of the ex-Soviet nations, yet this is the most important indicator of the maturity of society. The new shopkeepers and mafiosi groups that are grabbing State property will not form a class of civilized businessmen soon, although the latter have begun to emerge here and there. Thus, for quite a long time, all the post-Soviet countries will be in different stages of the transition period to modern society. The West will have to help them to undergo real reforms in its own interest, to avoid graver global problems. Meanwhile, the larger Newly Independent States will go on creating large problems for the world and the smaller States will create equally large problems.

All of the aforesaid applies almost equally to Georgia and the other new States. Naturally, differences between the post-Soviet countries exist. Social geography, "the study of social relations in space and the spatial structures that underpin those relations" (Johnston et al. 1994), is to some extent able to explain these differences. The geographer in general can show the spatial background of a nation's formation, spatial differences in the economy, population, sociopolitical mentality, culture and traditions, which together with the legal base and institutions are major internal factors of social change in a country. He can focus on the spatially manifested problems that arise from these differences. He can help to understand the nation. Economy is the foundation of a State, but what sort of economy a country can build depends less on natural resources than on human resources, on the qualities of the population. Surely these qualities are not something God-given forever; they change in time. For instance, in the second half of the twentieth century, the Chinese, considered to be one of the most conservative nations have achieved in different countries miracles of economic success. But without knowledge of the ideological background on which the discipline and persistence of the Chinese culture is based, not everything about their economic life can be explained. On the other hand, Confucius was born and taught in a certain sociogeographical environment, which influenced his way of thinking. Likewise, neither were Protestant ethics born in a vacuum.

In the case of Georgia, attention must be paid to certain cultural, historical, and geographical factors. The emergence and development of the nation were influenced by the natural environment (mountainous relief, moderate climate, etc.) and by the political context. Even more importantly, one must focus on certain sociocultural and historical factors that explain the social structure, the way of life of the modern population, and the possibilities of economic development, although these factors are not peculiar to Georgia, nor do they cover all possible explanations.

Introduction

First, the existence for a long period of a purely agrarian society, whereas merchants and artisans belonged to peoples of a different faith, was a factor in the social structure and it affected mass consciousness; peasants who worked hard for several months and then spent quite a long time doing nothing became a factor in the rural way of life.

Secondly, the social structure of the population was much affected by the nature of industrialization. In Georgia, as in almost all the Soviet republics, it began in the 1930s, straight into large-scale machine production; it did not follow logically from artisans' workshops and manufactures, as happened in most of western Europe. So the first generation of workers in this part of the world were not former artisans, but former peasants; in small Georgian towns, miners and factory workers still have land allotments and psychologically remain farmers until their dying day. In asserting this, I do not imply anything negative. The same things can be observed even in the industrial countries. However, it must be added that in the USSR, the country where the "dictatorship of the proletariat" was announced to be the political basis of the State, the workers were never paid enough to make their profession prestigious; the children of these "worker-farmers" dream of becoming doctors, lawyers, or at least traffic policemen.

Thirdly, permanent external and internal wars in the Middle Ages promoted the creation of a sizable class of warrior nobility. Their ethos, emphasizing "boldness, deliberate outbursts of non-rational violence and showy grand gestures" (Kuper 1989), although typical of all persons belonging to this class irrespective of their country of origin, became the stereotype of a Georgian in the nineteenth century, and this *damnosa hereditas* is likely to last into the twenty-first century.

Fourthly, Orthodox Christianity, the religion of the majority of Georgians, in allowing more personal freedom, proved to be a relatively weak social instrument in the upbringing of the younger generation from the point of view of self-discipline, especially during the Soviet era when the role of Church diminished to practically nothing. Religion, along with the natural environment, which did not require large collective efforts to achieve appreciable economic results, influenced the weakness of the collectivist mentality and promoted the marked individualism of this nation. Again, I do not suggest that individualism is negative. I agree completely with a classic view of English social theory that "the conceptions of society and the individual are correlative conceptions through and through" and that "the ultimate end of society and State as of the individual is the realization of the best life" (Bosanquet 1899: 180–81). I would just add that an over-hasty rush of individuals to the "best life" may leave society far behind.

Fifthly, a characteristic peculiar to the majority of the "Soviet nations" (again, not least the Georgians) was what could be called a "mythologized mentality", manifested mostly in a faith in the exclusive historical heritage (sometimes – even "mission") of any of these nations. Soviet ideology emphasized "culture – national in form and socialist in content", but in fact attention was paid only to the "national form", as nobody knew what "socialist content" was. Each nation, even the numerically smallest, put its efforts into searching out the deepest roots in its

Introduction

history. Since the history of neighbouring nations often intersected, instead of pure academic interest this research involved State policy. As the claws of the Communist Party became weaker, this kind of mentality became a catalyst of ethnic conflicts, which in their turn led to many misfortunes and hampered State-building.

A sixth sociogeographical factor also cannot be given a one-sided appraisal. Wine could (and still can) be consumed in large quantities in Georgia; that was impossible in the Muslim countries lying in the same climatic conditions, where grapes are also grown. "Wine is the property of high civilization" wrote an historian of Ancient Greece (Bonnard 1957). That's right. But the widespread stereotype that wine-drinking peoples produce too many talented men along with too many laggards, boasters and irresponsible individuals, is probably not very far from the truth as well. Familiarity with Georgian literature of the nineteenth and twentieth centuries gives the impression that this stereotype is based on something real.

The English philosopher, Roger Scruton, begins his essay *In defence of the nation*:

> It is neither polite nor politic for those brought up in the Western liberal tradition to defend the "national idea" as the foundation of political order. Or rather, you can defend that idea on behalf of others – at least if they are engaged in some "struggle for national liberation" – but not on behalf of your community and kind. Loyalties, if they are not universalist, must be expressed superstitiously, in the self-depriving language of one confessing to a private fault. (Scruton 1990)

Taking this "warning" into account (although Scruton himself does not seem to follow it), I did my best to avoid mentioning "the Georgian national idea" and tried to be as critical as possible of my own people. But alas, belonging to the nation that just a couple of years ago was considering itself oppressed and fighting for self-determination, it is not so easy to be fair to everyone. At least I admit that the Georgians are neither better nor much worse than any other people. They have their weak points, but also their positive characteristics as well, just as any other group on Earth, which is called a Nation. From this point of view, what Joseph de Maistre said in 1811 is true of the Georgians also, "*tout nation a le gouvernement qu'elle merite*"!

The purpose of this book is to give a reliable picture of the modern social geography of Georgia. It seems that today this can be achieved more easily than an economic geography of the country. In part this is because the economy of this once-flourishing Union Republic, then a shop window for the nationalities policy of the Communist Party (especially for the comrades from developing countries of "socialist orientation", who obviously very much liked "Georgian socialism", because most of the time was spent with a glass of wine in the hand!), nowadays lies in ruins and lacks an adequate industrial infrastructure. More importantly, it is

Introduction

because serious structural changes in the economy of the country will be needed to link it to the world economy and, in this event, many of the present economic branches may become obsolete. In contrast, linguistic, religious and ethnic differences are more conservative. The city-dwellers in this part of the world will have a different way of life from that of the rural population for quite a long time, and social problems will not be overcome so fast.

When in 1979 a new term for human geography, "economic and social geography", was officially adopted in the USSR (previously it was called simply "economic geography") and a new stage in the development of social geography started in the country (Lavrov et al. 1984), it was the result of more attention being paid to the social sphere in the Soviet Union. To no less an extent it was a response to Western geographers' rising interests in the social problems of their own countries. Especially influential were books by some British geographers, including Harvey (1973), Smith (1973, 1977), Jones & Eyles (1977), Coates et al. (1977), Herbert & Smith (1979), among others, together with several articles of the "radical geographers" and their magazines.

However, in the USSR there remained serious dogmatic limitations to the development of the social sciences. The existence of social problems was completely ignored. For example, it was official dogma that crime under socialism was just "a residue of capitalism" and its level must be constantly decreasing; the figures remained secret, naturally. Therefore, when sociologist A. Gabiani and the present author were lucky enough in their efforts to avoid the stamp "for official use", and published in open press the first Soviet book on the geography of crime (Gabiani & Gachechiladze 1982), which today seems rather trivial, it was in those days considered a great achievement and even "a new direction in the Soviet social geography" (Konstantinov 1985). It was not customary to write on the territorial disparities in the welfare of different areas – the Communist Party alleged that it did everything to bring welfare to everyone in every region. Reality did not support this thesis, at least not in Georgia (Gachechiladze 1982, 1987). But it should be said in all fairness that disparities in wealth between regions, and even more on the personal level, were far less than they are now and will continue to be on our way to a market economy.

It was in practice forbidden in the USSR before *perestroyka* to speak about potential ethnic tensions – all the Soviet peoples were brothers! The situation has changed dramatically since 1988, and thus, when I drew a map of potential ethnic conflicts in Georgia (Gachechiladze 1989, 1990c), it just defined facts already known to society, but a prominent Russian geographer considered it worthwhile to accord it a positive review (Preobrazhenskiy 1991).

Of course, it is rather hard to write a social geography of a country where civil wars are raging. It is difficult to gather up-to-date social statistics from all regions, but the years 1989–90, for which regional information is available, are not ancient times. Enduring social trends that have appeared in recent years, and some foreseeable social problems, are also discussed in this book.

Introduction

Organization of the text

The book consists of two parts. In Part One, a general geographical and historical background of Georgian social problems is given. In the Part Two, some specific sociogeographical problems are discussed. The book is an introductory text, with no intention to go deep into theory.

In the first chapter, a short account of the geographical location, space and resources for economic and social activities are discussed. Georgia's straddling of probably the best current routes connecting Europe and Central Asia by land and sea have been widely discussed in the local press. No less important is the situation of the country at a political crossroads as a new State between the southern flank of NATO (Turkey) and Russia, which, one may note in passing, does not make its situation safer. Proximity to certain nations has left its mark on the social, political and economic life and activity of the country as a whole, and to a large extent has determined regional differences in the local way of life (i.e. mountainous and lowland regions, West and East Georgia). The administrative–territorial division of the country and principles of the social regionalization are briefly discussed and, in the same chapter, an account of the social regions of Georgia is given. In following chapters, information often will be examined in both text and maps in terms of this network of social regions.

An historical–geographical background is absolutely necessary to understand the contemporary social and political geography (Ch. 2). Problems of ethnogenesis, the emergence and settlement of nations, acquire utmost importance in multinational States. The prolonged medieval phase predetermined Georgia's backwardness in the European model of development. The democratic ethic that was just about to develop in the first decades of the twentieth century was abruptly cut short by Sovietization. The author considers it important to give an account of the key historical events and those trends that help to illuminate the modern geographical pattern of Georgia, the ethnic and social structure of its population and its political geography. It is only a short account; the English-speaking reader can obtain more detailed information on the history of Georgia from Ronald Grigor Suni's book *The making of the Georgian nation* (1988). Recent years are discussed by Jonathan Aves in *Paths to national independence in Georgia, 1987–90* (1991). A comprehensive account of regions of Georgia is given by Roger Rosen in *The Georgian Republic: an independent tradition* (1992). As James Bater wrote: "in developing the thesis that a sense of history is prerequisite to understanding the contemporary geography of the Soviet Union, it is important that 1917 not be seen as a hard and fast watershed" (Bater 1989). This applies to the Republic of Georgia as well; although no longer a part of the now extinct USSR, the mark of the Soviet legacy will be carried by this NIS for quite a long time.

Two chapters are dedicated to the geography of population. Chapter 3 deals with the dynamics, location and structure of the population of Georgia. The peculiarities of Georgia's internal migrations lead to the depopulation of some mountainous regions. External migrations will promote a substantial loss of population

Introduction

(especially the "brain drain"). The urbanization of the country followed the model of the socialist countries, with hypertrophic growth of the capital city (the problems of which will be discussed in a separate chapter).

In Chapter 4, the national and religious structure of the population is described. Apart from the Georgians, who along with the Abkhaz are the autochthonous population of the State (i.e. the earliest inhabitants of this territory), quite sizeable minorities have settled in the country at different times. Georgia cannot be considered a mono-national country. Geographical location of the ethnic groups and the sequence of their settlement explain many of the internal problems of contemporary Georgia.

One cannot fathom the formation of the cultural environment without considering the role of religion. Belonging to the Christian world meant for the Georgians a natural inclination towards Europe, albeit eastern Europe. At the same time, in Georgia there are also other confessions than Georgian Orthodoxy. Although there are not (and historically have not been) any conflicts on purely religious grounds, differences in inter-ethnic relations such as mixed marriages, or in cultural traditions (sometimes even at the level of sub-ethnic groups), or in demographic behaviour may be explained only with reference to the religious realities.

In the second part of the book some spatial aspects of the modern social life of Georgia are examined. The major problems of society are discussed in Chapter 5. The comparative significance of these problems to modern Georgia has been estimated on the basis of public opinion surveys carried out during 1992–4.

The overall welfare of the people has nowadays become an even more distant dream than it was at the end of the 1980s, the period for which the geographical pattern of some social indicators is discussed (Ch. 6). Incomes, expenditure, savings and so on were not, and are not, equally distributed in all regions; differences were attributable to the urban or rural, mountainous or lowland location of the territorial communities, to the branches of economy peculiar to the area, and so on. It appears from survey data that the population of Georgia has quite a good geographical perception of the real wealth of the regions.

Deviance, discussed in Chapter 7, naturally has a tendency to uneven geographical distribution. The cities and seaside regions of Georgia appear to be the major areas of crime, drug addiction, and so on. But rural areas also have their peculiarities. In spite of the inadequacy of Soviet moral statistics (an inadequacy inherited to a large extent by the NIS), it was possible to study the regional level and structure of crime at the end of the 1980s. The dynamics and structure of crime in recent years are also considered. Some geographical peculiarities of drug-addiction and drug-trafficking are considered in the same chapter.

The social problems of a large city, one that has not yet become a capitalist city, but already is not entirely socialist either, are discussed in Chapter 8, which examines the problems of the Tbilisi Metropolitan Region, comprising the cities of Tbilisi, Rustavi and neighbouring smaller towns and intervening rural areas.

Chapter 9 describes from a geographical perspective a social problem that has

Introduction

great political significance. Ethnic tensions, which have taken such a tragic turn in the Caucasus, did not appear accidentally and are connected with the spatial location of the agents of these conflicts. A "third power" (Russia, or sometimes parts of Russia), not always clearly seen outside Georgia, is also involved in the conflicts. Thus, a wider geographical context must be examined. Historical and politico-geographical factors of already-existing ethnic tensions are considered and an account of potential conflicts is also given in that chapter.

The author is aware that the above topics do not cover the full array of the sociogeographical problems of Georgia, but he is bold enough to think that the questions discussed in this book can help one to come closer to a human geography of this young State.

PART I

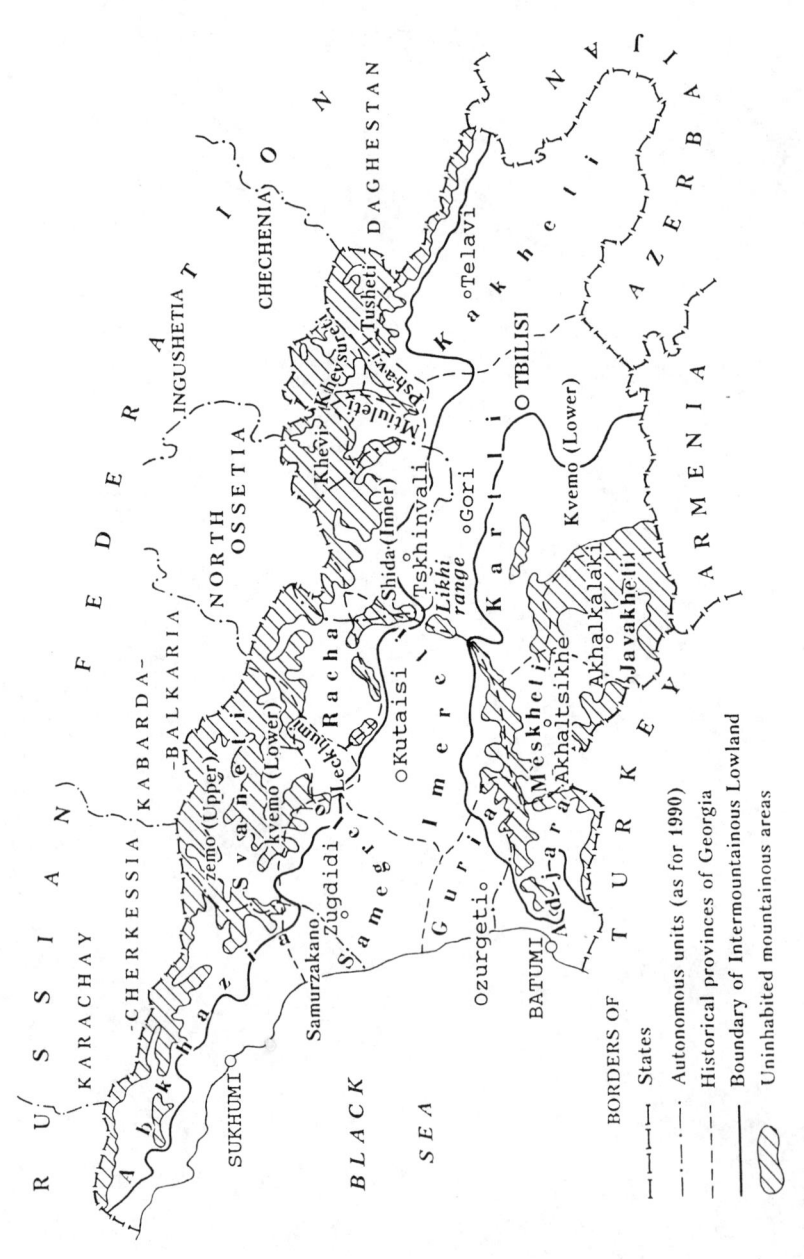

Figure 1.1 Georgia.

CHAPTER 1
Location, territory, resources, regions

The geopolitical situation

Among the newly coloured areas that appeared on the world map after 1991, there is one on the eastern shore of the Black Sea, south of the Great Caucasus Range. If one looks more attentively at this small area, called "the Republic of Georgia", one will see that it is situated in a rather important place. Of course, it is neither the centre of the world, nor even of the Caucasus. As two friendly Belgians recently warned Georgia, "its meaning for the rest of the world is not an absolute but only a relative one" (Blancoff-Scarr & Blancoff 1993).

But from the regional point of view, Georgia's geopolitical location is worth mentioning. On the south it borders Turkey, a member of NATO, and to the north and east it borders Russia, the country that since the seventeenth century has fought with the Ottoman Empire ten times and which has perpetually pushed the latter to the south. Now, for the first time in the past two centuries (with a short exception in 1918–21, when both the traditional adversaries had serious internal and external problems and for a while became "friends"), these countries have no common border. A buffer State has appeared between them (Fig. 1.1).

To understand Russia's geopolitical interests in Georgia, one must take into account that after the loss of important seaports in the Ukraine and of 312 km of Georgia's coast, the former metropolis of both these countries, Moscow, has been left with only a short littoral and one important port, Novorossiisk, on the Black Sea. Nevertheless, Russia's Minister of Defence officially announced its strategic interests in the Black Sea area (Lomsadze 1993, Rowell 1993b). Additionally, the Black Sea shore was a traditional vacation region for Russians from northern areas; easy access to this resort paradise is very important to Russia. Through Georgia are carried on economic and other contacts of Russia with Armenia, its strategic ally in the Caucasus; Armenia is understood by some experts to be the "key" (for Russia, presumably) to the Middle East (Vostrikov 1994).

Russia, in spite of its internal dissensions, thanks to its immense population, territorial and mineral resources, military strength, and long tradition of statehood, will be able to recover fastest of all the post-Soviet States from the heavy blow of 1991. If Russia resurrects its "World Mission", especially if the "Versailles Syndrome" develops and brings neo-imperialist forces to power, Georgia in some form (not necessarily as an annexed country) will be of even more interest to Russia (Kashia 1992). A Russian observer recently wrote frankly, "only Georgia among the Transcaucasian republics is objectively capable of serving as the foothold of Russian influence in the region. Neither Azerbaijan nor Armenia fit this role, first of all because of their geographical location, and secondly because in the context of the permanent Nagorno–Karabakh crisis, Moscow for a long time has carried out a "pendulum policy" towards the belligerents" (Anin 1994). This quotation is only one version of Russian foreign policy, but the "Monroe Doctrine of the East" has already been declared (Kampfner 1993).

Responsible and realistically thinking Georgian politicians understand this geopolitical reality, however unpleasant it is. It is obvious that without normal economic relations with Russia and, even more, without Russia's political will, this Newly Independent State will be constantly on the brink of disintegration, as the former Metropolis still possesses too powerful levers to bring it about, as the opening of the 1990s proved with the utmost cruelty (Emelyanenko 1993). Public opinion in Georgia understands the vital nature of good relations with Russia (Gachechiladze 1993).

On the other side, Russia also needs a politically stable and friendly neighbour in the south. The disintegration of Georgia might be a dangerous precedent for Russia itself, which also faces similar problems. The Russian Federation along its new southern border on the Great Caucasus Range includes the potentially turbulent, multi-ethnic north Caucasian region, with its arbitrarily delimited borders between autonomous units, all of which recently declared themselves to be republics. These borders, under the communists who delimited them, were regarded as administrative ones; now they have become "interrepublican". The peoples of that region have already started the vital battles for space with each other. Some look with hatred and some with hope either towards their Metropolis, Russia proper, or towards their politically new southern neighbour, the Republic of Georgia. Georgia is larger than any of them and in addition possesses part of the Black Sea littoral. In the ethno-territorial conflict between the Ossetians and Ingush that led to the ethnic cleansing of the latter, the Ossetians entirely relied upon Russia, whereas the Ingush expected at least moral support from Georgia. A north Caucasian Turkic people, the Balkars, having a potential territorial dispute with their immediate neighbours the Kabardians, have much warmer attitudes towards Georgia than do the latter, who are linguistically close to the Abkhaz and therefore consider Georgia "the enemy". Of course, these statements are oversimplifications of "ethnic relations". But the majority of north Caucasian autochthonous peoples cannot forget that they were conquered by Tsarist Russia and some of them were nearly exterminated under communist Russia. A strong positive feeling still persists in Georgia towards the north Caucasians in general, who are considered to be kindred in culture and even in origin. This feeling was not entirely overshadowed, even by the participation of some north Caucasians in the civil war in Abkhazia on the side of separatists. In fact, in the recent war in Abkhazia many volunteers from the "Confederation of the Peoples of the Caucasus", an organization formed within Russia in 1991 from peoples who are all citizens of Russia, took part against the Georgian side with the final goal of getting access to the sea for the so-called "Confederative State", which presumably will be created mostly out of the territory of the Russian Federation (see Ch. 9). Without taking into account this geographical context, most ethnic conflicts in the Caucasus might be incorrectly considered merely as clashes of bloodthirsty criminal gangs, even if armed with heavy weaponry, including aircraft.

After being compelled to ignore for more than half a century, when the Soviet-Turkish border was firmly closed, the existence of a large and important neighbour to the southwest, Georgia rediscovered Turkey. This has happened after 1988, when the border was opened and a customs post was set up in the village of Sarpi, on the Black Sea shore. After the independence of Georgia was restored in 1991, this gate was opened wider. This has had a multifaceted significance for both countries; immediately after the opening of the Sarpi gate, all the cheap (i.e. State-subsidized) goods disappeared from shops all over the Transcaucasus as if a vacuum cleaner had gone through it. Then flows of smuggled non-ferrous metals from all over the former Soviet Union and timber from the forest reserves of Georgia began to move towards Turkey. Conversely, a stream of food, garments and hard currency started to flow from Turkey. Many people from Georgia and other post-Soviet States, who participated in this scarcely legal barter trade, in spite of the undesirable implications, did get acquainted with some sort of market economy, something that was absolutely impossible under Soviet power. This group of people at least disabused themselves of such stereotypes as "cruel Turks with yatagans", "parasite capitalists", and so on, which had been a speciality of Soviet propaganda. Popular sentiment in Georgia has become quite friendly towards Turkey.

The existence within the Georgian nation of a Muslim sub-ethnic group, the Adjars, and within Turkey of the quite numerous Georgian-speaking Turkish citizens (often close relatives of the Adjars), as well as of other Turkish citizens of north Caucasian and Abkhaz descent, on the one hand facilitates contacts between these countries, but on the other hand may cause some social and political problems for both Georgia and Turkey.

According to the Treaty of 30 July 1992, Turkey and Georgia recognized the stability of their existing border and took responsibility for preventing any activities on their territories by organizations, groups or individuals with the aim of breaching the territorial integrity of the other country (Article 13). Although official Ankara strictly follows this article, popular sentiment in Turkey is more pro-Abkhaz, considering them as "the Muslim side" in the recent internal conflict in Georgia; that is entirely incorrect, the conflict had no religious character. They also see the Abkhaz as "pro-Turkish"; that is not entirely correct (see Ch. 9). Some Turkish citizens of Abkhaz or Circassian origin illegally participated in this internal conflict of a neighbouring country. There were reports of the former settling in those areas from which ethnic Georgians were cleansed by the separatists. However, it is obviously in the interests of Turkey to have a politically and economically stable State between itself and a still potentially dangerous superpower.

To the south of Georgia is Armenia, a Christian country, albeit of a different faith from Georgian Orthodoxy, which historically shared fortunes not very favourable to either country. Armenia has rather tense relations with its Turkic neighbours. If not officially declared, at least popular Armenian sentiment makes territorial claims to Turkey and to Azerbaijan. Armenia has been at undeclared war with the latter since 1988 over Nagorny (Mountainous) Karabakh. Land routes linking Armenia with its northern ally, Russia, and Western countries have to pass through Georgia, as Armenia has no access to the sea. Therefore, normal relations with Georgia and, moreover, safe roads inside the latter are of vital interest to Armenia.

For centuries Georgia, which had a slightly safer location as it was not entirely situated on the direct invasion routes of nomadic tribes, gave refuge on its territory to the Armenians. In the nineteenth century, Armenians arriving from eastern Anatolia were welcomed by the new masters of Transcaucasia, the Russians, who let them resettle in the southern and coastal areas of Georgia. A large influx of Armenians came during the First World War, when they were completely uprooted from the eastern provinces of the Ottoman Empire and had to find refuge in the Transcaucasus and elsewhere. In the communist era, many Armenians settled in the coastal areas of Georgia, notably in Abkhazia (see Ch. 4).

Along the border with Armenia, in the historical Georgian province of Javakheti, a substantial Armenian population is now located. Will it provoke a new outburst of irredentism? The geographical context in this case seems to be of great significance.

To the southeast Georgia borders Azerbaijan, a traditionally friendly country, very helpful at critical periods of recent Georgian history. During its civil wars, when Georgia's contacts with Russia via direct roads were temporarily cut off by separatists, most of its passenger and cargo flows were operated using Azerbaijani railways and highways. In return, Azerbaijan uses the Georgian Black Sea ports. There are no mutual territorial claims between these countries, but the existence of a small Georgian minority in Azerbaijan and, even more, of a large and rapidly growing Azeri community in bordering areas of southern Georgia could be used by some irresponsible nationalistic forces in either country, or even by a third country, as an instrument of provocation. Once again, the geographical setting is important.

Access to the Black Sea gives Georgia a real advantage in comparison with the other Transcaucasian and Central Asian republics of the former Soviet Union. For them all, as well as for Iran, the shortest and technically least difficult routes for transit (no serious mountain passes) lie through Georgia to its sea ports of Poti and Batumi. Georgia pins its hopes on the incomes from transit and the consequent restructuring of its economy. Naturally, real benefits could be achieved only after long-term political stabilization in Georgia and, equally, if Russia did not oppose such a development, which would obviously make Georgia more independent economically.

Although the economic advantages of Georgia, deriving from its transport-geographical location, might be significant, its geopolitical location is not as positive as some local commentators sometimes suggest. Georgia's territory might be important in strategic terms to other, for the most part neighbouring, powers, but that does not fully guarantee the safety of Georgia itself. It should be noted that Georgia clearly widens the frontiers of "actual Europe". From a physical-geographical point of view it is on the edge of Asia, although the physical frontier between Europe and Asia is rather vague, but from a cultural point of view Georgia has always tended to be closer to the West and persists in being a European nation.

Administrative–territorial division

The Republic of Georgia almost entirely inherited the complicated administrative–territorial division of the Georgian SSR. Since some later changes, discussed below, affected this division in rather odd ways and since the new Constitution was still in preparation when the present book was being written, the situation discussed further in the book will be that of 1989, the last year of relative political stability and the year of the last population census, according to which data are given (Fig. 1.2).

Georgia comprised three autonomous units of different legal levels: two Autonomous Republics (ASSR), Abkhazia and Adjara, both on the Black Sea coast, and one Autonomous Region, South Ossetia, in the eastern part of the country. The Autonomous Republics were considered by the Constitution of the Georgian SSR (modelled on that of the USSR) as States, with their own constitution and government. Autonomous Regions were administrative units without a constitution or government, but with an autonomous legislature, or Regional Council (*saolko sabcho* in Georgian, *oblastnoy soviet* in Russian).

The country was also divided into smaller administrative territorial units. These were Cities of Republican Subordination (CRS), a rough equivalent of the British county Boroughs, and Districts (*raiony*), rural and intraurban. The 14 CRS comprised the large cities (over 100 000 population) of Tbilisi, Kutaisi, Rustavi, Batumi and Sokhumi, the medium-size urban settlements (40–70 000 population) of Gori, Poti, Zugdidi and Tskhinvali, and five small towns having chiefly industrial significance, the mining towns of Tkibuli, Tkvarcheli and Chiatura, or recreational significance, Gagra and Tskaltubo. This last group were also centres of rural districts as with the exception of Tkvarcheli they managed quite extensive rural areas, officially termed "Territory Subordinated to the Town Council". The official boundaries of CRS Poti included a small rural area, in fact unpopulated and mostly occupied by bogs and lakes. Within the city of Tbilisi there were ten intraurban districts.

There were in Georgia 65 rural districts. On average 1000 km^2 in area, they varied in size from Abasha in the Western Lowland with 320.5 km^2 to Mestia in Western Kavkasioni with 3044.5 km^2. By population, the districts varied from

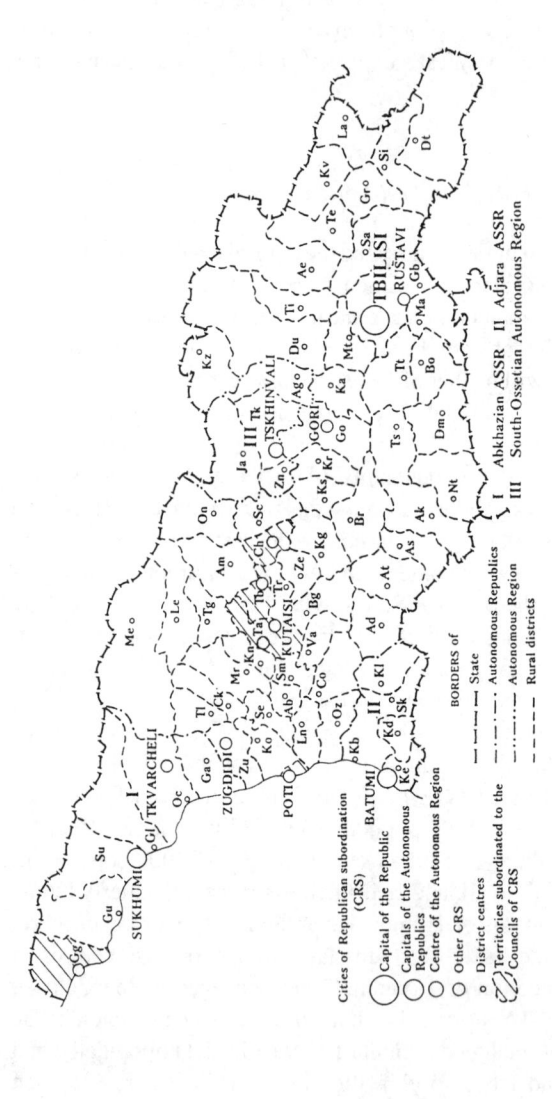

Figure 1.2 The administrative territorial divisions of Georgia (as of 1 January 1990).

Abbreviations

Ab Abasha	Br Borjomi	Gl Gulripshi	Kl Khulo	Ma Marneuli	Se Senaki	Tk Tskhinvali
Ad Adigeni	Ch Chiatura	Go Gori	Kn Khoni	Me Mestai	Si Signaghi	Tl Tsalenjikha
Ae Akhmeta	Ck Chkorotsku	Gr Gurjaani	Ko Khobi	Mr Martvili	Sk Shuakhevi	Tr Terjola
Ag Akhalgori	Co Chokhatauri	Gu Gudauta	Ks Khashuri	Mt Mtskheta	Sm Samtredia	Ts Tsalka
Ak Akhalkalaki	Dm Dmanisi	Ja Java	Kr Kareli	Nt Ninitsminda	Su Sokhumi	Tt Tetritskaro
Am Ambrolauri	Dt edoplitskaro	Ka Kaspi	Kv Kvareli	Oc Ochamchire	Ta Tskaltubo	Va Vani
As Aspindza	Du Dusheti	Kb Kobuleti	Kz Kazbegi	On Oni	Tb Tkibuli	Zn Znauri (Kornisi)
At Akhaltsikhe	Ga Gali	Kd Keda	La Lagodekhi	Oz Ozurgeti	Te Telavi	Zs Zestafoni
Bg Bagdati	Gb Gardabani	Ke Khelvachauri	Le Lentekhi	Sa Sagarejo	Tg Tsageri	Zu Zugdidi
Bo Bolnisi	Gg Gagra	Kg Kharagauli	Ln Lanchkhuti	Sc Sachkhere	Ti Tianeti	

I Abkhazian ASSR   II Adjara ASSR
III South-Ossetian Autonomous Region

Kazbegi in Eastern Kavkasioni with 6500 to Marneuli in the Eastern Lowland with 124 000. The rural districts were subdivided into 942 Village Councils (*sasoplo sabcho*), 46 Towns of District Subordination and 52 Townships. District centres were mostly selected from these towns and townships. Districts carried the names of their administrative centres.

The Abkhaz Autonomous Soviet Socialist Republic (Abkhazian ASSR) comprised an area of 8700 km^2 (12.5 per cent of the territory of Georgia), with 536 000 population (9.8 per cent of the national total). It had three CRS (Sokhumi, Tkvarcheli and Gagra) and five rural districts.

The Adjara Autonomous Soviet Socialist Republic (Adjara ASSR) had an area of 2900 km^2 (4.2% of Georgia), with 393 000 population (7.2%). It included one CRS (Batumi) and five rural districts.

The South Ossetian Autonomous Region had an area of 3400 km^2 (5.4 per cent of Georgia), with 98 000 population (1.8%). The region comprised one CRS (Tskhinvali) and four rural districts.

This administrative-territorial division was theoretically to be almost completely maintained to 1995. Minor changes since 1989 comprised the amalgamation of Zugdidi and Gori Rural Districts with their respective CRS. City and village councils were retitled *sakrebulo* instead of *sabcho*. Actually, more serious changes had occurred. The most important of these relate to some of the Autonomous units. There are no "ASSR", but officially the same areas are regarded as the Autonomous Republics of Adjara and Abkhazia. In the latter case, following the bloody civil war of 1992–3, the political status of the area is not yet clear (see Ch. 2). *De facto*, the province is not subordinate to the authority of the Tbilisi government. Quite an important change relates to the South Ossetian Autonomous Region. The history of the designation, attempts to change its status and the abolition of this Region are discussed in Chapter 2. It can be summarized here that in September, 1990 the Regional Council of South Ossetia unilaterally declared the territory of the Region a "Soviet Republic" within the USSR. In December of the same year the Supreme Council of the Republic of Georgia abolished the South Ossetian Autonomous Region. After the civil war that followed and ended in a cease-fire by mid-1992, part of the former Autonomous Region appeared to be directly subordinated to the Tbilisi government (Akhalgori district, enclaves of the Georgian-populated villages in the Liakhvi river valley), whereas the other part does not recognize central power and calls itself a "Republic". The "jurisdiction" of the latter covers the CRS of Tskhinvali, adjacent Ossetian-populated villages, and most of the Kornisi and Java districts. In both cases (Abkhazia and South Ossetia), the status is to be determined after negotiations.

Apart from the official administrative-territorial division, division of the country into historical provinces, mostly coinciding with the Kingdoms and Principalities of the late Middle Ages (see Ch. 2) is a tradition of continuing viability. In the eastern part of the country, embracing the basin of the River Mtkvari (Kura), flowing to the Caspian Sea, are Kartli (the core area of Georgia, giving its name to the entire country), Kakheti, Khevi, Mtiuleti, Pshavi, Khevsureti, Tusheti,

Meskheti and Javakheti. Of these, the most populated and economically developed are the lowland provinces of Kartli and Kakheti. In western Georgia, comprising the basins of several rivers flowing to the Black Sea, there are the historical provinces of Imereti, Guria, Samegrelo, Adjara, Racha, Lechkumi, Svaneti and Abkhazeti (Abkhazia) (Fig 1.1). Some of these provinces in their turn are traditionally subdivided into "lower" and "upper", in accordance with their physical-geographical location (e.g. there are Lower and Upper Svaneti, Lower and Upper Racha) or in some other way (e.g. Inner and Lower Kartli, Inner and Outer Kakheti), etc. This traditional division has been used for social regionalization in the present book and is considered by some political parties of this country as the basis of the future federative structure of Georgia or at least as the basis for administrative-territorial reform.

Space for economic and social life

Georgia, which covers 69 700 km^2, is by no means the smallest country in Europe or Asia. Its territory equals that of the Republic of Ireland and exceeds such countries in Europe and Asia as the Netherlands, Belgium, Croatia, Switzerland, Denmark, Sri-Lanka, Israel, and Kuwait, among others.

The country is a mountainous one; land below 600 m comprises only 31 per cent of the total surface, but in it are concentrated nine tenths of its population and economic activity. Land between 600 and 1800 m makes up 44 per cent of the territory, and above 1800 m 25 per cent. Apart from a handful of tiny villages, there is no permanent population in the highest area. Especially mountainous areas lie along the northern and southern borders.

According to surface character, Georgia is divided into three major geographical zones (Fig. 1.1): the Northern Highlands (in Georgian – Kavkasioni), the Intermontane Lowland, and the Southern Upland.

KAVKASIONI

The northern border of the territory settled by the Georgians (or the forefathers of the nation) for at least the past three millennia has followed the Great Caucasus Range with maximum heights exceeding 5600 m. The Range is a natural border not only from a physical point of view, defending the Transcaucasus from cold northern winds, but also a border in a cultural and political geographical sense; to the south and north live peoples mostly belonging to different linguistic families and sometimes even to different religions, although the standard cliché that "north Caucasus is the World of Islam, while South Caucasus is the World of Christianity" is an oversimplification. The Caucasus Range was always the natural border of Georgia with its northern neighbours. In the areas of ethnic interpenetration, which was inevitable since the relief was not an insurmountable barrier, nowadays the major ethnic conflicts occur. These areas were by no means the scene of perpetual ethnic clashes; relations between the different ethnic groups had quite often been friendly, but the geographical setting proved to be an important factor in conflict. A nationality from the north Caucasus, the Ossetians, some centuries ago settled on the southern slopes, within the Georgian Kingdom of Kartli, and later spread onto the lowland areas of Georgia, whereas the majority of their kinsmen remained in the north. In case of the Abkhaz, living in the Transcaucasus, all their closest linguistic relatives (the Abazins, Adigheans, Kabardians, Cherkess, Shapsugs) reside north of the Range. The major highway through the central part of the Caucasus from times immemorial followed the valleys of the rivers Aragvi (flowing to the south) and Terek (flowing to the north), across the Jvari (Cross) pass (2379m). In the eighteenth century the road was named by the Russians the "Georgian Military Highway". The northern border for the Georgians along this Highway during the past two to three millennia was marked by the narrow gorge of Daryal. The name derives from the Persian *"Dar-i-Alan"*, in Georgian *"ovsta kari"*; in both languages it means "the gate to the Alans/Ossetians". A new road over the Caucasus, with an automobile tunnel under the Roki pass, was opened in September, 1988. The road directly linked the areas in north Caucasus and Transcaucasus settled by the Ossetians. The construction of this road and tunnel served first of all political, then economic reasons (see Ch. 9).

Because of the rough surface and cool climate, Kavkasioni possesses rather limited possibilities for agriculture. The major wealth is in summer pastures and meadows. Hence, the principal activity of the highlanders is still animal husbandry; in east Kavkasioni, transhumance sheep-breeding used winter pastures in the lowlands of east Georgia or in the north Caucasus, where in the Soviet period Georgia rented large areas from Dagestan. After political instability embraced the north Caucasus as well, this route of transhumance became unsafe. In west Kavkasioni the major branch of economy is cattle-breeding, as there are no winter pastures for sheep in the densely populated western lowlands. The potential wealth of Kavkasioni is in its abundant resources for recreation – forests, mineral waters, gorgeous landscapes – although their development will need large investments and enough time. The mineral resources of Kavkasioni are non-ferrous metals and arsenic. Hydro-energy resources are substantial.

On the whole, Kavkasioni is the least populated geographical zone of Georgia (four per cent of the total) and is constantly losing population, which migrates to the lowland rural areas and urban places of Georgia and the north Caucasus. The provinces of Racha, Khevi, and the former South Ossetian Autonomous Region provided large flows of out-migrants from Georgia during the twentieth century.

In the Middle Ages, the historical provinces of Kavkasioni, while preserving some kind of cultural autonomy, were administratively subordinated to the political units located in the lowlands, with the exception of the mountainous Upper Svaneti, which always maintained its liberty based on the clan system and which had no feudal lords. The provinces of Khevi and Mtiuleti came under Kartli, those of Pshavi, Khevsureti and Tusheti under Kakheti, Racha under Imereti, Lechkhumi and Lower Svaneti under Samegrelo. This "highland–lowland" link was mutually helpful; the lowland areas were naturally wealthier, but the mountains were safer place of refuge during the not uncommon invasions and served as a constant reservoir of human resources.

THE INTERMONTANE LOWLAND

The intermontane lowland of Georgia comprises about 40 per cent of the country's territory, but it is home to almost 88 per cent of Georgia's population. The lowland is narrowest in its central part and widens out to east and west. It is divided by the Likhi Range, which serves as the major watershed between east Georgia (the Caspian Sea basin) and west Georgia (the Black Sea basin). Consequently, the intermontane lowland consists of eastern (Iveria) and western (Kolkheti) parts. The eastern lowland comprises the historical provinces of Kartli and Kakheti, western embraces the historical provinces of Imereti, Guria, Samegrelo and the littoral regions of Abkhazia and Adjara.

In earlier times the Likhi Range served as a frontier between Georgian feudal States or as a line delimiting the zones of influence of Rome and Iran, Byzantium and the Arab Khaliphate, the Ottoman Empire and Persia. However, for intra-ethnic contacts, the Likhi Range was no serious obstacle and on both its slopes the same Georgian language is spoken, although in different dialects. The subtropical climate of the Kolkheti lowland is humid. This makes the landscape green and attractive. But until the twentieth century, the land-short, boggy, malaria-infected west Georgia was always poorer than the eastern part, which possessed more land available for agriculture and had a healthier climate. The population in the Middle Ages avoided settling in most of the swampy littoral. There are no islands in the vicinity of Georgia. The Black Sea littoral within Georgia has just a handful of bays, suitable for ports. Thus, the Georgians were never good sailors. In contrast, the Kartvelian Lazi people, living to the southwest within modern Turkey, had many close contacts with the sea.

The introduction of maize in the seventeenth century gave a staple product to the population of west Georgia, which had previously consumed other, less productive cereals. But the real flourishing of the area was connected with the introduction of subtropical crops, tea and citrus fruit, from the late 1920s and the stable demand for them from an immense Soviet market, closed to any competition from abroad. The striving for the "tea independence of the USSR" brought the western lowland of Georgia, where 95 per cent of Soviet tea and up to 100 per cent of citrus fruit was produced, a high level of prosperity and outstanding welfare by Soviet standards. The swamps have been partially drained, malaria has been completely extinguished. However, nowadays the envisaged integration of Georgia within the world economy will involve the necessity of painful structural changes in the agriculture of the area.

The eastern (Iveria) lowland possesses on the whole a drier climate than west Georgia; practically everywhere plants need an artificial water supply, and some 400000 hectares are irrigated. But the soils are fertile and allow good quality grain and grapes to be grown. In historical times, the arable land was sufficient for quite a large rural population. Hence, the eastern lowland was always richer and more populated than the western one. Agriculture in east Georgia was always mixed, but during the Soviet period it became more specialized in viticulture (Kakheti province) and fruit-growing (Kartli province) for the all-Union market.

In east Georgia, the literary Georgian language developed and for a long time this part of the country was the real guardian of Georgian statehood. The capital city of Tbilisi is situated on the Iveria lowland. Being more vulnerable than the Kolkheti lowland to external aggression from the Middle Eastern powers (Arabs, Mongols, Persians, etc.) during the Middle Ages, this part of Georgia suffered serious losses in population. The vacant land was settled by immigrants from outside. This led to the contemporary multi-ethnicity of the area. All the large cities of Georgia and all the manufacturing industry are located in the Intermontane Lowland zone of Georgia. A dense transport infrastructure is capable of serving international traffic as well.

THE SOUTHERN UPLAND

The southern upland of Georgia is much less elevated than Kavkasioni, although its peaks reach 3000m. This is one of the most seismic areas of Georgia. The climate being rigorous, the territory lacks forest, especially on the Javakheti Plateau. Nevertheless, its wide plateaux and valleys are relatively better settled than Kavkasioni, although they include just eight per cent of the total population of Georgia. Summer pastures and meadows give a good fodder base for animal husbandry. At the end of the nineteenth century, the potato was introduced as the staple product of the area. In the Mtkvari valley fruit-growing became important. However, on the whole the Southern Upland is a relatively poor area of Georgia. Some rural parts of it are overpopulated; for example, there is a very high density of population on the arable land in mountainous Adjara. The Southern Upland lacks large industrial enterprises.

Georgia is more open to the south than to the north; natural barriers are practically absent here. Hence, the border has been more mobile in this part of the country (see Figs 2.1 to 2.4). This led to ethnic and religious diversity, most clearly manifest (apart from Abkhazia) along the southern border of Georgia, where in some districts the ethnic minorities that settled here from the seventeenth to nineteenth centuries are numerically dominant (see Ch. 4).

Natural resources for economic development and their use

The natural environment of Georgia is varied and the resources for economic development are quite rich, but from the point of view of the modern world economy, Georgia lacks the most important commodity – sources of energy. Oil, extracted in Kakheti province, meets five per cent of domestic demand; coal, from Tkibuli and Tkvarcheli mines, provides up to 50 per cent; there is no gas so far discovered. Power capacities of the rivers of Georgia (more than 25 000 in all) are substantial; they amount to 18 200 000 Kwt, mostly in west Georgia. So far less than 12 per cent are exploited. The largest hydroelectric power station is on the River Inguri.

On the whole, the country is rich in water resources. Water, including mineral and fresh spring water, is considered to be the major wealth of Georgia. In some places spas were developed, which were famous all over the USSR, notably Tskaltubo, Borjomi, Sairme, Tsaishi, Menji, and Tbilisi. They are capable of acquiring a world reputation, if reconstructed and advertised in a proper manner (Resorts 1989).

Mineral resources are varied, but not large enough. The most important of them are the best quality manganese ores, which have been extracted in Chiatura since 1879 and which for some time gave the Russian Empire a world monopoly of its exports before the First World War. They are now practically exhausted; predominantly low quality ores are left, although even their extraction is profitable. Nonferrous metal ores (copper, zinc, lead), which are extracted in Kazreti and Kvaisa, together with arsenic, are substantial, but only on the regional level. Among raw materials for the chemical industry worth mentioning are barite, diatomite, talcum, bentonite clays, and for the building materials industry, limestone, marble, basalt, teshenite, tufa, and so on.

Forests entirely belong to the State, which in practice means that they are protected merely formally. They make up 37.4 per cent of the total territory, reaching in some districts of west Georgia as much as 70 per cent. The forests in this mountainous country have soil-protecting, water-saving, climate-regulating, and aesthetic-recreational functions. From the end of the 1950s until the beginning of the 1990s was the "Golden era" of Georgian forestry; the rural population got cheap gas fuel (natural or condensate) and almost gave up cutting wood for domestic needs, except in the remote mountain villages. Lumbering was restricted as well.

However, the energy crisis since 1992, which followed the dramatic price rise of fuel imported from the other post-Soviet States (notably gas from Turkmenistan, and petrol from Russia and Azerbaijan) and the persistent lack of energy in rural areas because of the economic and political instability, led to an increase in wood-felling. In Armenia practically all forests have been cut down in recent years as a result of the energy blockade following the war over Nagorno–Karabakh; since the border is not protected, the citizens of the neighbouring country have been cutting wood in the adjacent peripheral areas of Georgia as well.

Georgia possesses considerable land resources for developing mixed agriculture. It is considered that land is insufficient for the simultaneous production of staple products for domestic needs and for export products (Jaoshvili 1993). Actually this is more the result of socioeconomic factors, notably bad resource-management, than of demographic pressure; the population of Georgia is not increasing very rapidly. Under Soviet power, Georgia received cheap (State-subsidized) grain, meat, and milk and produced instead much more expensive tea, citrus fruit, tobacco, grapes, and other fruit, some of which could be grown only in the soil and climatic conditions of this southern republic of the USSR. But if at the end of the 1980s, a kilo of tangerines bought no less than three litres of petrol, after world prices began to influence what was once "all-Soviet economic space", it emerged that one litre of petrol would buy two to three kilos of tangerines. Cheap staple products, apart from gifts on a short term basis from some Western governments, will no longer be available. This inevitably will lead to dramatic changes in the land-use structure.

Eradication of vineyards and tea plantations is already observable. Instead, cereals or vegetables are sown. The lack of fuel restricts the use of mechanical equipment, whereas the farmers have almost entirely got rid of oxen and horses over the past three decades. This left a large area uncultivated in 1992–4. Of the total area of the country, 21.7 per cent was tilled in 1940 and just 14.8 per cent half a century later; in 1990, 704000 hectares were arable and 326000 under perennial crops (*Georgia in figures*, 1991). This decrease was due partially to urban sprawl, but more to misuse of the land. As the land was in State ownership (i.e. "belonged to everybody and nobody") and all types of production and even agricultural operations were planned "from above" (the Communist Party local, district, republican committees), neither farmers nor managers had personal incentives to rationalize land-use in the *kolkhoz* and *sovkhoz* (collective and State farms). Small private allotments of collective farmers and employees of the *sovkhoz* had much higher productivity than the large plots of *kolkhoz* or *sovkhoz* land (Kekelia 1988).

These private plots, covering 13 per cent of the arable and 20 per cent of the land under perennial crops, produced in 1989 51 per cent of maize, 41 per cent of grapes, 45 per cent of potatoes, 64 per cent of citrus fruit, 76 per cent of other fruit. The private sector has produced 30 per cent of eggs, 51 per cent of meat, 58 per cent of milk and 63 per cent of wool (*Georgia in figures* 1991). Although conceding that land-use is clearly better and labour more efficient on the private plots, one must mention an additional "small cunning", peculiar to all the Soviet Union, to explain these "remarkable results of market economy", in reality the "second" economy. The individual farmers used additional land that did not belong to them; for example, shepherds grazed their sheep along with those belonging to the *kolkhoz* on the State-owned pastures. According to reports, the "State sheep" were vulnerable to all kinds of disease, wolves hunted them specially, whereas the private sheep suffered no losses. Land privatization began in 1992, although it proceeds slowly and with many complications, including even some fatal outcomes as the result of quarrels over land redistribution. Paradoxically it was easier to take away the land from everybody than to return it to the peasants after 70 years of complete State-ownership. Restructuring of agriculture and its adjustment to the needs of the market are envisaged. This will not happen in the near future; a more evident trend now seems to be a return to subsistence agriculture. But it is clear that such a development will be a temporary phenomenon and those remaining in the rural area will be compelled to become capitalist farmers rather than remain traditional peasants. This will happen first in the lowland areas. Georgia's natural resources, if used properly, are sufficient, in general, to sustain the local population and even provide products for export.

Social regions

It is obvious that there must be regional differences of social life in a mountainous, multi-ethnic and semi-urbanized country. Several schemes for the regionalization of Georgia have been scientifically argued. The best known and widely used is the division of the country into eight Standard Economic Regions carried out by Professor Giorgi Gvelesiani (1965). He divided the country according to the principle of internal economic ties, emphasizing the transport infrastructure. Thus, adjacent lowland and highland areas were united in single regions. That is a logical approach for an economic regionalization.

But social processes do not proceed in the same way, social life is not universal, social values differ in the lowland and highland areas, in rural and urban districts, in areas with different ethnic composition. Social regionalization, in essence, is a classification according to similarities of social indicators. These similarities are created by the social groups, "the bearers of the functions and creators of spatial structures" (Maier et al. 1977). The criteria for identifying the social regions of Georgia were: ethnic-cultural differences; physical environment; the predominant character of labour; the way of life of the population (especially differences in urban and rural areas); existing borders (historical, physical, State, and administrative) (Gachechiladze 1990b).

It appeared that many of the historical provinces of Georgia accord with the above-mentioned criteria of social regionalization, and display a high degree of cohesion. At the same time, some neighbouring historical provinces revealed such similarities that it was senseless to consider them as separate Social Regions. On the contrary, some historical provinces had substantial internal differences. All the cities and some larger towns in Georgia differ significantly from the rural area whereas most of the small and medium towns hardly could be distinguished from the adjacent countryside, judging by the way of life of their inhabitants and other criteria.

Social regions were needed analyze social processes in Georgia, as the 79 units of the existing administrative-territorial division were too many, and the eight units of economic regionalization were too few and too generalized, to permit adequate regional comparisons of some social indicators. Figure 1.3 demonstrates

Table 1.1 Key indicators for the social regions of Georgia, 1989.

Social regions	Population in 1000s	% of total population	Urban population (%)	Population in higher education (%)	Population density pers/km	Major ethnos (%)*	Income per cap. (rouble)	GDP** per cap. (rouble)
Urban social regions								
Tbilisi	1247	23.1	100.0	24.9	3564	G-66, A-12, R-10	1682	1050
Kutaisi	232	4.3	100.0	16.8	3020	G-91, R-4	1120	1602
Rustavi	159	2.9	100.0	12.1	2624	G-65, R-13	1222	993
Batumi	137	2.5	100.0	15.6	7058	G-66, R-15, A-10	1598	1703
Sukhumi	119	2.1	100.0	19.6	4565	G-42, R-22, Ab-13	1837	682
Gori	68	1.2	100.0	16.6	5844	G-77, O-12	1207	1475
Poti	51	0.9	100.0	10.6	4704	G-73, R-20	1735	1645
Zugdidi	50	0.9	100.0	13.8	2557	G-93, R-4	3945	...
Tskhinvali	42	0.7	100.0	20.0	4704	O-75, G-16	1901	1045
Rural social regions								
Imereti	534	9.9	33.1	7.6	85	G-96, R-2	1058	885
Kvemo Kartli	449	8.3	24.9	6.2	67	Az-53, G-25, Gr-10	1059	1268
Kakheti	441	8.2	22.7	8.6	39	G-82, Az-8	1100	1249
Rural Abkhazia	406	7.5	31.6	7.6	47	G-47, Ab-19 1204, A-16, R-12	1204	1075
Shida Kartli	355	6.6	30.4	6.9	66	G-84, O-8	1173	971
Samegrelo	310	5.7	21.9	6.6	72	G-97, R-2	1084	...
Rural Adjara	256	4.7	17.4	5.6	89	G-92, R-4	1180	953
Meskheti-Javakheti	196	3.6	30.8	7.2	38	A-63, G-30	952	696
Guria	158	2.9	28.6	8.3	78	G-93, R-3	1084	1473
Western Kavkasioni	74	1.4	20.6	7.7	10	G-98	1012	684
Eastern Kavkasioni	59	1.1	35.6	8.1	12	G-94, O-4	1544	982
"Rural Tskhinvali"	56	1.0	12.7	7.0	15	O-60, G-39	501	648

Source: 1989 Population Census data; Georgian branch of Gosbank of the USSR.
* A=the Armenians; Ab=the Abkhaz; Az=the Azeris; G=the Georgians; Gr=the Greeks; O=the Ossetians; R=the Russians.
** Data as for mid-1970s. Source: Melkadze, 1978.

Location, territory, resources, regions

Figure 1.3 The social regions of Georgia.

the 21 social regions of Georgia and Table 1.1 illustrates their differing parameters.

There are nine urban social regions distinguished; the CRS Tbilisi, Kutaisi, Rustavi, Batumi, Sokhumi, Gori, Poti, Zugdidi and Tskhinvali. These are cities and large or medium-size towns that differ very much from the adjacent rural areas.

Twelve rural social regions have been distinguished, half of which completely coincide with a historical province of the same name (Kakheti, Imereti, Samegrelo, Guria, Abkhazia, Adjara). Three rural social regions aggregate smaller mountainous provinces: East Kavkasioni, comprising the historical provinces of Khevi, Mtiuleti, Pshavi and Khevsureti; West Kavkasioni, comprising the historical provinces of Svaneti, Racha and Lechkhumi; Meskheti–Javakheti, comprising the two historical provinces of the same name. Kartli, the largest historical province, actually the heartland of Georgia, extends over four urban social regions (Tbilisi, Rustavi, Gori, Tskhinvali) and three rural social regions: Shida or Inner Kartli (with a predominantly Georgian population), Kvemo or Lower Kartli (with a mixed, predominantly Azeri population) and the "Rural Tskhinvali Region" (with a dominant Ossetian population). This last social region covers the rural part of the former South Ossetian Autonomous Region. Until the status of the area is officially established by the forthcoming Constitution of the Republic of Georgia, this temporary (albeit, I admit, artificial) name is used in this book. In the following text, especially in Part II of the book, this network of social regions will be used as the spatial base for the study of various social problems in Georgia.

CHAPTER 2
The historical–geographical background

Language and the identification of the nation

First one must begin with the language, one of the most important components of self-identification of a nation. According to modern linguistic theory, there is a separate Kartvelian linguistic family that consists of literary "*kartuli*" (the Georgian alphabet does not use capitals), or Georgian proper, and the unwritten languages "*svanuri*" (svan) and "*zanuri*", which in turn is divided into "*megruli*" (megrelian) and "*lazuri*" (laz) (Gamkrelidze & Ivanov 1984). The speakers of all these languages, living in Georgia today, form a single nation using Georgian proper as the literary language. There are also *lazuri* and *kartuli* speakers in some other countries, notably Turkey (see Ch. 4). There is also a theory of a single Caucasian or Ibero–Caucasian linguistic family, comprising the Kartvelian linguistic group along with groups of north Caucasian languages. The nation is known to the Middle Eastern peoples as *Gurji*, with phonetic variations such as *Djurz*, *Gurz*, *Kurj*, *Gorji* and *Gürcü* among different languages (Djaparidze 1993). To the west Europeans they are Georgians, to the Russians and the other Slavs *gruziny*. All these names seem to be derivations of a single name. Lang (1966: 18) argued that, "the Armenians and ancient Persians called the Georgians of the Eastern region *virk* or *Wyrshn* respectively, the *vir* element giving rise to the name Iveroi or Iberians, used by Greeks and Romans". There are other scholarly explanations of the existence of such a variety of names for a single nation (Paichadze 1993). However, the self-identification of the Georgians is not connected with any of the above, being *kartveli* (pl. *kartvel-ebi*). The Georgians call their country *sakartvelo* ("the place of Kartvelis").

From no later than the fifth century AD, written Georgian has used its own phonetic alphabet, differing from Latin or Cyrillic. During the Middle Ages, the Georgian script underwent a transformation, although the old script is still used for some ecclesiastical texts. But the language has shown rare stability. Unlike, for example, Anglo–Saxon or ancient Slavic, almost everything written some 1500 years ago is easily understandable, even to children of 14 or 15, who study ancient Georgian texts in school.

The historical–geographical background

Ancient and medieval Georgia

One can speak of the geography of settlement of the Kartvelian tribes in Transcaucasia since at least the second millennium BC, in the late Bronze and early Iron Ages (Muskhelishvili 1980). These tribes later organized into early States, which had intensive contacts with contemporary countries. Especially important were contacts with the Ancient Greeks, whose famous legend of the Argonauts is connected with the West Georgian kingdom of Colchis. Such a kingdom, populated by the Kartvelian tribes, really existed from the sixth century BC, called *kolkheti* in Georgian. Later, in its place arose the kingdoms of Lazica and Egrisi, taking their names from the dominant Kartvelian tribes of *lazi* and *egri/megreli* (Fig. 2.1).

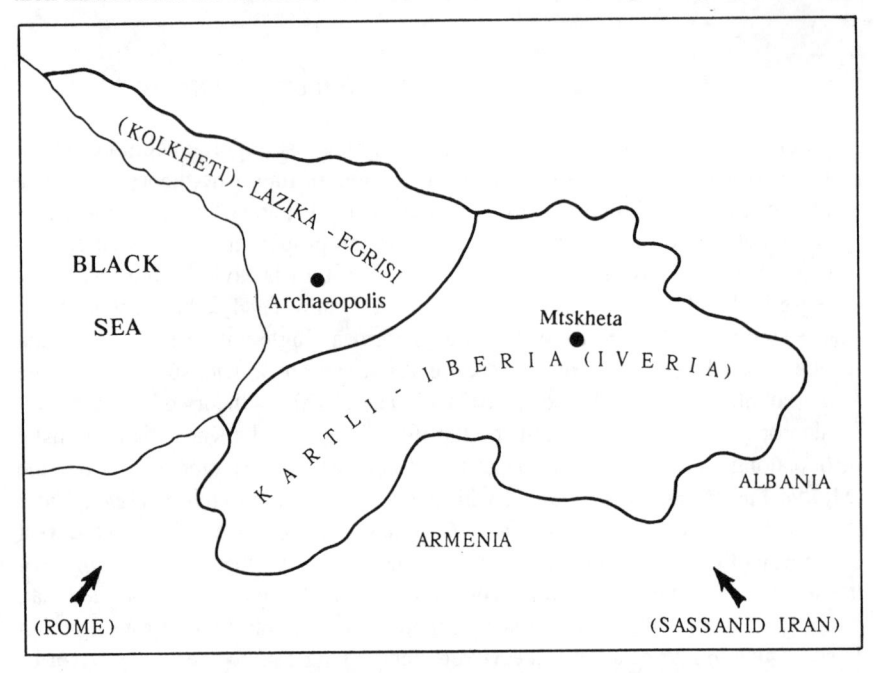

Figure 2.1 Georgia in the first to fourth centuries AD.

At the turn of the fourth and third centuries BC in Eastern Georgia, the *karti* tribes formed the Kartli kingdom, known to the Greeks and Romans as Iberia (Iveria). Their capital was Mtskheta. The *karti* tribes, who resided in the upper and middle valley of the River Mtkvari (known to the rest of the world from the Greek as Cyrus, and now as Kura) and its tributaries, were numerous and powerful enough to spread to the western part of the country. They penetrated into the area of the *zanuri*-speaking population, dividing it into the two linguistic zones of *megruli* in the north and *lazuri* to the south. By the end of the first millennium BC, Georgian proper (*kartuli*) entirely dominated in eastern Georgia and also in a substantial part of West Georgia. The capital of Kartli from the fifth century AD was moved from

Mtskheta to Tbilisi, just 20 miles to the south, down stream on the River Mtkvari.

A Georgian scholar, Otar Lordkipanidze, argues that the true beginning of Georgian civilization must be attributed to the existence of the Kingdom of Kartli from the third century BC (Lordkipanidze 1990). Naturally, the historical process was not going on in isolation from the outer world; Scythians, Cimmerians, the settlements of the Milesian Greeks, Persians, Rome, Byzantium, the north Caucasian peoples, Armenians, Arabs, Turks and others were in more or less intensive contact, either military or peaceful, with the Georgians and their States, and they left their traces on the latter's language and culture – and vice versa.

The most important factor on the way to the formation of a single Georgian nation was the adoption of Christianity. Christianity first became the State religion in East Georgia, which had to defend itself against the attacks of Sassanid Iran, where the State religion was Zoroastrianism. Kartli preferred to have ideological unity with the major foe of Iran, Christian Byzantium, and this geopolitical reason induced King Mirian of Kartli and his Queen Nana to grant a favour to a Cappadocian woman Nino, who is believed to be responsible for the conversion of Georgia. The traditional date for the adoption of Christianity in Georgia is 331 AD. The names Nino and Nana have since been widespread female names in Georgia. So is Mary (Mariam), as the Virgin Mary is recognized by the Georgian Church to be the patron of the country. Among male names, the most popular down the centuries were George (Giorgi), since in popular sentiment St George is considered to be the true patron of the nation, and David, because the Bagrationi dynasty, ruling from the ninth to the nineteenth centuries, claimed descent from King David of the Old Testament.

The official baptism of West Georgia, where there were Christian communities even earlier than in Kartli, occurred later, in the sixth century. In Kartli, public worship traditionally was in the Georgian (*kartuli*) language, into which the Holy Bible was translated. Its canonized Georgian text was finally adopted in the tenth and eleventh centuries. Literature in Georgian began to develop from the fifth century. The characteristic style of church architecture had also been developed. All these were later exported "ready-made" to West Georgia and there the Georgian Bible was much better understood than the Greek Bible used in West Georgia until the tenth century. This linguistic transition in worship became an important factor in national consolidation on the basis of the Georgian language.

It must be stressed that in the Middle Ages the social significance of religious affiliation was far more important than ethnic affiliation. From this point of view it is worth mentioning that, for the later self-identification of the Georgian nation, it was crucial that the Georgian church leaders at the beginning of the seventh century refused to belong to Monophysitism, which the Georgians shared with the Armenians and Albanians, and by the decisive change to the Chalcedonian faith, Greek Orthodoxy, which made Georgia closer to Byzantium and alien to Sassanid Iran, which was more liberal towards the Monophysites (Javakhisvili 1979). Georgian-speaking Monophysites, who remained in some rural areas of Georgia or for some reason later converted to this faith, were until recently considered by

The historical–geographical background

the majority of Chalcedonian Georgians as *somekhi* (Armenian). The Albanians referred to here are the Caucasian Albanians, who lived in the area of modern Azerbaijan; later their languages (akin to those of the north Caucasus) and statehood became extinct, assimilated by their more powerful and viable neighbours, mostly the Oguz Turks, who migrated to this territory from the eleventh century. In the seventh century, East Georgia was conquered by the Arabs, but Islam failed to supplant Christianity. Islam was more successful south of Tbilisi and especially in neighbouring Albania, lying to the south and closer to the major routes of the Arabs.

In the mid-tenth century, a Georgian hagiologist Giorgi Merchule formulated a definition of the ethnic territory of the Georgians that became axiomatic in medieval times. "Georgia consists of those spacious lands in which church services are celebrated and all prayers said in the Georgian (*kartuli*) tongue". Within a century or so after Merchule enunciated his doctrine, the area where the Christian (Chalcedonian) liturgy was followed in Georgian comprised the whole territory of present-day Georgia.

It must be said that this ethnic self-identification might have been impossible if some "sense of unity" of the different tribes that were merging into a nation had not existed. It has been argued that this sense existed even before the baptism of Georgia, despite sub-ethnic differences (Gordeziani 1993).

As in western Europe, where the growth of "nation-States" was in progress from the ninth to the fifteenth centuries, a similar process proceeded in Georgia. Its political unification began on the eve of the ninth century. The first part of the Transcaucasus to be free of the Arabs and Byzantium, the masters of most of western Georgia, appeared to be a peripheral area north of Sokhumi, where the *abazg* principality (called "*abkhazeti*" in Georgian) emerged in the eighth century. At the end of that century, the principality expanded into West Georgia, and became the kingdom known as "*abkhazta samepo*" (Abkhazian Kingdom), after the ruling Abkhaz dynasty, who made Kutaisi the capital of the realm, in the fertile central part of western Georgia (Fig. 2.2).

An almost similar extension of the name of the ruling dynasty over the larger territory occurred in Britain in the same century. When the King of Scots, Kenneth Macalpin, got the Pictish throne, the new united kingdom became known to the outer world as "Scotia", although the Picts outnumbered the Scots, and the capital, Scone, was situated in "their part" of the new realm (Mackie 1964). In the case of Georgia, the name of the kingdom in West Georgia (Abkhazeti) was transferred in foreign sources to that of the united Georgia, Sakartvelo; in tenth- to thirteenth-century Persian, Arabic, Greek, and Russian the whole of Georgia was termed "Abazgia" or "Abkhaz" (Djaparidze 1993, Lomouri 1993).

As a prominent Abkhaz historian wrote: "In the Abkhazian Kingdom, the majority of the population was composed of the Kartvelian element, which also occupied the largest and the leading part of the territory of the realm. Moreover, this element appeared to be more advanced from the socio-economic and cultural points of view. Thus, Georgian proper gradually achieved general prevalence as

Ancient and medieval Georgia

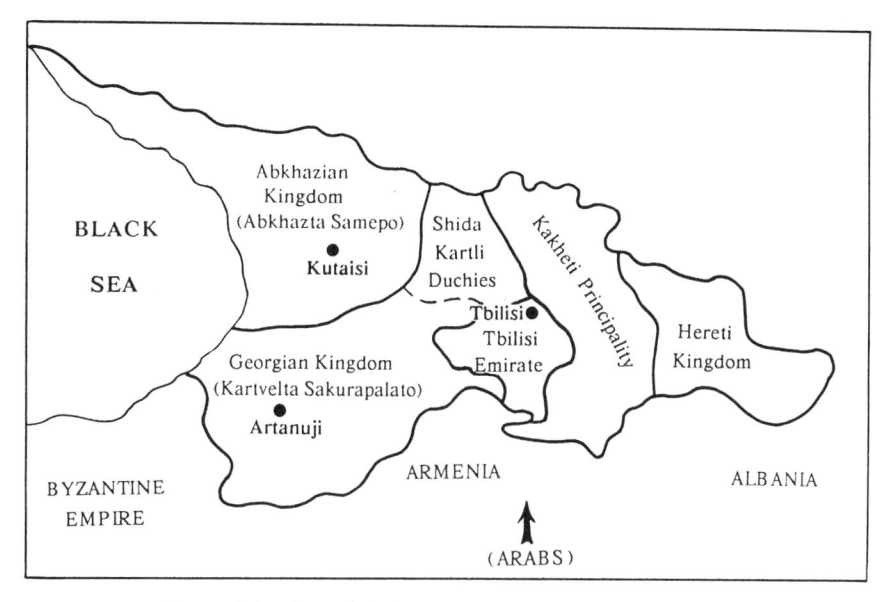

Figure 2.2 Georgia before unification in the ninth century.

the major language of literacy and culture in the whole Abkhazian Kingdom and supplanted Greek, which had been used before for these purposes in Abkhazia proper, in particular" (Anchabadze 1976: 53).

Abkhazta samepo fought with the other States in the area of modern Georgia, in a typically feudal manner, to enlarge the boundaries of the realm, but in practice promoting the unification of Georgia (Anchabadze 1959, Melikishvili 1973). The peaceful unification of Georgia occurred in 978, when, as a result of dynastic inheritance, the Abkhazian Kingdom and the Kingdom of the Georgians ("*kartvelta samepo*", called earlier "*sakurapalato*") merged under the House of Bagrationi, the Kings of the Georgians. The self-styled name of the united kingdom from the early eleventh century became Sakartvelo (Georgia). The sovereigns of the united kingdom had their throne first in Kutaisi and from the twelfth century in Tbilisi. They enlarged the realm at the expanse of most of the Transcaucasus (Fig. 2.3). In the united Georgian kingdom the people would doubtless have spoken different languages, but the only literary and ecclesiastical language was Georgian proper.

The strongest impetus to the consolidation of the nation in a unified State was given by the reign of King David IV *agmashenebeli* (the Rebuilder, 1089–1125; Metreveli 1986). He was the contemporary of the English kings William II Rufus and Henry I. This vigorous king joined to his realm the last lands inhabited by Georgians, which had not been earlier connected to Sakartvelo. These included the Tbilisi emirate, the last Muslim enclave remaining from the Arab occupation. Tbilisi became the capital of united Georgia in 1122, since when it has always played the role of the major city of Georgia, even when the country was disunited. Indirectly,

The historical–geographical background

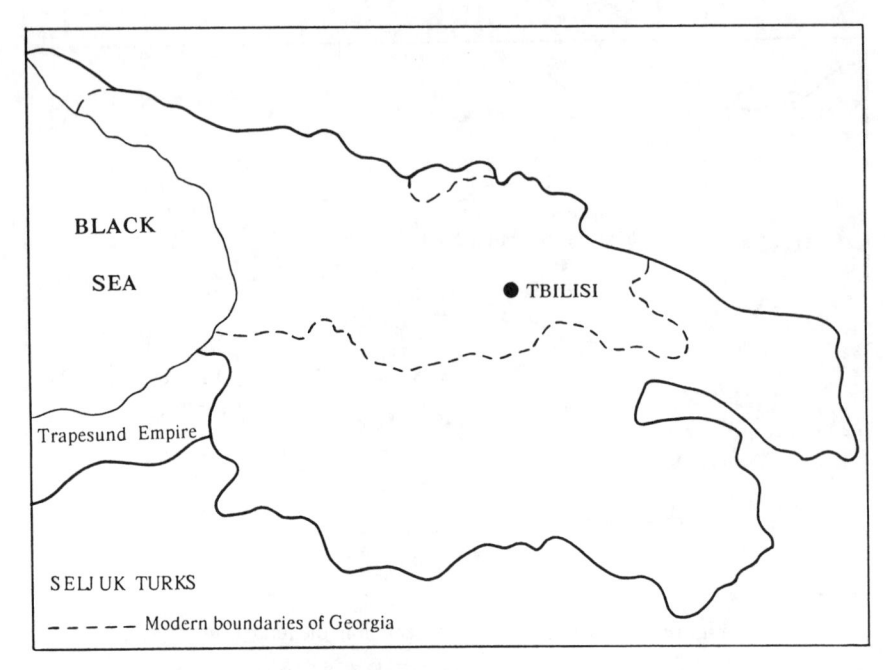

Figure 2.3 A unified kingdom – Sakartvelo – in the thirteenth century.

the success of the Georgian kings was assisted by western Europe; the crusades diverted the major forces of the Muslim rulers from an ever-expanding Georgia.

In their empire the Bagrationi monarchs followed a policy of religious tolerance and their Christian (Orthodox and Gregorian), Muslim and Jewish subjects could feel quite comfortable. Medieval Georgia, in its political and cultural development and social structure, resembled Europe, obviously influenced by Byzantium. As David Lang (1966: 116) points out, "all the familiar terms of Western feudalism had their equivalents in the social system of medieval Georgia". The medieval culture of Georgia reached its height in the twelfth to thirteenth centuries (Lordkipanidze 1987).

At the beginning of the thirteenth century, according to the most likely estimates, the population of the realm, which in those days was almost equal in size to England and Wales, was 2 400 000–2 500 000 (Kakabadze 1920: 40; Jaoshvili 1984: 49). Of these, 1 800 000 lived in the area of modern Georgia (Jaoshvili 1984: 50), a comparable figure with that of contemporary England (Russell 1948). Some authors rather groundlessly argue that the population of the united Georgian Kingdom reached 4 500 000 or even more.

The Mongol invasion put an the end to the expansion of Georgia and promoted the disintegration of the country. Apart from paying heavy tribute and participating in the Mongol military campaigns, in 1250 Georgia, where the kings were officially left on the throne, were given two new ones, cousins of Bagrationi blood, by the Mongols. Later this led to the break-up of the country: one branch of the royal dynasty remained in Tbilisi, while the other settled in Kutaisi in West Georgia, which has since then been called Imereti – literally "the country on the other side [of the mountains]". Later the country was again reunited, albeit temporarily. Powerful internal and external factors worked for feudal disintegration and in the fifteenth century the country finally broke up. For a very long time Georgia sank into a deep political, economic and cultural stagnation, typical of feudalism. Unlike the countries of medieval Europe, where the three elements of political compromise – towns, feudal lords and the church – divided power among themselves (the best example is the English Parliament) and consequently promoted the development of strong centralized nation-States, in disunited Georgia there was not the necessary balance of power among the same elements. The towns were too weak and were deprived of rights, the feudal lords were too strong, and the church was nominally subjugated to the crown and politically less active.

Even so, if normal conditions for the economic development of the towns had existed, sooner or later the structural approach of the European model of development was theoretically possible. In practice this was not achievable, not least because of geographical factors. The discovery by west Europeans in the fifteenth century of routes to India and the New World for a long time made the eastern Mediterranean, and even more the Black Sea basin, remote from western Europe. In the Hellenistic period, the Transcaucasian region had a much more central position in the world than it did 15 to 17 centuries later, by which time the major trade routes had moved far away. Georgian towns lost all incentives for development.

A no less important factor in the serious backwardness of Georgia at the end of the Middle Ages compared to the European model of development was its disadvantageous geopolitical location. On the southwest, its neighbour was the powerful Ottoman Empire, which by the mid-fifteenth century had absorbed Byzantium and its outlet, the Trapezund Empire, a Greek State with a substantial kartvelian (lazi) population. Armenia, which had lost its independence in the eleventh century, found itself under the absolute rule of several Turkic khans. Persia had been disunited for almost eight centuries and did not itself present a political danger to Georgia, although that did not apply to the several Turkic and Mongol States on the Iranian territory. In 1502 Persia was united under the vigorous dynasty of the Safavids and began to expand towards the Transcaucasus. The small, Turkic-speaking khanates in the area of modern Azerbaijan, from the religious–cultural point of view, were closer to Persia, being all Shi'a Muslim. In the northern Caucasus, Ottoman influence was stronger, as the local peoples adopted Sunni Islam.

By the sixteenth century, Georgia was completely surrounded by the world of Islam and was drawn away from Europe. Of course, in practice relations with the Muslim peoples were not always hostile; often they were quite friendly and a fruitful mutual influence always existed. But the two Middle Eastern superpowers, which were perpetually at war with each other in the frontier areas, would have never permitted the appearance of a strong rival in the Transcaucasus, which served as a marchland for them both, least of all a Christian one.

The historical–geographical background

After the final break-up of feudal Georgia occurred in the fifteenth century, three kingdoms appeared, ruled by different branches of the Bagrationi dynasty: Kartli and Kakheti in the eastern part and Imereti in the western. The last included the nominally vassal, but actually semi-independent, principalities of Guria and Sabediano (Odishi). Sabediano in its turn embraced the two historical provinces of Samegrelo and Abkhazeti, the latter with a dominant ethnic Abkhaz population, who called themselves *Apsua* (Fig. 2.4).

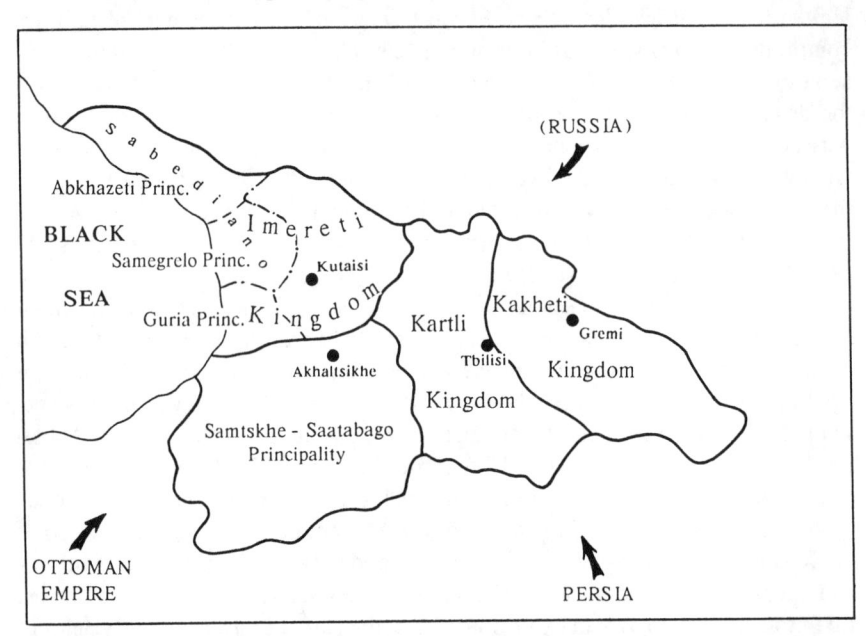

Figure 2.4 Georgian kingdoms and principalities by the mid-sixteenth century.

In the seventeenth century, the princes of Abkhazeti, the Shervashidze, became nominally independent from Samegrelo, but fell under Ottoman control and led perpetual wars with the princes of Samegrelo, the Dadiani, first for the territory between the rivers Kodori and Galidzga. After the conquest of this area and its Abkhazianization by the late seventeenth century, the marchland area moved farther southwards to the territory between the rivers Galidzga and Inguri, later called Samurzakano (Anchabadze 1976: 68); a fuller account is given in Chapter 4. In southwestern Georgia an independent principality of Samtskhe–Saatabago developed and for quite a long time it was the most flourishing economically and culturally. Within modern Georgia it comprised the historical provinces of Meskheti and Javakheti, but a large part of the principality lay farther south.

In every kingdom and principality, cultural development to some extent continued in the all-Georgian tradition. For example, in Samtskhe–Saatabago beautiful Georgian churches and monasteries were constructed in the fourteenth and fifteenth centuries. The idea of reunification never died out entirely, but every "strong ruler" considered himself "the Reunifier" and this always meant fresh bloodshed. The new kingdoms and principalities were not centralized States either; each strong vassal attempted to make himself independent. It is of note that all the monarchs of Georgian States and the nobility, if they followed the Christian orthodoxy, traditionally considered themselves "kartveli" (Georgian), whereas if they converted to Islam they were called *tatari*, "Tartars", the common Georgian name for all Muslim, predominantly Turkic, peoples living to the south.

In Georgia, loss of territory and religious changes followed. After a long war, the Safavids and the Ottomans in 1555 divided the Transcaucasus; western Georgia came under the sphere of influence of Turkey, eastern Georgia under that of Persia, although nominally the Georgian kingdoms were not abolished. The dividing line followed the Likhi mountain range. The Middle Eastern powers periodically reconfirmed this border, making the reunification of Georgia impossible.

In 1628 the Ottoman Empire completely incorporated the Samtskhe–Saatabago principality; it became Akhaltsikhe *pashalik* (Gabashvili 1957), deriving its name from its capital, which means "Newcastle" in Georgian. An Islamized Georgian princely family were made hereditary pashas. Georgian as a colloquial language was preserved in this province of the Ottoman Empire for quite a long time. The majority of the local Georgian (*meskhi*) population gradually Islamized and later adopted the Turkish language, although quite a few remained bilingual until the mid-twentieth century. The conversion to Islam in Samtskhe–Saatabago was largely the result of economic factors, but partly also of political factors. A Muslim feudal lord kept possession of the land, a Muslim peasant paid fewer taxes than a Christian one, whereas a convert had his way open to a political career (Abuladze 1989). While some of the population from Meskheti province found refuge in the inner Christian kingdoms of Georgia, others stayed and retained Christianity at the expense of converting to Catholicism. According to the "Capitulations" granted by the Sultan to the King of France, the latter was the protector of all the Catholics in the Ottoman Empire. If the local Georgians preferred converting to Catholicism, they were considered as *frangi* ("the French"), the common name in the Middle East for all west Europeans. To the present, the largest community of Georgian Catholics lives along its southern border.

In the seventeenth century the incorporation by the Ottoman Empire of the mountainous area of Adjara and adjacent coastal area north of Batumi (Kobuleti), earlier belonging to the princes of Guria, led to the gradual conversion to Islam of the local population. Their descendants constitute today the only Muslim Georgian community in the country. In contrast to the results of the conversion of Meskhetians, the population of Adjara and Kobuleti never abandoned its native Georgian tongue and avoided direct demographic influence. After the Russian–Turkish War of 1877–8, part of this population was persuaded to emigrate to the Ottoman Empire. Their quite numerous Georgian-speaking descendants still live in the Black Sea coastal area and the northwestern part of Asiatic Turkey.

A certain cultural renaissance occurred in East Georgia at the beginning of the eighteenth century. Under King Vakhtang VI of Kartli, a printing house was established in Tbilisi, which produced books in Georgian. A scientific commission was set up to edit and supplement the text of the Georgian Chronicle, "*kartlis tskovreba*"; the first dictionary of the Georgian language was compiled; the first detailed geographical description of the country (with a map) was written in Georgian by Prince Vakhushti, and so on.

In the same century, new attempts were made to reunite Georgia. In 1762, the Eastern Georgian kingdoms of Kartli and Kakheti were united under the crown of Erekle II, the representative of the Kakhetian branch of the Bagrationi. Moreover, the West Georgian dynasts, formally the vassals of the Sultan, recognized the authority of Erekle, in fact the only independent monarch in the Caucasian region. The neighbouring Muslim khanates within the territories of modern Azerbaijan and Armenia, nominally parts of the then weak Persia, also recognized the protectorate of the (East) Georgian monarchy. However, the Middle Ages were too long drawn out for Georgia and it turned out to be impossible for the small and divided country to escape from permanent crisis.

While in western Europe industrial development was beginning, Georgia remained purely an agrarian society. In the few towns, the traders and artisans were peoples of different faiths. There was not even the embryo of a national bourgeoisie. This hindered nation-building. International economic ties were restricted. The dangerous proximity of the economically and politically stagnating, but still powerful, Middle Eastern superpowers persisted. In spite of a moderate political and cultural progress, the general backwardness of the country against the European background became even more apparent.

At this time, the rapidly expanding Russian Empire, which underwent superficial Europeanization in the eighteenth century, seemed to Georgia a desirable ally, especially because for the Georgians, in contrast to almost all the other Caucasian peoples, Greek-Orthodox Christian Russia was co-religious. For a time, the interests of an imperialistic power and its future colony coincided. The Georgians were ready to support Russia's military actions against their own traditional adversaries: Persia, the Ottoman Empire and the north Caucasian (mostly Dagestani) highlanders. The last of these, with their perpetual small-scale but very painful raids into the lowlands of Georgia, were the major menace to economic and political stabilization in this country. The Georgian monarchs, who had earlier tried in vain to attract the attention of western Europe, saw in Russia an example of European culture, State order, and military strength.

The Russian domination

In 1783, special envoys from the (East) Georgian Kingdom signed a treaty in Georgievsk, a Russian stronghold in the north Caucasus, according to which the Russian Tsars were recognized as the protectors of East Georgia. In return King Erekle and his heirs were guaranteed the throne, the Georgian church was allowed to remain independent, and Erekle II was promised military aid, including that needed to reunite within his realm the Georgian lands under the jurisdiction of third countries.

However, the Empire did not fulfil the articles of the treaty. No military support was given to Georgia when it was attacked by Persia in 1795, and Tbilisi was eventually burnt to ashes in retaliation for Georgia's closeness to Russia. In 1801, in complete breach of the treaty, Tsar Alexander I unilaterally abolished the (East) Georgian Kingdom. Erekle II and his successor Giorgi XII were both dead by that time and the new heir was to be nominated by the Tsar himself. Instead, it was announced that the kingdom was annexed to the Russian Empire as a *gubernia* (province). The royal family was deported at once and the autocephality of the Georgian church was abolished in 1811.

In spite of the obvious violation of promises given, the incorporation of East Georgia into the Russian Empire went on relatively peacefully. There was no king left to lead a resistance, only pretenders who had no social base of support. On the whole, the Georgian nobility was content with its equalization in rights with the Russian aristocracy and the majority of their own free will entered Russian military service, many of them reaching the highest ranks. The common people were satisfied with the peace and order established in the country. However, at the same time the policy of Russification, which began at once, together with dishonesty and corruption among the new officials, sometimes led to strong discontent. At the beginning of Russian rule, popular uprisings took place, (e.g. in 1802, 1804, 1812, 1819–20) and there was a plot led by part of the nobility in 1832. But on the whole, Georgia appeared to be the most reliable strategic foothold of the Russian Empire in its Caucasian and Middle Eastern policy. The Georgians for the most part were the Tsar's loyal subjects.

The West Georgian States were annexed to the Empire later. Russia conquered the kingdom of Imereti by force of arms in 1810. The principalities that wisely "entered" the Empire preserved some autonomy for quite a long time, Guria until 1828, Samegrelo and Svaneti until 1857, Abkhazeti until 1864. Such a pattern of annexation affected the administrative–territorial division of Georgia within the Russian Empire. The former East Georgian (Kartli–Kakheti) Kingdom constituted the *Tiflisskaya gubernia* (Tbilisi province), which by the end of the nineteenth century was divided into nine *uezdy* (districts): Tbilisi, Gori, Telavi, Signaghi, Tianeti, Dusheti, Borchalo, Akhaltsikhe, and Akhalkalaki, together with an *okrug* (region) of Zakatala. West Georgia comprised *Kutaisskaya gubernia* (Kutaisi province), divided into three districts of the former Imereti kingdom (Kutaisi, Shorapani, Racha) and eventually incorporating also the former principalities of Guria (Ozurgeti district), Samegrelo (districts of Zugdidi, Senaki and Lechkhumi) and Abkhazeti (Sokhumi region – *Sukhumskiy okrug*).

In 1828 Russia annexed from the Ottoman Empire the historical Georgian provinces of Meskheti and Javakheti, which then became Akhaltsikhe and Akhalkalaki districts respectively within Tbilisi province. By the Berlin Treaty of 1878, the Batumi region (*Batumskiy okrug*), comprising the Georgian province of

Adjara (with Kobuleti), was annexed and subordinated to Kutaisi province. Between 1878 and 1918, some other territories of medieval Georgia were also part of the Russian Empire.

Thus, the Russian Empire accomplished the "gathering of the Georgian lands", which had been the dream of the Georgian people, who always will be grateful to Russia for this. However, the "unification of Georgia" was by no means the conscious aim of the rulers of the Empire. The Imperial Government emptied the territory for its own loyal colonists. For example, after annexing Meskheti and Javakheti provinces, everything was done to persuade the Muslim population (mostly Georgian speakers) to leave. The same was attempted in Adjara and, with much more success, in the former Abkhazeti principality, from which almost the half of the Abkhaz population left between 1866 and 1878. All of these people emigrated to the Ottoman Empire. To replace them, a Christian but non-Georgian population was resettled in the area, including Armenians and Greeks from Turkey, Russian *raskolniki* (religious minorities such as the Dukhobortsy and Molokane) and veteran soldiers, German and Estonian colonists. Ossetian peasants were allowed to move from both slopes of the Caucasus to the fertile lowlands of Georgia. Thus, the basis of the modern ethnic mosaic in this country was established. From the economic point of view, Tsarist Russia considered Georgia a typical colony, a supplier of raw materials and a market for goods produced in the central provinces of Russia (Gachechiladze et al. 1984). The Georgian historian S. Chkhetia cited the Russian magazine *Syn otechestva* (*The Son of Fatherland*) for the year 1835: "As a colony of Russia, the Transcaucasus must not have a manufacturing industry, i.e. without destroying that which already exists, building of new factories must not be permitted" (Chkhetia 1942: 224). This kind of policy dominated during the whole nineteenth century, and at the beginning of the twentieth century there were in Georgia no more than 30 factories, mostly in the light and food industries, with the largest being the railway repair workshops in Tbilisi. However, this restrictive policy did not apply to the extractive industries, and Russia became the world monopolist in manganese ore exports, thanks to the Chiatura deposits of West Georgia.

The social structure of the population changed very slowly. As in the Middle Ages, the Georgians were again either aristocracy (intellectuals and the many army officers almost entirely belonged to the nobility), or peasants (see Ch. 3). The bureaucrats were Russians, Russified Germans and Poles. Bourgeois were rare among the Georgians; trade remained the monopoly of the Armenians. R. G. Suni wrote:

> . . . the Armenian merchants and craftsmen of Caucasia's towns benefited from the new security provided by Russian arms and, while competing with privileged Russian traders, orientated themselves away from the Middle East and towards Russian and European commerce. In the process they laid the foundation for their own fortunes and their future as the leading economic and political element in Russian Georgia. The peasantry of Transcau-

casia was forced in the meantime to submit to new exactions as its status became increasingly similar to that of Russian peasants. (Suni 1988: 63)

The maintenance by the Armenians of economic domination in the Transcaucasus during the whole period of Russian rule was a major reason for ethnic-based class tensions in the area. In Azerbaijan this even lead to bloodshed in 1905. The Georgian nobility, rather careless and non-industrious, and still thinking in feudal terms that their major business was war (and large feasts between wars!), very often became dependent on Armenian creditors and usurers, and tended to blame on them all of their misfortunes. This commonly happened in Tbilisi province. The government did not care, as it meant that there was no Russophobia! It must be added that there were no true ethnic conflicts between the Georgians and Armenians either. On the contrary, inter-ethnic marriages between the elites were not rare; the gentlemen liked the rich dowry and the merchants liked their grandchildren to have a title.

The Empire did not recognize the existence of a single Georgian nation (Antadze 1973). The 1897 census enumerated 11 ethnic groups of "kartvelian origin", albeit officially admitting that "the peoples constituting the Kartvelian or Iverian group to a considerable extent embrace a homogeneic whole" (Troïnitsky 1905: XXVI). Nevertheless, the process of national consolidation gradually went on, especially intensifying in the second half of the nineteenth century, when in 1872 a railway connected the eastern and western parts of Georgia. Tbilisi, recognized by all the sub-ethnic groups to be the major city of the Georgians, began to draw migrants from all the provinces. As the centre of Russian Caucasia, seat of the viceroy, and multi-ethnic in population, Tbilisi was not regarded as a city "belonging" exclusively to a single historical province of Georgia, although geographically it is within Kartli province. This psychologically facilitated Georgians from different areas to count Tbilisi "their own capital". They even called it simply "*kalaki*" ("the Town"). By the end of the nineteenth century, it consolidated its role as the major centre of Georgian culture; out of nine magazines and newspapers published in the Empire in Georgian in 1901, eight were published in Tbilisi (*Kavkazski Kalendar* 1902). After the Emancipation of the Serfs (1864–71), migration from the Western mono-ethnic Georgian districts to urban and rural areas of East Georgia intensified. These movements contributed to the greater consolidation of the Georgian nation.

The level of literacy among the Georgian population increased. Moreover, they wrote using the original alphabet and read a literature written a millennium earlier. This hampered their Russification, even if a few representatives of the nobility changed the endings of their surnames into the Russian style with the ending "-ov", instead of the typical -dze, -shvili, -ia, and so on, which were preserved by the common people and by the gentry, mostly of Kutaisi province, and even if the Europeanization of social life via Russia became irreversible. In an effort to weaken the national revival of the Georgians in the last decades of the nineteenth century, the Russian government tried to use a more subtle plan than plain suppression. This was "care for the cultural development of all the ethnic minorities", which showed itself in attempts to introduce teaching in the primary schools and public worship in the other Kartvelian languages, Megrelian and Svan, which had never before been used for these purposes. This plan was spoiled by decisive resistance from the Georgian intelligentsia belonging to the same sub-ethnic groups, who realized that the fulfilment of this plan would have meant the dismembering of the incipient national unity achieved with such difficulty (Gogebashvili 1912).

The same type of plan in the Sokhumi region appeared to be more successful. Here, instead of the Georgian liturgy traditional since the tenth century, Russian liturgy and education in primary schools were introduced. Weidenbaum, an officer of the Caucasian viceroy, wrote in a confidential report at the beginning of the twentieth century:

> The Abkhaz language, which lacks an alphabet and literature, is obviously doomed to disappearance in the more or less near future. The question is: which language will replace it? It is clear that the role of champion of cultural ideas and definitions must be played not by Georgian, but by the Russian language. It seems to me that the introduction of a written Abkhaz language must not be an end in itself but only a means to weaken, in the case of church and school, the necessity of Georgian language and for its gradual change to the State [i.e. Russian] language. Otherwise, we take a risk of creating above (the claims of) Georgian and other autonomies, a (claim of) Abkhazian autonomy in addition. (Anchabadze 1976: 96)

Since the Abkhaz are a distinct people, with their mother-tongue differing from Georgian, it was up to them to decide what language to use for study and for worship. Just a short comment must be added; the fulfilment of the plan led to the gradual Russification of the Abkhaz and their alienation from the local Georgian population, with whom they shared a common historical heritage. The latter idea was closer to the Abkhaz nobility (Menteshashvili 1990). But as the new Abkhaz intellectuals, brought up in Russian language and culture, became more influential, the "image of alien" (successfully transformed into that of "foe") was projected on to the Georgians. Later, under Soviet power, this image was consolidated and generations of Abkhaz were brought up with a hatred for the Georgians.

Naturally, raising the educational level would have led to strengthening the national feelings of every ethnic group of the Empire. Many of the Georgian intelligentsia, educated in Russian and west European universities, successfully popularized ideas of patriotism. From the government angle this could be criticized as "nationalism". Actually the idea of the autonomy of Georgia within the Empire was quite popular with the majority of intellectuals, who insisted that the Georgievsk Treaty articles had not been fulfilled. In addition, there were more radical ideas seeking the restoration of full independence.

The political culture of the population grew. In spite of the later communist propaganda, which described the Russian Empire as an exclusively police State, it was less anti-democratic (especially in its last years) than its Bolshevik successor. Most of the political parties under the Tsar were legal. The population of West Georgia was politically more active than that of the eastern part. For example, the province of Guria was almost entirely seized by the ideas of Social Democracy, to such an extent that even Lenin admired the existence in Georgia of "the most efficient Party organizations" and he called the peasant movement in Guria "the most advanced" (Lenin 1905: 368, 391). Lenin could not have foreseen that the majority of the Georgian Social Democrats, who later won many supporters in both Georgian gubernias and became very influential in the All-Russia Party, would take the side of the Mensheviks, his more liberal opponents in the Party. Among the Georgian Bolsheviks (i.e. the members of the radical faction of Lenin) only Joseph Jugashvili (better known by his party pseudonym – Stalin) later became a prominent figure.

The First Republic

The revolutionary cataclysms of 1917 in Russia and the sudden fall of the Empire created unexpected conditions for the appearance of new States in the outlying regions of the agonizing Empire. After the defeat of Russia in the war and the signing of the separate Treaty of Brest–Litovsk in March 1918, independent States emerged in the Transcaucasus (Georgia, Armenia and Azerbaijan). Naturally, the Central powers stimulated this process; before its final defeat in the war, Germany assisted Georgia in particular in the State-building process, of course with its own interests in the mind. As the best organized and most numerous political party, the Social Democrats (Menshevik faction) had the honour to head the independent Georgian State declared on 26 May 1918. Although according to their internationalist ideology, the Social Democratic Party of Georgia would not have followed the line of secession from Russia, the chaos in the former Empire obliged them to turn into patriots. Such a duality to some extent hindered their efforts in State-building. On one side, they had to fight for its borders and to suppress separatists; on the other, the common Marxist ideology made them consider the Bolsheviks still their "Party brethren" (albeit gone far astray!). In fact the Bolsheviks were carrying out subversive activities, such as organizing uprisings in the areas settled by the Ossetians, out of their desire to annex Georgia to the "Brotherhood of the Proletariat" (i.e. Soviet Russia) and to follow the path of "World Revolution".

Nevertheless, the actual ideological basis of the government of the Democratic Republic of Georgia (the official name of the State) was European-style democratic socialism, which differed in its essence from the Russian model of socialism. Georgian democratic socialism, taking into account the realities of the country, was mostly orientated to the middle classes of society as its means of support, whereas the Bolsheviks considered them their major enemy (Surguladze 1991: 202).

Article 6 of the Declaration of Independence of Georgia, stated that "within its boundaries the Republic equally guarantees all civil and political rights to its citizens irrespective of their nationality, religion, social status and sex". Later this phrase reverberated within the Constitution of Georgia adopted on 21 February 1921. According to this Constitution (Article 107), autonomy was again guaranteed to Abkhazia, a right that was already recognized by the Georgian government in 1918 (Menteshashvili 1993), to Adjara ("Muslim Georgia") and to Saingilo (i.e. the Zakatala region, now part of Azerbaijan). The same day, the Constituent Assembly adopted "the Statute of the Autonomous Rule of Abkhazia", according to which Abkhazia was granted full rights of managing its internal affairs, as long as it remained an inseparable part of the Republic of Georgia (Surguladze 1992: 209). However, the Constitution of Georgia had no chance to start operating, as in just four days (sic!) after its adoption, Tbilisi was occupied by the attacking Red Army of the Bolsheviks.

The defeat of Germany and its allies in the First World War untied the hands of the Entente in the Middle East. But the European powers had shown no active interest in the Transcaucasus, other than the oil-rich Baku area, chiefly because they still considered the new States to be within the sphere of influence of the Russian Empire, albeit called now "RSFSR" or "Bolshevik Russia". Thus, Great Britain and France passively watched the Bolshevik expansion to the south.

Nevertheless, on 7 May 1920 the independence of the Democratic Republic of Georgia was recognized by Soviet Russia. The treaty was signed in Moscow with the consent of Lenin and, only after this act, *de jure* recognitions followed from Great Britain, France, Japan, Italy, Germany, Belgium and others. Previously, Georgia had been recognized only by Argentina. The USA never recognized the independence of Georgia. Soviet Russia, by Article 4 of the Treaty, officially recognized the borders of the new State to comprise the following former parts of the Russian Empire: Tbilisi and Kutaisi provinces, including Sokhumi, Batumi and Zakatala regions (Surguladze 1991: 339). Thus, Georgia was officially restored within its historical and ethnic boundaries. However, just as a century earlier in the case of the Treaty of Georgievsk, Russia (now Soviet) very soon violated the Moscow Treaty. Using as an excuse a feigned "popular uprising" in the disputed area between Armenia, already under Soviet rule, and Georgia, Bolshevik Russia attacked the country from different sides. This invasion was hypocritically called "help to the proletariat in revolt", even though the workers fought in the Georgian army. On 25 February 1921, Tbilisi fell. The Socialist Soviet Republic of Georgia was proclaimed. Nominally, the Georgian SSR was considered an independent State up to the end of 1922, when it was incorporated into the Transcaucasian Federation, one of the founders of the Soviet Union. In practice, it was ruled from Moscow. The Social Democratic government, which proved unable to organize proper resistance to the Bolsheviks, emigrated to France in hope of securing political support from the European powers, but in fact merely received sincere condolences.

The three years of independence, in spite of being so short a time, and in spite of serious economic and political difficulties, had great political and cultural significance. There were serious achievements in the sphere of education. More than a thousand new schools were opened and textbooks in the mother tongue were published, the University and Conservatoire were established in Tbilisi, the first Georgian opera was staged, the national theatre revived. From the political point of view, it was important that the territorial integrity was internationally recognized.

Communist Georgia (the Second Republic)

After Sovietization, the boundaries of Georgia were changed, but not in its favour. Almost 16000 km^2 of its territory were ceded to neighbouring States, along with 300000 population.

Even worse results followed the formation of State-type structures within Georgia. Apprehending attempts to restore the independence of Georgia, Moscow created its "delayed action mines". A secret report of the Russian Military Attache, General P. Sitin, to the Russian Government (dated 22–30 April 1921, disclosed in 1993) laid firm foundations to suppress Georgian aspirations to restore its independence. It urged that the most reliable measure would be "the dismembering of the Republic of Georgia into a number of autonomous units; the smaller these units, the more they will be subject to the influence of the RSFSR" (Sitin 1921). It seems that this advice was well followed by the Kremlin. The declaration on 4 March 1921 by the Abkhaz Bolsheviks of a separate Soviet Socialist Republic was encouraged. The Abkhaz numbered at that time about 50000 people, who were by no means a majority in the area. However, at the end of the same year, with the consent of Lenin (who was still in good health), the Abkhazian SSR was once more attached to Georgia as a "treaty Republic". The Constitution of the USSR of 1924 (Basic Law 1931) did not recognize Abkhazia as a "Union Republic" and treated it in fact as an autonomous republic within Georgia, a status that was made official in 1931.

It is worth noting that in the early stages of Soviet power there were other "States" such as the Crimean SSR, the Terek, Don, Stavropol and Odessa Soviet Republics, the Far Eastern Republic, the Khorezm and Bukhara Peoples Socialist Republics, which were later, while Lenin was still alive, abolished or given lower status (Daines 1993). The modern Nakhichevan Autonomous Republic within Azerbaijan until the mid-1930s had been called "Nakhichevan Socialist Soviet Republic" and was considered to be a protectorate of Soviet Azerbaijan (Article 52 of the Constitution of the latter; Vinogradov 1933). Thus, the change in status of Abkhazia within Georgia was not an extraordinary event for the Kremlin, carried out by "Georgian Stalin who decreed that Abkhazia was to be subordinated to Georgia only in 1931!" (Hewitt 1993b).

According to an agreement between Moscow and Ankara, an Autonomous Republic was created in Adjara. Paradoxically for the atheist Bolsheviks, the basis was confessional, not ethnic; the local population were the Georgian Muslims.

The strongest antipathy amongst the Georgians was caused by the creation in north-central Georgia of an Autonomous Region (oblast) for the local Ossetians, who totalled about 65 000 in the area, as a reward for their great zeal in the struggle for Soviet power against the legal government of the Republic of Georgia. The small Georgian town of Tskhinvali, inhabited mostly by Georgian Jews and Christians, was made the centre of the oblast. Although the designation of the autonomous areas of Abkhazia and Adjara was guaranteed by the Constitution of Georgia of 1921, the Ossetians were not considered by public opinion as deserving territorial autonomy, since they were relatively recent migrants from their north Caucasian homeland, where the majority of them still lived, and by that time, 1922, Soviet Russia had not given that homeland any autonomy at all. North Ossetia was designed only in 1924. One of the arguments was that Ossetians had never lived in Tskhinvali before. The other arguments (signed, incidentally, by the People's Commissar for Internal Affairs of the Georgian SSR, a Bolshevik himself) included such geographical ones as "inaccessibility of the territory", "the absence of internal economic ties and of an integrated geographical region", "the scattered character of the Ossetian settlements", and so on (From the History, 1991: 60–73). None of these arguments affected the final decision of the Kremlin, and the Autonomous Region was created. It was given the name "South Ossetia", stressing that it is the southern part of a "single Ossetia", whereas "the territory was not Ossetia at all but primordial central Georgia, where the Ossetians gradually became the prevailing population in recent centuries. Primordial Ossetia is the so-called North Ossetia", as a neutral, non-Georgian expert on ethnic relations has written (Arutyunov 1992: 71).

A modern Turkish scholar comments of these territorial manipulations:

... like its predecessor Russia, Soviet policy (in Georgia) was to encourage ethnic differences and for this purpose, several political jurisdictions were created on the basis of ethno-territorial distinctions. Although this division created a sense of political and ethnic distinctiveness among minority elites, it also turned them into machines of patronage along ethnic lines and discouraged nation-building. (Tashan 1993)

The internal policy of early Soviet rule in Georgia was disastrous. Up to 1500 churches, mosques and synagogues were closed in the 1920s, their property seized, and the number of clergy dramatically decreased. Private property of land was abolished and the Bolsheviks encouraged the poor peasants to take the land from the nobility and rich farmers and to drive them out of their dwellings. Repressions against the intellectuals increased. The Red Terror reached an especially large scale after the anti-Bolshevik uprising of August, 1924. Although the revolt began simultaneously in different parts of the country, its leadership was arrested at an early stage and the uprising was suppressed in blood. It provided a good excuse also to blot out the nobility. Later, the mass purges of 1937–8 were once again directed against the remnants of the Georgian nobility and intellectuals, although many Communist Party functionaries were also obliterated. In Georgia tens of thousands of people were shot or banished, although the exact figures have never been disclosed. Representatives of all the nationalities suffered from the Bolshevik terror; no ethnic group was left intact.

In order to weaken the "obstinate Georgian nationalists", the three Transcaucasian republics were united into a Federation in 1922. The authorities of the Federation, located in Tbilisi, were not permitted to be mono-national, nor could they use the language of any one of the largest, but not dominant nationalities, Georgian, Armenian or Azeri Turkic. The official language could only be Russian. The inevitable internal controversies would have never allowed any possibility of the Federation uniting against the Centre. Thus, in this case the famous Roman motto, without losing its essence, changed in superficial appearance to "Unite and rule!".

A leading group of Georgian Bolsheviks objected to Stalin's idea of weakening the Soviet Republics and paradoxically were supported by Lenin (1922), who by then was mortally ill. Later, the majority of these Georgian Bolshevik "*natsional-uklonisty*" ("nationalist-deviators") were shot as "enemies of the people" and "spies of international imperialism". However, when the Soviet power felt itself strong enough, once again by Moscow's decision, the Transcaucasian Federation was dissolved (1936).

According to all versions (1924, 1936, 1977) of the Soviet Constitution, all the Union republics were nominally declared to be "sovereign States", which had "entered the Union by their own will" and had the right of "free withdrawal" from the Union. "The Imperial authorities considered the 'sovereignty' of Georgia (as well as of all the other Union Republics) an annoying formality, the full legal abolition of which was inexpedient from a tactical point of view" (Shevardnadze 1993a). However, that very same article in the Soviet Constitution legalized the division of the USSR into 15 independent States in 1991.

It would be unfair not to mention that the Soviet Union, perhaps against the conscious will of its rulers, actually helped to forge most of the new nations. It is a different question to what extent they are mature and viable now that independence has been acquired. As an American expert concluded in his book, "Against the original expectations of many observers, the most complete consolidation of the Georgians as a nation came in the first seven decades of Soviet power" (Suni 1988: 318).

In the Soviet republics, the same sort of ethnodemographic policy of population intermixing was carried out as in the frontier provinces of the Russian Empire, but this time more intensively. From the end of the 1920s and the beginning of large-scale industrialization, in all the non-Slavic Union Republics the proportion of Russians, Ukrainians, and Byelorussians sharply increased. The last two groups, outside their republics, Russified very fast. This increase in the number of Slavs was aimed at the "reinforcing of the working class". As a result, the proportion of ethnic Georgians in the republic's population, as well as that of ethnic Abkhaz in the Autonomous Republic, decreased dramatically in the 1930s (see Fig. 4.1).

It is unjust to blame this "demographic expansion" on the Slavic, or any other, peoples. This very policy eventually led to the almost complete depopulation of the core area of Russia proper, yet did not give any advantages to the ethnic Russians on a personal level. "The unitary Soviet State, with its ideologized line promoting 'the flourishing and growing together of nations' has in general had to 'pay' for the union in terms of a diminished investment in the social benefits and culture of the dominant ethnic group" (Tishkov 1991: 211). At least in the Soviet Transcaucasus, the quite numerous Russians did not feel themselves to be an exclusively privileged people, as representatives of the "Nation-Conqueror".

Nevertheless, on the highest State level – in Moscow, in the army, in the sphere of foreign relations – all the *"Natsmeny"* (*natsional'niye menshinstva*, or non-Russian national minorities) had their very restricted quota and had to know "their place". Stalin, of *natsmen* descent himself, understood that he was building the Russian State, and he admitted, by acquiescence, that the Soviet Union was the direct successor to the Russian Empire. This became more apparent during and immediately after the Second World War, when even the most violent anti-bolshevik emigrants from Russia recognized in Stalin the true torch-bearer of the cause of the Tsars.

Industrial development, a very progressive process in essence, in the Soviet Union served first of all the policy of centralization and militarization, without which the very existence of the USSR was impossible, since it was not built on the basis of the mutual interests of its citizens or ethnic groups. With the political target of the total integration of the country, the CPSU ("Centre", "Kremlin", "Moscow") artificially interwove the economic ties between the Union Republics to make their economic and, thus, political independence impossible. The 1990s have demonstrated "the magnificent results" of these efforts; most of the Newly Independent States (NIS) cannot achieve "economic independence". Georgia, poor in natural resources and, moreover, involved in endless internal conflicts, found itself in a very poor economic position.

From another point of view, industrialization under communist rule bequeathed the NIS quite a substantial industrial infrastructure and also promoted major changes in the social structure of the population. In Georgia these changes were revealed in a massive growth of the working class at the expense of the peasantry, albeit the latter is still large in number. The proportion of white-collar workers has increased. Social mobility has intensified. The educational level of the population has risen (see Ch. 3).

In spite of the happy news in Party newspapers that the "nationality problem in the USSR is solved forever", ethnic relations were aggravated. Each ethnocratic elite tried to accumulate on "its territory" the maximum material wealth. Each national intelligentsia continued to bring up its people in the spirit of patriotism. The vigilant Communist Party often detected forbidden "nationalism" in this activity and punished the guilty. The peculiarity of Georgia was that, at least nominally, the State language was Georgian, a survival of the independence of 1918–21. The constitutions of the majority of the other republics lacked a similar article.

In practice this never meant that the only official language was Georgian. On the contrary, Russian was more extensively used; in the Abkhaz and South Ossetian autonomous areas, Russian was the actual official language. But that article in the constitution was considered to be an instrument to resist assimilation. In April 1978, in course of public discussion of the proposal for a new constitution for the Georgian SSR, which was modelled on the 1977 Soviet constitution, it was discovered that this very article on the national status of the Georgian language was absent. Public opinion understood this as the next step to Russification. For the first time in the history of the USSR, thousands of people organized a political demonstration in Tbilisi on April 14, which ended with the full satisfaction of the demands of the demonstrators – the article was restored.

Joy in the "national victory" was darkened very soon. The Abkhaz demanded the annexation of the Autonomous Republic to the RSFSR and the introduction of Abkhaz and Russian, without Georgian, as the State languages of Abkhazia. According to the population census of January 1979, the Abkhaz made up 17 per cent of the total population of the Autonomous Republic, whereas the Georgians constituted 43 per cent. The latter were not asked where they preferred to live. On this occasion the Kremlin "conceded" to Georgia, leaving its boundaries intact. In fact, the initiation of new border delimitation might have been a bad precedent in the multinational country. At the same time, Georgian was left as one of the State languages in Abkhazia, although in practice almost never used as such. To satisfy the other side, an Abkhaz State University (with teaching predominantly in Russian) and State television in the native language were opened (Slider 1985). Unofficially, additional quotas were given to the ethnic Abkhaz in crucial governmental positions and in the local Party leadership. The proportion of representatives of the titular nationality in these positions exceeded 50 per cent. In a bureaucratic State this meant real domination of one ethnic group in all the spheres of economic, social and political life.

All this might have been considered quite a fair decision. People, even the least numerous, must have opportunity to study and to watch TV in the language they prefer, whether native or any other. They must manage their own affairs. But these concessions did not satisfy the Abkhaz ethnocracy, while making the Georgians even more suspicious. The roots of alienation were already very deep. In 1989 the claim for the secession of Abkhazia was repeated again. This led to open conflict.

The weakening of centralized power in the USSR during *perestroyka* inevitably provided an opportunity for the rise of national movements. Such a multinational State as the Soviet Union could have existed only under harsh one-party control. Lenin understood this and so did his best disciple Stalin. It was not able to transform peacefully into a democracy; it seems as if Gorbachev did not want to understand this. Where national feelings secretly seethed in the people, as in the Baltic republics, Georgia, Armenia, Moldova, and the Western Ukraine, national movements came out from underground earlier and correspondingly received the worst retaliatory blows.

The reverberations of the Tbilisi tragedy of 9 April 1989, when the break-up of a mass rally by units of the Soviet Army and the All-Union Ministry of Internal Affairs resulted in more than 20 deaths and hundreds of casualties, shattered the image of the Soviet leaders following the narrow path of democratization and gave strong arguments to their opponents. The worst blow was suffered by the Communist Party of Georgia, which completely lost face, while the national movement, comprising among its leaders quite a few influential populists and demagogues, won many new supporters among people who earlier had been rather neutral. On 28 October 1990, for the first time in the USSR, multiparty elections to the Supreme Council were held in Georgia. The Communist Party of Georgia was defeated. The largest opposition bloc of radical parties, "Round Table – Free Georgia", for whom the people voted as the alternative to the "hated communists", came to power. Only later it became clear that the people of Georgia had to pay dearly for their loyalty to the new populist leaders, who were ignorant of the real possibilities for the economic development of the country, and who drastically worsened relations with Moscow and the local ethnic minorities (Jones 1993b).

On the eve of the elections, the communist leaders of the South Ossetian Autonomous Oblast decided that it was the best time to raise the status of the oblast, and on 20 September 1990 they unilaterally declared the creation of a "South Ossetian Soviet Democratic Republic" (later renamed "Republic of South Ossetia"), within the USSR. As the act contradicted the existing Constitutions of the Georgian SSR and the USSR, the next day it was abrogated by the Presidium of the Supreme Council of the Georgian SSR (still communist-dominated), and even Moscow did not openly support the South Ossetian cause. On 11 December 1990, the Ossetian leaders passed a resolution subordinating all local State and legal structures to the USSR (Appeal 1990). The newly elected Supreme Council of Georgia (non-communist dominated), after formally trying in vain to persuade the Ossetian leaders to abandon their course towards actual secession, hurried the same day to abolish the autonomous unit totally. Thus, the stubbornness of the politicians led to a bloody ethnic conflict where the victims, as usual, were the ordinary people.

The restoration of independence and after (the Third Republic)

After a nationwide referendum on 31 March 1991, when an absolute majority of the population voted for independence, the Supreme Council of the Republic of Georgia (the country's new name) passed the Restoration of Independence Act on 9 April 1991. However, this Act acquired real international legal significance only after the official denunciation of the Union Treaty of 1922, which occurred in Alma-Ata on 22 December 1991, when the Soviet Union was formally dissolved. The 12 Union Republics (the three Baltic republics had seceded some months earlier) became independent and 11 of them, without Georgia, announced the formation of the Commonwealth of Independent States (CIS). At that very moment, Georgia became involved in the gravest internal political crisis. A split among the irresponsible leaders of the ruling bloc led to a destructive military confrontation in the centre of the capital – the "Tbilisi war" from 21 December 1991 to 6 January 1992 – and to the ousting of President Gamsakhurdia. The victorious side formed a Military Council, which declared that it was taking all power into its hands.

This war was the natural result of the lack of political culture and democratic traditions, apart from the subjective factors of the actual leadership, which by its declarations and actions isolated itself from the international community and alienated influential circles within the country. The conflict can to some extent be ascribed to the revenge of the former political elite, which was too rapidly removed from the helm by the new people. The latter were "considered 'parvenus' or 'provincials' by the established cultural elite, who resented the loss of their own status as the voice and conscience of the people" (Jones 1993b).

However, suspicions about a "skilful control of the process" from the outside also cannot be entirely ruled out. Both sides were obtaining arms from the Russian armed forces still quartered in Georgia, and the side preferable to the Russians received more (Batiashvili 1994). In any case, the political results of the action cannot be given a single explanation such as "a revolt against provincial fascism", "a military coup", "a mutiny against legal government", "a struggle for power", and so on. All these and some other labels carry some applicability. But from the point of view of the overall development of society, the worst is that the taboo on bloodshed has been abrogated and other mechanisms of deterrence demolished, at least for time being. Once the acting Military Council of Georgia realized that it was unlikely to receive recognition from the international community, an invitation followed to Edouard Shevardnadze, the former Minister of Foreign Affairs of the USSR.

Shevardnadze returned to his homeland in March 1992, to head the newly established State Council. The common people, who felt that the country was on the brink of chaos, heading into political, economic and social catastrophe, put all their trust in this political figure and almost unanimously voted for him as the Chairman of the new Parliament in the 11 October 1992 Parliamentary elections. Later, he was elected by the Parliament as Head of State as well. The elections formally restored democracy in the country. The problem of finding a way out of international isolation was speedily solved. The "Shevardnadze factor" secured recognition of the independence and territorial integrity of Georgia on the international level and by all its neighbours. The country was received as a member of the United Nations and the CSCE. The Western world gave it substantial humanitarian and other support to avoid mass famine over the following several years.

Meanwhile, it appeared next to impossible to halt the dangerous trends in the country's economic development. Crisis was inevitable, because the established economic system had collapsed and the country was too dependent on the import of energy sources. Economic ties with Russia were virtually cut off and not only because of Georgian actions. Once Russia imposed world prices on its fuel and raw materials, which had been imported earlier at very low price, the industrial output of Georgia more than halved. By the end of 1993, it had dropped to the

1964 level and was continuing to fall. Transport, industry and agriculture were seriously hindered by the shortage of fuel. Export opportunities diminished dramatically. The introduction of the new Russian currency pushed Georgia out of the ruble zone, while the provisional local currency, introduced as the alternative from 5 April 1993, proved to be weak and hyperinflation ruined the population. Unemployment has grown immensely.

It is worth noting *en passant* that Georgia might have been more viable as a purely agrarian society. For example, the "1918 model" of independent Georgia, where more than 80 per cent of the population were rural and mostly self-subsistent, where electric energy was restricted to the capital city, and where transport was by railway using local coal, oxen or horses, was economically in a much better position than the "1991 model" of independent Georgia, where more than half the population was urban, agriculture was highly specialized in industrial crops orientated only towards the Soviet (i.e. Russian) market and thus politically vulnerable, and electricity production and transport were dependent entirely on expensive imported oil and gas.

The activity of Georgia at the international level and its obvious inclination, based on current global realities, to carry out a foreign policy, which if not more pro-Western was at least more balanced, were probably in themselves a cause of jealousy at the centre of the former Empire, which would not be anxious to have a "too independent" new neighbour in the south. The very "Shevardnadze factor" probably created a negative attitude to Georgia on the part of the Russian generals, as they could not forgive him his decisive role in the ending of the "Cold War" and the withdrawal of Soviet Army from eastern Europe and Afghanistan.

With all its other neighbours, Georgia signed full-scale treaties and normalized its relations in 1992 and early 1993; Russia, as a condition of signing such a treaty, stipulated serious concessions by Georgia in its internal affairs, using the ethnic tensions as an excuse. Signing a full-scale treaty with Russia on 3 February 1994 became possible only after Tbilisi had finally to kneel before Russia after its defeat in the civil war in Abkhazia, a defeat that would have been less probable were it not for the Russian involvement. Under this Treaty, Russian military bases in Georgia are to be given legal status.

In all fairness it must be admitted that Georgian political leaders and parties themselves prepared a fertile soil for the seeds of internal ethnic conflicts and foreign power involvement. This was more particularly the case with the early national leadership, which did everything possible to cut the ties with Russia and to alienate the strongest participant in the geopolitical game in the Caucasus. Unluckily, the series of political errors did not end with the ousting of that leadership. The Military Council restored the Constitution of 1921, which had never been formally abrogated, but which contained some anachronisms that actually made its operation impossible. To some extent it created grounds for "legal nihilism" in the country. Internal political issues deteriorated. Despite the halting by mid-1992 of the bloody conflict in former South Ossetia ("Tskhinvali region") after major concessions on the Georgian side, including inviting in Russian peace-keeping forces, a solution of the problem was simply postponed. The efforts of the new government in Tbilisi to establish peace in the country, such as a total amnesty to political adversaries, appeals for national consensus and reconciliation with the supporters of the previous government, were all in vain. Independent Georgia has not lived a single day in peace, and the shadows of its territorial disintegration have become darker.

In the autumn of 1991, elections to the Supreme Council of the Abkhazian ASSR had been held. By an amendment of 27 August to the Electoral Law, introduced with the consent of President Gamsakhurdia, a certain gerrymandering on an ethnic basis was perpetrated during the elections. Of 65 constituencies, 28 were created specially for the ethnic Abkhaz candidates, 26 were for the ethnic Georgians and the remaining 11 were for the other ethnic groups (Law of the Abkhazian ASSR 1991). This meant that the 43 per cent "Abkhaz constituencies", representing 18 per cent of the electorate, were three to five times smaller than those of the Georgians or "the others"; 40 per cent of the constituencies represented 46 per cent of the ethnic Georgian population and the 36 per cent of the voters constituted by the other ethnic groups were even more underrepresented, with only 17 per cent of constituencies.

Taking advantage of the internal unrest in Georgia, the ethnic Abkhaz members of the Supreme Council of the Autonomous Republic, in direct violation of their own Constitution and without consent of the ethnic Georgian members of the Supreme Council, on 23 July 1992 passed the Law of the Restoration of the Constitution of the Abkhazian SSR of 1925. The constitutional changes required a two-thirds majority of deputies, whereas the act was passed by a simple majority. By Article 4 of the restored Constitution in its original version, "The SSR of Abkhazia, united on the basis of a special Union Treaty with the SSR of Georgia, enters through it the Transcaucasian Socialist Federative Soviet Republic [extinct since 1936] and as a part of the latter enters the Union of Soviet Socialist Republics". To say nothing of the anachronism of this Constitution, it must be added that according to official data, this version of the constitution was never published and had not acquired legal force (Toidze 1994).

Even earlier, in preparation for armed conflict, the leadership of the Autonomous Republic started building mono-ethnic (Abkhaz) military units, directly subordinated to the Chairman of the Supreme Council. Customs procedures were introduced on the River Inguri, the border of the Autonomous Republic with Georgia. The self-proclaimed Confederation of the Peoples of the Caucasus, based in the Russian Federation, supported the separatist cause inside Georgia (see Ch. 9) and started to gather its troops in the area. All these steps were presumably directed to provoke the Georgian leadership to commit a political error. In the prevailing conditions, such errors were easily predictable. The command of the poorly disciplined armed forces of Georgia, where the most important positions were held by non-professional military, had just got rid of the previous government and did not completely obey the new civil government either.

In August 1992 the Georgian National Guard was given some obsolete armoured weaponry from the arsenals of the former Soviet Army, as the quota allotted to this NIS. Russian military intelligence knew to whom and when to give the arms, and fatal steps followed very soon (Batiashvili 1994). The legitimate aim of the State to take control of transport communications within one of its provinces (Abkhazia), which were constantly cut off by supporters of the former president, was fulfilled in a clumsy manner by the Georgian military forces (Mikadze, Shevelyov 1993). Beginning this action was manna for the Abkhaz separatists, allowing them to accuse the Tbilisi government of the "invasion of a sovereign State" (sic). As a Russian author has argued, the start of war was desirable to the Abkhaz leaders, who were inspired by, and relied upon, the real help of some influential forces in Russia connected with the Supreme Council of the Russian Federation, in opposition to their own President, and even more closely connected with the former Soviet, now Russian, military–industrial complex (Chervonnaya 1994).

It must be admitted that the Abkhaz leadership met the conflict quite well organized, and were masterly in using the controversies between Georgia and Russia. On the other hand, the Georgian leadership was not unanimous in its decisions, Georgian society as a whole and the ethnic Georgian community in Abkhazia in particular, were torn in a bitter internal strife between the supporters of the ousted president, the so-called "Zviadists", and their adversaries. This made the demographic superiority of the Georgians in the area of conflict a mere formality. Ex-President Gamsakhurdia relied upon promises, later proved to be false, from the Abkhaz side that they "will not touch his supporters in Abkhazia". Consequently, he prevented his quite substantial forces, as well as the bulk of the Georgian population in Gali and Ochamchire districts, from participation in the war on the side of "the Tbilisi junta forces". The deceived people of those districts had to pay with their property and even with their lives for their confidence in such promises.

Instead, Gamsakhurdia stirred up the Georgian civil war, which entered its final stage on 15 September 1993. This action, synchronized with a major offensive by the separatists, played a decisive role in the 1993 campaign in Abkhazia. The Georgian civil war took place mostly in the West Georgian provinces of Samegrelo, Imereti and Guria, which suffered the worst. Some towns – Poti, Senaki, Abasha, Samtredia, Khobi and Khoni – and many villages changed hands several times, and were destroyed and looted. This ruined the population of a once flourishing area, although fatalities and casualties were minimal; no general battle was fought. The government troops were victorious and the Georgian civil war in effect ended in November 1993. One of the major factors in this outcome was the official support given by the Russian Federation to the Tbilisi government, after the latter declared the adherence of Georgia to the CIS (see below), and the subsequent landing of Russian marines in Poti. Although not actually participating in the warfare, the presence of these troops demoralized the supporters of Gamsakhurdia, who had earlier been confident that certain influential military groups in Russia supported only them.

The civil war in Abkhazia, which began on 14 August 1992, turned out to be the worst event in the contemporary history of Georgia. Its visible results were a massive loss of life on both sides, a ruined economy, the destruction of Sokhumi, the regional capital, and hundreds of thousands of internally displaced persons (IDP). The local population, often related to one another, became bitter enemies.

From a geographical point of view, it is worth mentioning that the Georgian armed forces never actually entered the major areas of Abkhaz settlement, apart from six or seven villages situated along the major roads. The centre of the separatist movement, Gudauta, was left intact during the whole war. The city of Sokhumi was mostly destroyed by Russian military aviation and artillery in the Abkhaz service, while the city was in Georgian hands. The majority of the city's population before the war had been Georgian. For most of the war, the Georgian forces were in control of the littoral area southeast of Sokhumi, where ethnic Georgians were the vast majority. Control of the border with the Russian Federation was lost by the Georgian side in the early stages of the war. Although nominally controlled from the Russian side, this border was easily penetrable by armed forces (Russian Cossacks, ethnic north Caucasian volunteers, mercenary officers from the former Soviet Army), military supplies and economic aid from various, perhaps non-governmental, organizations in Russia. Without these very substantial supplies and aid, the separatist cause was doomed to defeat.

Dramatic demographic changes took place in Abkhazia in 1993. On 16 September 1993, the separatists and their allies breached the cease-fire, brokered by the Russian government, and captured the regional capital Sokhumi on September 27. The major reasons for the defeat were the serious shortcomings of the Georgian civil and military leaders (Batiashvili 1994). After the rest of the territory of the Autonomous Republic was occupied by the separatists, more than 200000 ethnic Georgian civilians, from both urban and rural areas, fled the inevitable massacre in panic, mostly on foot, through narrow and steep mountain passes over 2600m above sea level, where at least 400 children, women and elderly people died from exhaustion, starvation and cold. This was the only available route, as the roads in the lowland area were blocked by the Georgian civil war. According to foreign eyewitnesses, those ethnic Georgians that dared to stay in their dwellings were mercilessly slaughtered, their houses either burned down or settled by the north Caucasian and other "volunteers" fighting on the side of the Abkhaz (Chelnokov 1993, Rotar 1993a). At the same time there were also reports of examples of selfless assistance by the local Abkhaz, Armenians and Russians to their Georgian neighbours.

The civil war in Abkhazia was seen by most experts as an "ethnic conflict". But perhaps it was most accurately described by a Russian observer as a "thrilling military–political operation, with an Abkhazian bias, for the "voluntary" involvement of Georgia in the Commonwealth of Independent States (CIS)" (Anin 1994). On 8 October 1993, Georgia, in stalemate as a result of the disastrous civil wars, had to declare its incorporation within the Russia-dominated Commonwealth of Independent States. Georgia was the last of the former Union Republics to do this, apart from the Baltic Republics, which are protected by the Western powers. The act has not received equal approval from the different political parties in Georgia, but it seemed at this tragic moment of the country's history, that its people would have supported any reasonable measure that could lead to peace and security. Many resolutions of the UN Security Council, in which separatism, the violation of the territorial integrity of a UN member-country and demographic cleansing were condemned, led to no practical results.

In May 1994, an agreement was reached between the Georgian and Abkhazian sides and the Russian Federation on a start to the return of the IDP to Abkhazia and on some other issues aimed to normalize the situation. Russian military forces on behalf of the CIS started to carry out peace-keeping functions and in the first stage actually made the River Inguri a heavily guarded border between Georgia and its province of Abkhazia.

The UN Security Council, after some hesitation, agreed with the interested side (Russia) to carry out peace-keeping functions in a neighbouring country, and the UN sent its observers to the area. But because of mutual distrust, the restoration of the demographic status quo and, even more, the achievement of a full political solution, will take long time. It is clear that the peaceful solution of internal conflicts will be the major prerequisite for a return to normal political, economic and social life in the country.

CHAPTER 3
Population

According to the last Soviet all-Union population census of 12 January 1989, the population of Georgia present at the census 5 456 000, the permanent population being a little less at 5 401 000. In terms of population, Georgia almost equals Scotland and exceeds such European nations as Denmark, Ireland, Norway, Finland, Slovakia, Lithuania, Latvia, Estonia, Moldova, Slovenia and Albania. Among its neighbours, Georgia has a slightly larger population than Armenia, but has fallen behind Azerbaijan since the early 1960s. Its population is 11 times smaller than that of Turkey, with the gap tending to widen, and 30 times smaller than the Russian Federation. Among the 15 former Soviet Union Republics, Georgia with 2 per cent of the USSR population was in seventh place.

Population dynamics

According to an estimate at the beginning of the nineteenth century, the population of Georgia within its modern boundaries was 785 000 (Jaosvili 1984: 69). By the end of that century, the population had more than doubled, reaching 1 900 000. During the twentieth century, the population experienced substantial growth (Table 3.1, Fig 3.1), save for the end of the 1910s, when influenced by the First World War and the fall of the Russian Empire, and again in the 1940s, when the Second World War caused heavy loss of the male population of Georgia, estimated at 210 000–220 000 (Natmeladze 1993: 46), even though its territory was not occupied by the Nazis.

The fastest growth of population was observed during the interwar period; from 1926 to 1939, annual growth amounted to 23.6 per thousand, because of continuing high birthrate and rapidly falling mortality rate, and also significantly because of the large flow of in-migrants from the other Soviet republics. Over the past three decades, a decline in population growth rate has become increasingly apparent; between 1959 and 1989 the annual growth rate was 8.8 per thousand.

In recent years, as a result of the collapse of the USSR, out-migration of population, including that of ethnic Georgians, has been gaining ground. In addition, the permanent internal wars since 1990 and the total economic crisis in the country

Population

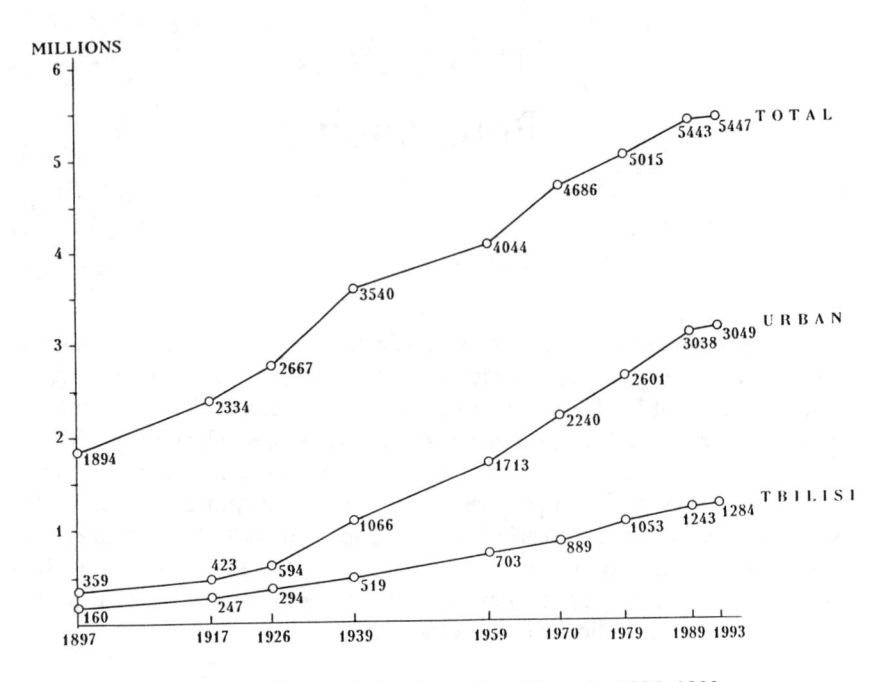

Figure 3.1 The population dynamics of Georgia, 1897–1993.

Table 3.1 Population dynamics of Georgia (1897–1993)(available population figures)

Years	Total	Urban		Rural		Male	Female
	1000s	1000s	%	1000s	%	%	%
1897	1894.2	359.0	19.0	1535.2	81.0	53.4	46.6
1913*	2601.0	666.0	25.6	1935.0	74.4	...	...
1920*	2408.0	481.0	20.0	1927.0	80.0	...	...
1926	2666.5	594.2	22.3	2072.3	77.7	50.5	49.5
1939	3540.0	1066.2	30.1	2473.8	69.9	49.9	50.1
1959	4044.0	1712.9	42.9	2331.1	57.6	46.1	53.9
1970	4686.4	2239.8	47.8	2446.6	52.2	47.0	53.5
1979	5014.8	2601.0	51.9	2415.0	48.1	47.0	53.0
1989	5443.4	3035.8	55.8	2407.6	44.2	47.4	52.6
1991*	5464.2	3073.0	56.2	2391.2	43.8	47.5	52.5
1993†	5447.1	3048.8	56.0	2398.3	44.0	47.5	52.5

Source: Population Censuses.
* [Population, 1991]
† Estimate of the Committee of Socio-Economic Information of Georgia

have also affected the trends in population dynamics. In the 1990s an absolute decline of population can be observed, from 5464000 in 1991 to 5407100 by 1 January 1995 and in all likelihood it will decline even more in the immediate future.

Geographical distribution of population and urbanization

The mountainous terrain means that only 36.1 per cent of the area of Georgia is really inhabited (Jaoshvili 1968: 181). Ninety per cent of the population live in the intermontane lowland at elevations not exceeding 1000m above sea level. The population is unevenly distributed between East and West Georgia, with 57 and 43 per cent respectively. The eastern part includes 64 per cent of the urban population, because Tbilisi, the largest metropolitan region, is situated there. Rural population is distributed more equally: 52 per cent in West Georgia and 48 per cent in the eastern part of the country.

Among the rural Social Regions, the most populous are Imereti (9.9% of the total), Kvemo Kartli and Kakheti (8.2–8.3%), whereas the least populous are the northern highland regions (Table 1.1). The uneven distribution of population is seen in Figure 3.2, showing population density by districts and CRSs. Average density in Georgia is 76 persons per km^2; in urban areas, highest density is reached in Batumi (7038 per km^2) and in rural areas, in Khelvachauri district (210 per km^2). In the capital city, Tbilisi, which has an official area of 365km^2, the population density in 1989 was 3564 persons per km^2. Density is over 100 persons per km^2 in the lowland areas of western Georgia and Kakheti province. The lowest density is in the mountainous Mestia district (western Kavkasioni), with 5.6 persons per km^2. However, if density is measured against the agricultural land, that same Mestia district, where land-hungry peasants till small plots of land, has one of the highest densities in rural Georgia.

The urban population of Georgia has grown steadily, especially in the second half of the twentieth century. Nevertheless, the rate of urbanization was not as high as in some neighbouring countries. For example, in the late 1930s the populations of Tbilisi and Teheran (Iran) were equal in number; half a century later, the latter was five times larger, with a population exceeding that of Georgia as a whole. Even in little Armenia, the population of its capital, Yerevan, which three decades earlier had been far less than that of Tbilisi, by 1989 almost equalled the latter.

The metropolitan centre at the apex of Georgia's urban hierarchy is Tbilisi with 1300000. It exceeds by more than five times the runner-up, the industrial city of Kutaisi (232000). The other large cities are Rustavi, an industrial centre within the Tbilisi Metropolitan Region (159000), the multifunctional cities of Batumi (137000) and Sokhumi (119000), capitals of Adjara and Abkhazia Autonomous republics respectively.

The medium-size cities comprise Gori (regional centre of the province of Shida

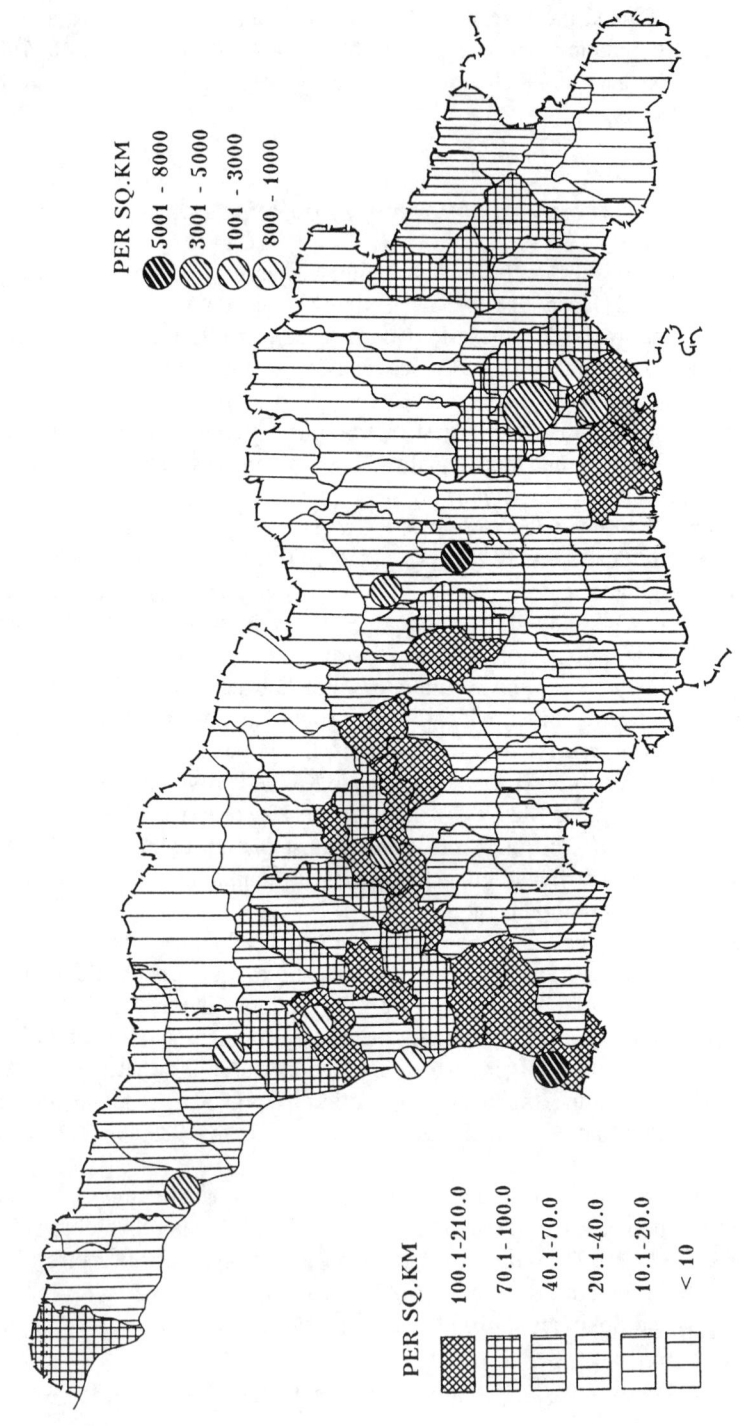

Figure 3.2 Population density, 1989.

Kartli), Zugdidi (regional centre of Samegrelo province), Poti (the major seaport of Georgia) and Tskhinvali (regional centre of former South Ossetia), each with 40000–70000 inhabitants. Gori and Zugdidi are industrial centres of nationwide significance; Tskhinvali is a multifunctional city.

Among the rest, comprising about a hundred urban places, the larger, with 20–35000 inhabitants, include the regional centres of historical provinces – Telavi (Kakheti), Ozurgeti (Guria), Akhaltsikhe (Meskheti) – and such industrial centres or transport nodes as Samtredia, Zestafoni, Chiatura, Tkibuli (all of them in Imereti), Khashuri (Shida Kartli), Marneuli (Kvemo Kartli), and Tkvarcheli (Abkhazia). There are many small towns, centres of rural districts, most of which hardly differ from the adjacent villages.

Rural settlements in Georgia number 4300 altogether. The average size is 533 inhabitants. In the highlands, especially the Kavkasioni zone, there are many hamlets. Large villages, of which there are more than 200 with populations of 2000–5000 and 21 with more than 5000 each, are found especially in Kvemo Kartli and Kakheti provinces and in the Kolkheti Lowland.

Trends in fertility, mortality and natural growth

The Georgians were not distinguished by a high birthrate even in the past. Some kind of family planning was practised even at the beginning of the twentieth century, to the extent that gentry facing impoverishment, and even wealthier peasants, tried to evade parcellation of their land by restricting the number of heirs. Nevertheless, families with five or more children were not rare, especially in rural areas.

In 1940 the crude birthrate was still high enough at 27.4 per thousand. By 1970 it had fallen to 19.2 and in 1989 amounted to 16.7. Meanwhile, the mortality rate remained more or less stable, 8.8 per thousand in 1940, 7.3 in 1970 and 8.6 in 1989. Thus, the crude rate of natural increase in the country decreased from 18.6 per thousand in 1940 to 8.1 in 1989.

By the end of the 1980s, the population growth rate in Georgia was at the average level of the then USSR, higher than in the Slavic and Baltic republics, but much less than in the Central Asian and the other Transcaucasian republics, Azerbaijan and Armenia. The ageing of the population and the decline in the proportion of children became the demographic characteristics of the majority of population, apart from some religious minorities (Ch. 4). This will negatively affect future population reproduction. The reduction in birthrate was affected by the significant increase in female employment, the advancement of women's education, and the process of urbanization, which in turn caused dramatic distortion of the sex:age ratio in some rural areas, especially in the mountains.

The mortality rate is gradually rising because of the ageing of the population and, in recent years, because of malnutrition, stress and lack of medicines caused by the deep economic and social crisis. Some diseases that had practically disappeared are returning; for example, an increase in the number of tuberculosis cases is reported. There are no reliable figures about AIDS, but it also may well have grown. According to official statistics, the major causes of death in 1992 were cardiovascular diseases (69%), malignant tumours (10%) and accidents (6%) (Report 1993). The recent bloody internal wars also seriously affected mortality.

In spite of some decline in the infant mortality rate, from 25.4 per thousand live births in 1980, to 15.8 in 1989, it is still higher than in the developed countries. As social spending has virtually stopped, supplementary feeding programmes are needed for pregnant and lactating women, otherwise infant mortality rate will go up again.

According to data of the Committee on Social–Economic Information of the Republic of Georgia, during 1992 there were 75 429 babies born in Georgia (13.8 per thousand), and 48 902 persons died (9.0 per thousand). The rate of natural increase thus constituted 4.8 per thousand. The natural increase of population is distributed unevenly (Fig. 3.3). It is highest, at more than 20 per thousand, along the southern border of Georgia. This is the area of settlement of predominantly rural ethnic and religious minorities, among whom the tradition of large families persists. In Bolnisi and Marneuli districts, where the Azeris are an absolute majority, one finds the highest crude birthrate in Georgia, 30 per thousand in 1985 and declining to 24–26 per cent in 1990, whereas the mortality rate is low at 6.0–7.7 per thousand. In the same districts there is also the highest level of infant mortality, at 40 and more per thousand live births, which probably indirectly influences the high birthrate.

Birthrate is also high among the Muslim Georgian population. The River Choloki is a distinct division between the two sets of demographic behaviour, although the people living on both banks speak the same Georgian and often have the same surnames. Those on the north, in Ozurgeti district in the historical province of Guria, are orientated towards small families; natural increase in 1985 was 8.5 per thousand. Those on the south bank, in the Kobuleti district in the historical province and Autonomous Republic of Adjara, have larger families and a natural increase of 17.5 per thousand. The only distinction between these communities is religious tradition: Orthodox Christianity in Guria and Islam in Adjara. However, there is a rapid convergence of these demographic patterns; birthrate has tended to decline in Kobuleti district as well.

In the Kavkasioni mountain zone as a whole, natural increase is very low, and since the early 1980s in some districts such as Ambrolauri, Oni, Kazbegi and Tsageri, depopulation has been observed. The same trend will soon become characteristic of other rural areas, even in the western lowland zone with a purely Georgian population. Meanwhile, in most of the urban areas, natural increase was close to the national average. But even here the deterioration of the economic situation affects vital statistics; natural population growth in Tbilisi declined from 7.4 per thousand in 1990 to 1.8 in 1993. In the 1980s, absolute population growth amounted to 50 000–55 000 annually, whereas in the early 1990s it had fallen to 10 000–15 000 and the trend is a further reduction.

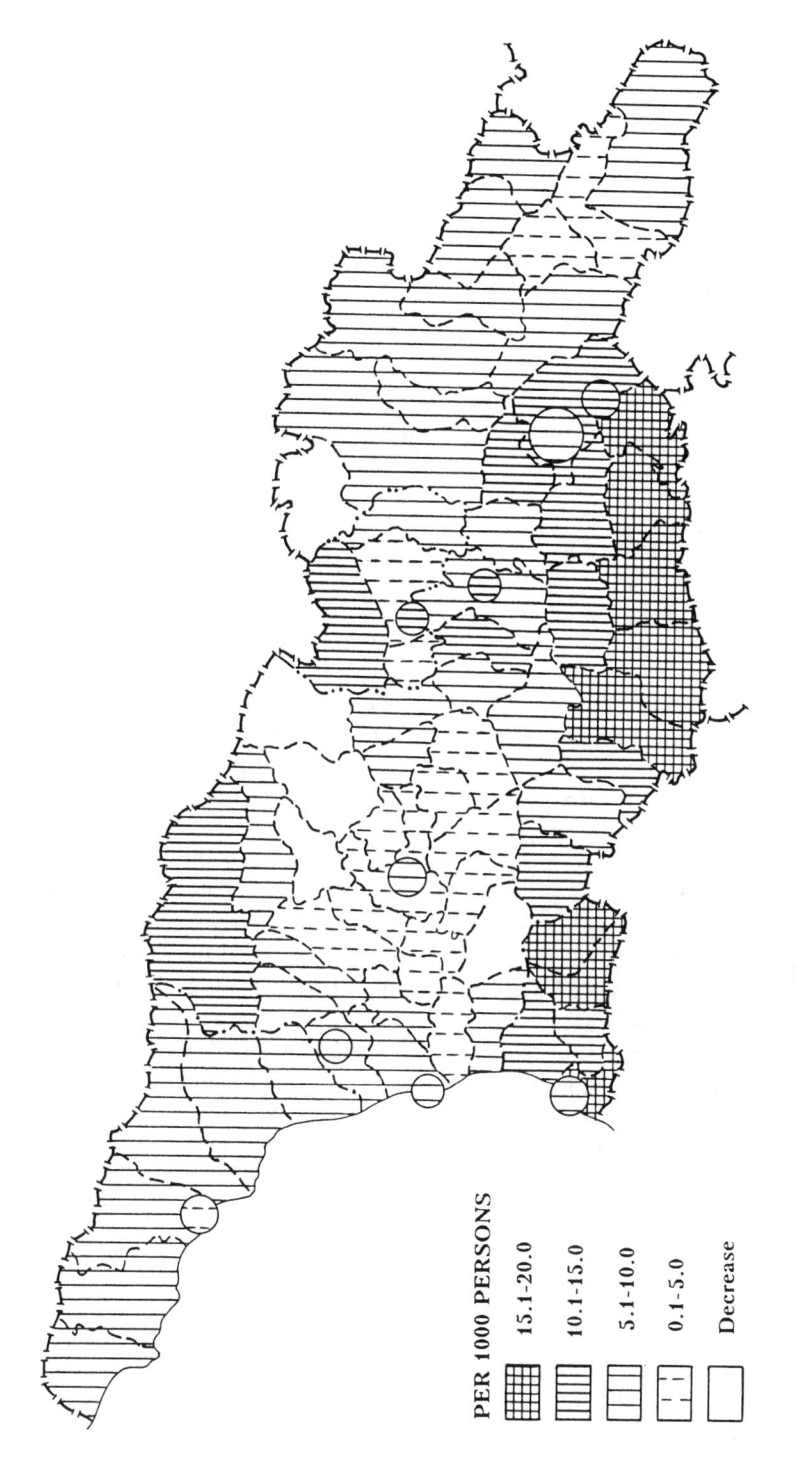

Figure 3.3 Natural population increase, 1989.

Population

Figure 3.4 Age pyramids, 1989.

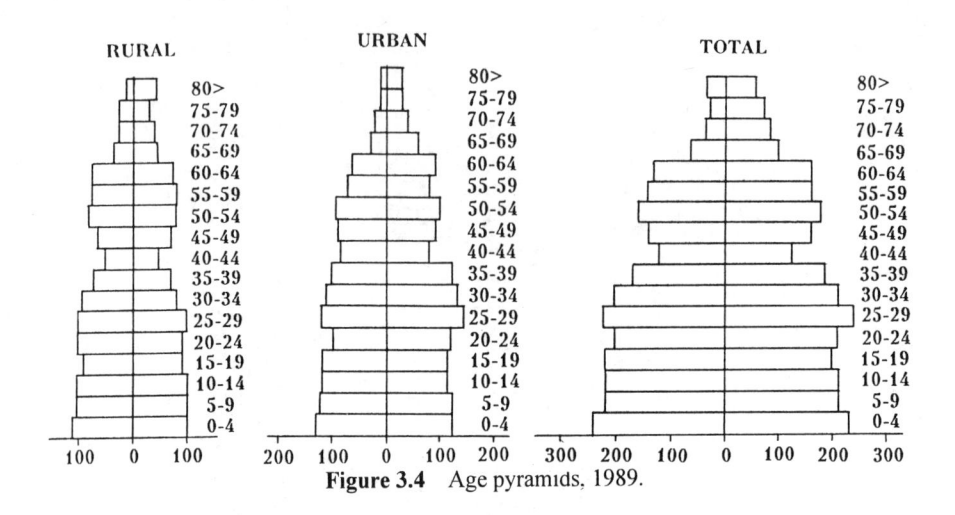

Sex and age structure

The sex structure of the population changed dramatically during the 1940s, as a consequence of the Second World War (Table 3.1). In 1959, women constituted 53.9 per cent and men 46.1 per cent; even almost a half a century after the war ended, in 1989, there were 277 000 more women (mostly elderly) than men.

The average age of the population increased from 32.5 in 1979 to 33.9 in 1989. It was higher in rural areas, especially of the female population, at 34.6 in 1979 and 36.3 in 1989. The age pyramid of Georgia's population (total, urban and rural: Fig. 3.4), illustrates an ageing population, especially in rural areas. In 1989 the percentage of population under 15 was 26.3, that of 15–64 year olds 64.8 and of elderly population over 65 8.9 per cent. These figures make Georgia appear in a more favourable position than contemporary European countries, where similar proportions were observed as early as 1950 (Noin & Woods 1993). But Georgia is moving too rapidly along the path of demographic transition and will probably equal Europe from the point of view of a diminished young generation and an increased number of the elderly over the next two decades, or even earlier, especially if the crisis should last longer and develop into a mass out-migration of young people. The official age of retirement is 55 for women and 60 for men. Accordingly, everyone between 15 and the retirement ages is considered to be of potentially economically active age, the "able-bodied ages". People of retirement age and older comprised 13.7 per cent in 1959 and 18.3 per cent in 1989. It must be added that most people continue to work after reaching retirement age.

In 1990, average life expectancy at birth was 76.3 for women and 69.0 for men, a larger gap than that of the developed countries. However, the figures were almost twice those of the 1930s. In the Soviet period, Georgia was world famous for longevity, and American and Japanese gerontologists spared no colour film shooting moustached, hale old men dancing folk dances on the stage and claiming to be more than 100 years old! It is hard to say whether the hale and hearty old men, predominantly from Abkhazia and other mountainous areas, will survive the severe economic crisis of the 1990s.

Family, marriage, divorce

The dominant traditional household in Georgia was the small family. Extended families have been gradually disappearing since the second half of the nineteenth century.

The matrimonial norm of the Georgians until the twentieth century was strict exogamy; marriage was forbidden between cousins closer than seven or eight times removed, even between persons with the same surname (Bromley 1988: 143). In rural areas, it was normal to marry a person from another community, often from another province; this was a factor in the formation of a single nation. These traditions are to some extent followed to the present day, although in urban areas, where kinship relations are much weaker, it became rather hard to determine the ancestry of the marriage partner, as the selection of the latter is mostly determined by love or affection. Marriage in recent times is not always preceded by asking permission of the parents. The tradition of dowry has mostly disappeared, especially in urban areas, but the tradition persists of celebrating crowded weddings with much wine consumed; in organizing such a feast, the parents are more useful than in advising on whom to marry.

One might note in passing the continuing burdensome family obligation to hold costly funerals, with a feast that is repeated both 40 days and a year later, especially in rural areas and, where city dwellers have their roots in a village, in urban areas as well. This "harmful tradition" (so labelled by the Communist Party that tried in vain to get rid of it) could have ruined each individual household, but for the assistance of relatives (kinship relations still remaining of utmost importance in such patterns of social life) and of the rural community, which made the burden bearable.

The average household size in Georgia is 4.1 people (4.0 in urban areas and 4.2 in rural). For the ethnic Georgians, a nuclear family with two children is modal, but there is now a tendency to have one child. Slavic households are smaller (2.8–3.1 persons), whereas those of Azeris are much larger (4.9 persons); the largest are Kurdish households with 5.1 persons. In recent decades the absolute number of marriages has been falling. In 1979 there were 52500 marriages registered, in 1990 36800, a decline from 10.0 to 7.4 per thousand population. The minimum age of marriage since 1956 has been 18 for both sexes, but in 1991 the Supreme Council (Parliament), lowered the legal minimum age of marriage to 16 for both sexes, with the object of increasing the birthrate. In fact, this result was not achieved; although some increase in the number early marriages has been observed, such teenage families have proved in general to be not stable enough (Totadze 1993).

Among males over 16 years of age, 70 per cent were married in 1989; 24.8 per cent never married, 2.7 were widowers and 1.5 were divorced. Among the female population, the respective percentage figures were 60.9, 17.4, 16.7 and 4.1. Many more widows and divorced women than men are unable to form new families.

The proportion of women who never married is substantially higher in urban areas, and is above the national average among Georgian women. One of the reasons given for the latter situation was ethnically mixed marriages (Totadze 1993), which Georgian males are more willing to enter. In 1989, 7.5 per cent of Georgian men were married to women of another nationality, predominantly Russians, Ossetians and Armenians. For Georgian women the proportion was 4.8 per cent, married predominantly to Armenian, Ossetian or Russian males. Among the Abkhaz, ethnically mixed marriages constitute almost a quarter, the spouse of another nationality being most often Georgian; other marriage partners are Russians, Armenians or Greeks. Overall, 12 per cent of Georgian households were bi-ethnic in 1989, a figure rising in Tbilisi to 17.8 and in Sokhumi to 29.8. The most closed to ethnically mixed marriages are Azeris, the most open are the Russians. In 1989, 55.9 per cent of married Russian women in Georgia and 42.9 per cent of men had a spouse of another nationality (*National Economy* 1991: 85).

In terms of the divorce rate, Georgia and neighbouring Armenia were in the last place among the Union Republics of the former USSR, with less than 1.1 per 1000 persons in 1990. But even such a low index seems very high in comparison with the equivalent figure in 1950, when 427 divorces were formally registered, only seven of them in rural areas (Totadze 1993). The reason lay in the USSR's active pro-natalist policy, outlawing abortion and fighting divorce. Divorces had to be announced in advance in an official document and heard in court, where there was a good chance that the court would refuse. Once such "totalitarian pressure" became lighter, the number of divorces substantially increased: 7796 were registered in 1990, less than ten per cent of which were in rural areas.

Figure 3.5 shows the variation in the stability of families: the ratio of divorces to marriages. It is apparent that rural areas, especially the mountainous ones, display more stability in marital status, and it seems that the old patriarchal traditions still persist. Urban areas, especially seaside resorts, have the most unstable families. Every third marriage ended in divorce in the cities, whereas in rural areas it was only every nineteenth.

One must note a substantial growth in the number of illegitimate births, from 4194 in 1980 to 16161 in 1989, when they formed 17.7 per cent of all live births, a change that affected rural areas as well. Demographers tend to explain this phenomenon by the distortion of the sex ratio, caused by the heavy out-migration of young males from the villages (Totadze 1993: 108). One of the explanations in urban areas, where the majority of such births occur, could be more trivial. Under Soviet legislation a single mother had some privileges, for example in applying for

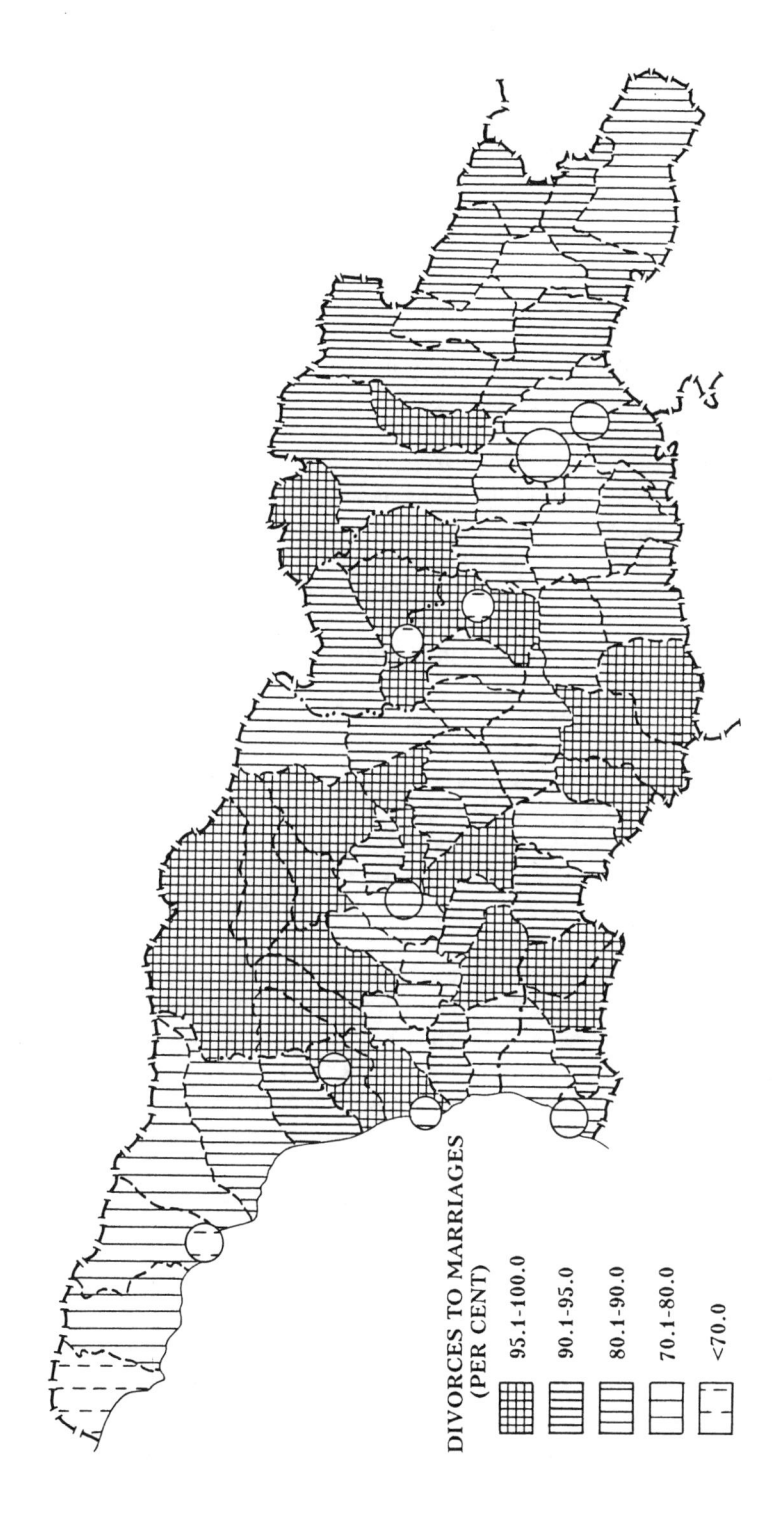

Figure 3.5 Stability of families: ration of divorces to marriages, 1989.

a free apartment. Thus, a family could receive greater benefit without registering the marriage. In general, however, this trend shows the advance in the emancipation of women.

Education

Until recently, schooling was compulsory in Georgia up to the age of 17, that is 11 years at school. Since 1993, education has been compulsory only up to 15, but full opportunities for free secondary education still exist. The number of full-time pupils in schools increased up to the 1970s; in 1971 it exceeded a million. Later it started to decline as a result of the changing age structure. In September 1990, 878 000 pupils attended primary and secondary schools, 56 000 pupils were in vocational schools, 43 000 in technical secondary schools and 104 000 students were enrolled in higher education institutions. School education was carried out in six languages: Georgian, Russian, Armenian, Azeri, Abkhaz, and Ossetian. The first two were the major languages of instruction, with 68 and 21 per cent of pupils respectively, in 1990.

There is at least one primary school in each rural settlement, and a vocational school in most of the district centres. Higher education is located in the larger urban settlements. Of 20 State institutions of higher education, all of them free, 12 were situated in the capital city of Tbilisi, including the oldest and most prestigious Tbilisi State University. Kutaisi and Sokhumi have two each, and Batumi, Tskhinvali, Telavi and Gori have a single institution. In recent years, polytechnics and some other institutes have acquired the status of university and there are now eight State universities in Georgia.

Feminization of the over-seventeen student population has been a social phenomenon, in a process like that proceeding in the countries of southern Europe (Noin & Woods 1993: 131). Even such subjects as chemistry and biology, to say nothing of the social sciences as a whole, have become "open territory" for female students in Georgia. Polytechnics have already started to complain of a shortage of male students, who have been successfully out-competed by the girls.

The most popular subjects, according to competition rates in the entrance examinations, are medicine, law, economics, and other social studies, followed by engineering, industrial training and agriculture.

In previous decades, many people acquired higher education in State institutions, where requirements for entry and teaching implied a real level of knowledge; such people numbered 613 000 in 1989. The distribution of persons with higher education reveals their over-concentration in the cities. In Tbilisi, of people over six years of age, 24.9 per cent had higher education. The runners-up were Tskhinvali, the centre of the former South Ossetian Autonomous Region, and Sokhumi, the capital of the Abkhaz Autonomous Republic, each with 20 per cent. The lowest proportion can be observed in the mountainous Adjara and other areas along the southern border and in rural areas in general (Fig. 3.6). To a certain extent these figures are indirect indicators of the level of the spatial social development.

As part of the "democratization of society and the switch to a market economy", 209 (sic!) commercial higher education institutions were licensed by a lavish Ministry of Education in 1991–2. Of these, 131 actually functioned, with a total enrolment of 33000 students in 1993; 83 of the institutions were situated in Tbilisi (Report 1994: 14). In fact they relied upon the skills and part-time services of lecturers in the State institutes, who were compelled to earn some extra money in the conditions of a dramatic deterioration of living standards. Some of such commercial institutions sprang up in small towns and even in villages, lacking any material or intellectual basis, but they generally had lower requirements for entry than the State ones. It is obvious that real competition on education market will bring about the closing down of the majority of such "universities".

Employment and unemployment

The most recent data on employment derive from the 1989 population census, which now is out of date, as the social change that has been going on is having the most dramatic affect on employment (and unemployment). Nevertheless, the situation at the end of the 1980s gives a portrait of society just before the change began (Table 3.2). In 1989, 48.8 per cent of the total population were employed, women comprising almost half (46.3%). Of the total employed, 36.5 per cent were

Table 3.2 Employment (1989).

	Thousands	%
Agriculture and forestry	676.4	25.7
Mining and quarrying	5.5	0.2
Manufacturing	552.1	21.0
Electricity, gas, water	59.4	2.3
Construction	201.0	7.6
Retail trade and public catering	140.5	5.3
Transport, storage and communications	206.4	7.8
Credit and insurance	12.5	0.5
Communal and social services	578.8	21.8
Consumer services	42.2	1.6
Education	241.0	9.1
Science and scientific services	60.1	2.3
Art and culture	48.2	1.8
Medical service & social maintenance	177.3	6.7
Administration	136.4	5.2
Communist Party, Komsomol, trade unions	18.1	0.7
Miscellaneous branches	69.6	2.6
TOTAL	2634.3	100.0

Source: Employment, 1991, I, 4–8.

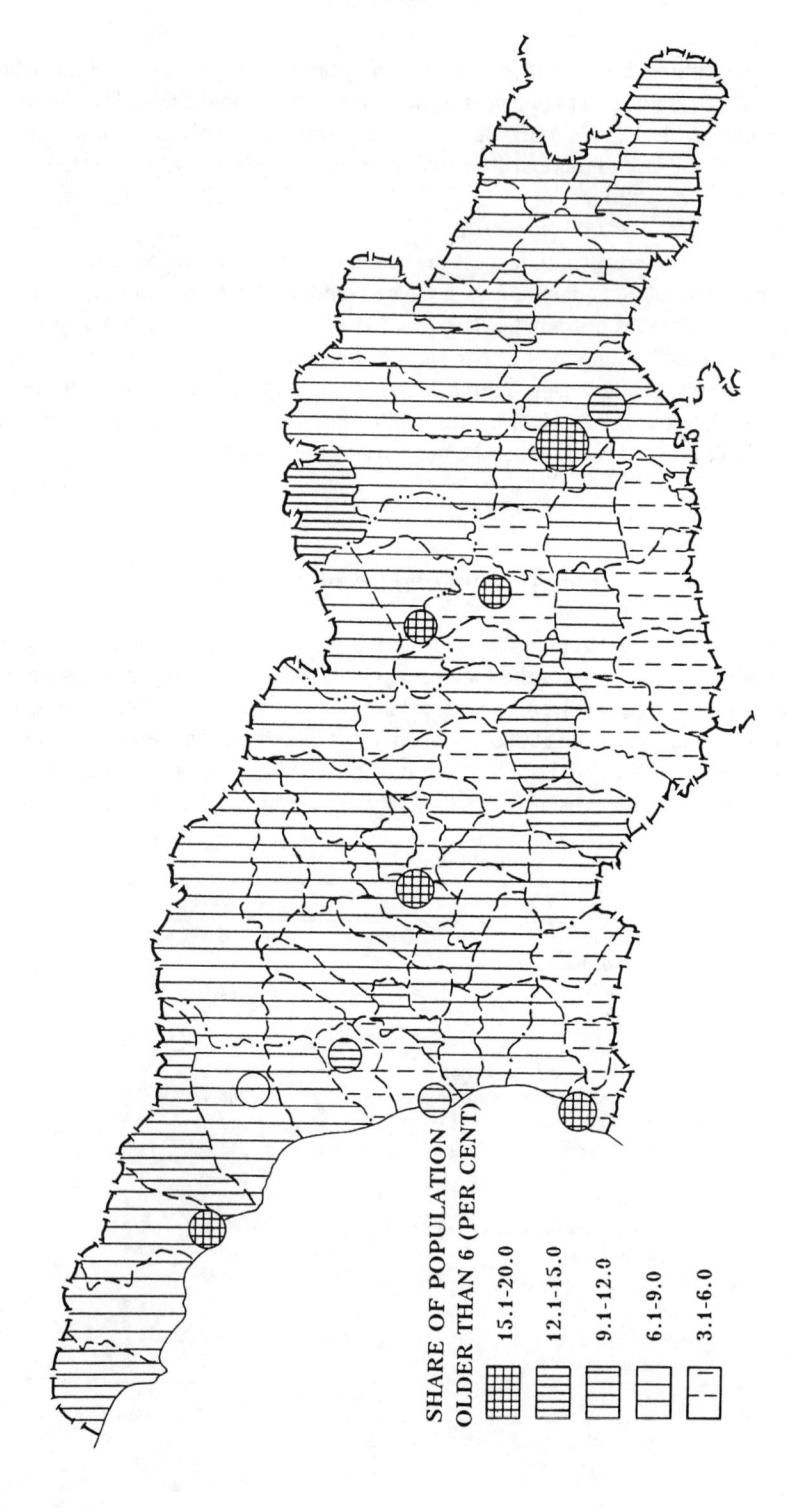

Figure 3.6 Individuals with higher education.

listed as engaged in "mental work", a growth of six percentage points since 1979. The rest, 63.5 per cent, were in blue-collar and manual jobs, "physical work". According to age structure, the majority of employed were represented by the most active age groups: 24.8 per cent were 20–29 years old, 25.6 per cent 30–39 years old and 18.6 per cent 40–49 years old; only 4.5 per cent of employees were under 20 years and 7.9 per cent over retirement age (over 60), most of these last being in part-time employment.

Industrialization caused substantial changes in the employment structure. Before the 1930s, Georgia was a predominantly rural and agricultural country and, even in 1960, 48 per cent were engaged in agriculture. After several significant industrial enterprises were built in the cities and larger towns (Tbilisi, Kutaisi, Rustavi, Batumi, Sokhumi, Gori, Poti, Zugdidi), employment in the industrial sector grew substantially.

Despite the decline in the absolute number of those engaged in agriculture, by 23 per cent during the past decade alone, it still remains the largest single branch of the economy. By numbers engaged in agriculture, Georgia exceeds the UK, but it is far behind the latter in labour efficiency. Although agricultural land was concentrated in large farms (the *kolkhoz* or collective farm, and the *sovkhoz* or State farm), their efficiency was low. This was not least because too many were employed, who were major consumers as well, to say nothing of the drawbacks of the Soviet planning and management system – and not only in agriculture.

During the 1980s, employment in manufacturing grew, especially in engineering, the chemical industries, and iron and steel. The largest branches, however, are still the food and other light industries.

Up to a quarter of the employed population is engaged in white-collar work. The large number of educational workers is explicable as there are up to 3500 schools, situated in almost every village, and there are other institutions as well.

The ratio of those engaged in science looks rather odd for a small country. These are scientific-academic jobs in higher education institutions and pure scientific jobs in the institutes belonging to different ministries and to the Academy of Sciences. The Academy is a scientific body typical of the socialist countries, with about 50 institutions, mostly located in Tbilisi. In Sokhumi, Batumi, Tskhinvali, Kutaisi, Abastumani and Zugdidi there are one or two institutions each. Some 30 000 are engaged in science and humanities altogether, of whom 9400 have Candidate of Science (PhD) degrees. Some 1500 have higher doctoral science degrees, the most prestigious titles in the USSR and its successor States. From 1970 to 1989 the number of scientists and scholars increased by 50 per cent, at a slower rate than in previous decades, but still appearing rather large. The number engaged in science can be explained by the official support and by the All-Union significance of research carried out in Georgia.

Those engaged in art and cultural services (1.8%) play an important role in the cultural development of society. Several theatres and film studios, as well as writers, musicians, painters, who are mostly to be found in Tbilisi, were well known and highly appreciated in the USSR and some of them yet farther abroad;

they formed the "pride of the nation". Almost the same can be said of a few sportsmen in the "prestigious sports", such as higher league footballers and chess players, officially amateurs, in practice professionals supported by the State. Every year Georgia provided dozens of world and European champions, especially in wrestling and female chess, and every four years four to seven Olympic champions, all contributing to the prestige of the Socialist State! It is questionable how long the independent, but impoverished, developing country will be able to go on financing the scientific institutions, art and culture. However, it is also true, since intellectuals are a major item of Georgia's real wealth that their loss would be a serious additional blow to the country. One can already observe a brain drain, to say nothing of some of the best footballers (another "pride of the nation"), who play in European clubs.

There were, in 1989, more than 100 000 medical workers in all, of whom 32 000 were medical doctors. By the average number of doctors per 10 000 population, Georgia with 59 far exceeded all the other Union Republics and was one of the leaders on a world scale. But the geographical dimension shows the inappropriateness of boasting of such an achievement. Almost half these doctors were concentrated in the capital city of Tbilisi, which had 131 doctors per 10 000 people, followed by the regional capitals Sokhumi, Tskhinvali and Batumi with 68–85 per 10 000. At the same time, quite extensive rural areas were left without adequate medical care.

Those engaged in administration, including central and local government, Communist Party management, police (militia) and so on, were almost 12 times as numerous as those in credit and insurance organizations. The latter occupations, without any competition under the Soviet centralized system, had no incentives for numerical growth. In the past few years, since the country started to move slowly towards a market economy, several banks and insurance companies have appeared, but so far with fewer employees. Administration, on the contrary, needed more and more recruits. In spite of frequent official campaigns to "reduce the *apparat* (managing staff)", managers were the fastest increasing social group. Between the censuses of 1979 and 1989, their number in the different sectors increased by 2.5 times, The number of functionaries in the Communist Party and "public organizations", by which was meant the Komsomol and official Trade Unions, increased by 214.2 per cent (Employment 1991, II: 6). In fact, a major part of this social group formed the "bureaucracy", the real ruling class of any Soviet or post-Soviet country (see below).

Georgians were less engaged in military occupations. In the Russian Empire, almost every Georgian aristocrat was happy to choose a military career, which made ethnic Georgian officers the most numerous group in the Russian Army after the Slavs. In the USSR on the contrary, Georgians tried to avoid military service. By then the aristocracy and their traditions had been successfully destroyed by the Bolsheviks, whereas the peasants or their urban descendants had no special affiliation towards a Soviet Army dominated by Russian language, not entirely understandable to them, and different social values. After 1956, when all national military units such as the Georgian Regiments were abolished, the number of ethnic Georgian officers became insignificant. The fruits of this were reaped after Georgian independence was restored and the country was left with just a handful of well trained officers. This made the process of building a national army long and rather difficult.

The generalized regional structure of employment is shown in Figure 3.7, which displays the proportions of those engaged in the primary, secondary and tertiary sectors (*Georgia–2000-Regions* 1987). The rural districts and CRSs of Georgia exhibit distinct clustering on the employment triangle, and five types of regions were singled out; three districts, marked by an asterisk on the map, could not be ranked with any of these types. The five types of CRSs and rural districts, by sectors of economic activity, are:

- secondary/tertiary (all cities)
- balanced/secondary (Zestafoni, Samtredia, Khashuri and Mtsketa rural districts with substantial industrial development)
- balanced (rural districts in lowland and less populated mountainous areas, where the agricultural sector was supported by the tertiary sector and white-collar workers composed a substantial part of employees)
- primary/balanced (better developed rural districts in the lowlands, predominantly within the limits of Tbilisi and Kutaisi Metropolitan Regions and the lowland part of the province of Guria);
- primary (purely agricultural areas, making up most of rural Georgia and found in every part of the country).

As for unemployment, under communist rule the very existence of the problem was denied. On the contrary, legislation in every Republic contained harsh laws against sponging. True, unemployment was curtailed by actual practice, in which a job that could have been done by one was done by several, the salary of each being relatively low, within the established upper limit. Moreover, the vast spaces of the then USSR, where there were always huge numbers of vacancies somewhere, gave at least a demagogic excuse for the existence of the "laws against parasites" referred to. But the reality defied the theory. People usually want to work where they live, but jobs are not always be available. Already under *perestroyka*, the existence of unemployment was loudly proclaimed. This particularly concerned the so-called "labour-excessive" republics – Central Asia, Azerbaijan and the autonomous republics of the northern Caucasus. Georgia on the whole did not qualify for this group, but in fact there were, and are, regions with high birthrates and relatively high population density on agricultural land, creating conditions of latent unemployment. For example, thousands of rural migrants from the districts of Kvemo Kartli were seeking temporary jobs in other rural areas or towns. Armenians from Javakheti province migrated annually to northern Russia, engaged there in highly paid construction works during the warm period of the year and returned home in late autumn. Hundreds of landless households from mountainous Adjara were to be resettled in other areas.

The huge migration of rural population was an indirect indicator of unemploy-

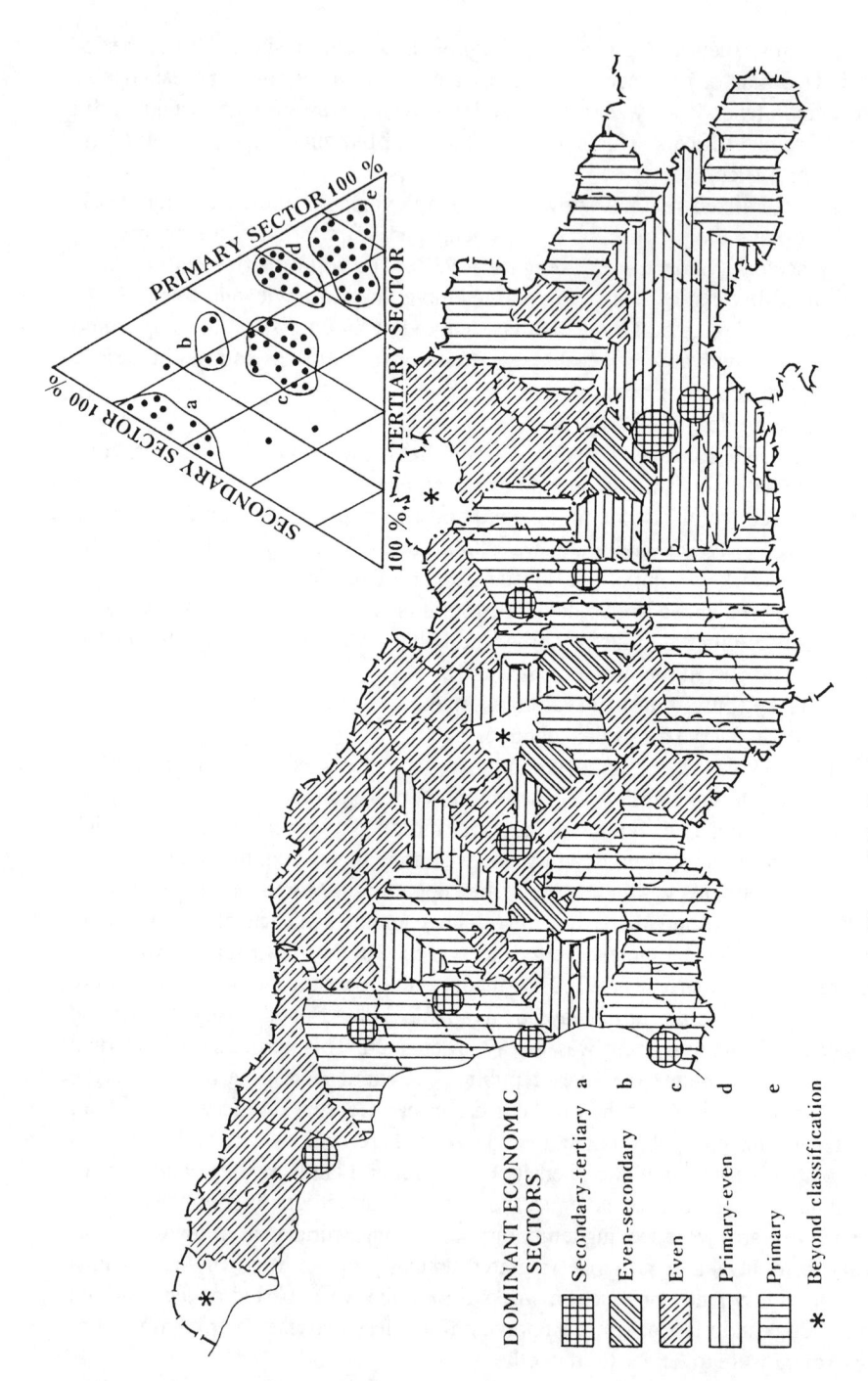

Figure 3.7 Employment structure, 1985.

ment, or at least underemployment, in rural areas. In the urban areas, structural unemployment was also revealed, especially among women with higher and vocational education; trained teachers and nurses had to wait in long queues for a job. Meanwhile, in some rural areas, there was a shortage of teachers. After independence was restored, and especially because of the severe economic crisis, unemployment has been recognized as a real social problem. According to the Ministry of Labour and Social Affairs, the number of people who were registered as actively seeking work in December 1993 amounted to 220 000, including 170 000 unemployed or 5.4 per cent of labour resources (Social–Economic 1994: 10). The highest unemployment index, exceeding 15 per cent, was in small and medium-size industrial towns and adjacent rural areas (Chiatura, Kaspi, Samtredia), and in areas affected by civil war (Zugdidi, Poti, Senaki, Abasha).

Real figures of unemployment presumably are higher. Because of shortages or even absence of fuel and raw materials, the huge industrial enterprises, which had earlier relied on co-operation with enterprises in the other Soviet republics (themselves now Newly Independent States, with their own problems), have had to halve or almost cease production, letting most of their employees go on "longer vacations", without pay. If not formally sacked, these people cannot register as unemployed. Unofficially, most of them find self-employment in petty retail trades, or various kinds of artisanship that permit them to survive the heavy transitional period to a market economy. However, elderly people are in real trouble. Figures of unemployment among the under-25s are not measured, but may be very high, because one can see many young people hanging about on the streets of every town and city. Having no jobs makes them lazy and pushes them towards deviance; the growing crime rate and drug addiction are not unconnected.

The current geographical pattern of unemployment is obscured by the presence in the central regions of Georgia of some 250 000 displaced persons and refugees who had to flee from Abkhazia, most of whom remain jobless. Once economic activity is renewed in this country, the trends in employment and unemployment will inevitably show changes, including spatial changes.

Social stratification and class structure

Stratification as a structural set of inequalities between different groupings of people was openly recognized in the Russian Empire, where all people knew that they belonged to a certain stratum or "class" (*sosloviye*), with unequal legal rights, regulated by the State. Among Georgians, according to the 1897 population census, the hereditary nobility comprised 5.29 per cent, while the same group among the total population of the Empire amounted to 0.97 per cent. Personal nobility and high-ranking officials without title formed 1.04 per cent (in the Empire 0.50%), the clergy 2.18 per cent (0.47%), hereditary and personal honorary citizens 0.21 (0.27%), merchants 0.17 (0.22%), petty bourgeoisie (*meshchaniye*) 3.55

(10.99%), and the peasantry 87.32 per cent (77.12% in the Empire). In each case the data also include the family members (Troinitsky 1905: LVI).

It is apparent that among the Georgians too large a percentage of people belonged to the privileged classes, and too large a percentage were peasantry. The middle class was very insignificant a hundred years ago, as it has remained up to the present. This explains much in the ethnic psychology and the trends of development. However, it must be said in all fairness that in the Russian Empire the Georgians were not an underprivileged ethnic group on the whole.

The communist ideology was more hypocritical. The workers were announced to be "the ruling class" and the dictatorship of the proletariat was proclaimed to be the foundation of the State, at least until the 1980s. The Communist Party was determined to build a society without class differences, but for the time being it recognized the existence of two classes: the working class and co-operative peasantry (*kolkhozniki* or collective farmers). The former "exploiting classes" were uprooted and some of their representatives even annihilated. For Georgia, this "class struggle" proved to be a disastrous process, as almost every tenth person in the nation belonged to the upper classes.

Along with the classes of workers, who were increasing in number, and co-operative peasantry, who were decreasing, the essential elements of the social structure of Soviet society were "social groups, among whom numerically the largest are the intelligentsia (specialists) and white-collar workers (non-specialists)" (Filippov 1988: 26). The intelligentsia were supposed to be all those with higher and specialized secondary education (ibid.). In addition, the existence of numerically insignificant social groups, non-co-operative peasants, artisans and clergy, was also recognized.

According to this scheme, 55.5 per cent of the total population was listed as working class in 1989; in 1959 it had been 31.7 per cent. The class of co-operative peasantry formed 13.2 per cent, down from 47.8 per cent in 1959. White-collar workers, including the intelligentsia, constituted 30.7 per cent as against 20.2 per cent in 1959. Other social groups amounted to mere 0.6 per cent.

In order to ensure growth of the "ruling class", many collective farms (*kolkhozy*), without the consent of the "owners of the land", were transformed into State farms (*sovkhozy*), the employees of which, yesterday's peasants, were turned into workers in an instant. In the typical rural districts of Akhmeta and Gardabani in eastern Georgia, not a single peasant remained as all the *kolkhozy* were converted into *sovkhozy* by an order from Tbilisi, which in its turn received the order from Moscow. The collective farmers never objected. As they did not really own the *kolkhoz* land, it suited them better to receive a guaranteed salary from the State, irrespective of what grew in the field. Quite a few of the *sovkhozy* in Georgia were subsidized by the State. The farmers also kept the small personal plots of land that everyone engaged in agriculture was entitled to maintain. More than 668 000 households, including 319 000 *sovkhoz* workers, owned such plots in 1982 (Kekelia 1988).

It has been recorded that 625 000 hectares of land were in fact privatized by

November 1993 (Social–Economic 1994: 23), although the Law of Land Reform was not yet adopted. This figure seems rather large, and clearly there will be a sizable number of small peasant farms, which will be less marketable than large farms. For the moment this privatized land will help to sustain the lives of rural households and will to some extent help the city dwellers as well, but in a long-term perspective the persistence of a large peasantry may affect the pace and character of social change in Georgia.

The intelligentsia as a single social group never existed. In fact only scholars, higher education institution lecturers, artists and writers were referred as the "intelligentsia" proper. Sometimes reference was made to the "intelligentsia of mass professions" (schoolteachers, medical workers, other professionals), or the "technical intelligentsia" (engineers). But ever-increasing numbers of people with professional training, especially since the late 1970s, preferred to do blue-collar jobs. This was officially forbidden, since "the State had paid for preparing the specialists!", but it was more profitable for a man with a diploma of higher education in his pocket, which formally labelled him intelligent and which permitted him to seek promotion, to be a taxi driver or to serve in a wholesale store, than to be a schoolteacher.

Classes depend on economic differences between groupings of individuals, on inequality in the possession and control of material resources. In practice, neither of the two classes in the USSR, and thus of course in the Georgian SSR, possessed anything apart from personal belongings, among which a house and a car were the most expensive items. The land, mineral resources, factories and so on belonged to the State. The State was run by top executives of the Communist Party, who directly controlled productive resources. Thus, the real ruling class in Soviet Georgia, as elsewhere in the socialist countries, was bureaucracy.

Many professional managers appeared. In reality they emerged not from business life but from the party hierarchy. The standard process for a young ambitious person was to become a Komsomol (Young Communist League) functionary, thereafter moving to the Communist Party local, district, city, regional and central committees. With the acquisition of more experience, for which higher education was a major prerequisite (hence its exclusive social prestige), the person would become a high-ranking manager in an industrial enterprise, State company, or ministry. The *nomenklatura*, the official register of high-ranking Party functionaries together with these managers, became the foundation of the ruling class in the USSR, a process that was practically universal in all the Soviet republics.

Theoretically, these people are able to manage effectively only in conditions of one-party rule and State-ownership of everything. In practice, another process was affecting the development of the new ruling class. From the mid-1950s in Georgia and in the USSR as a whole, the shadow, or second, economy began to appear. Illegal businessmen (called in Russian "*dyelets*", pl. "*dyeltsy*"), who not uncommonly were the managers of formally State-owned enterprises, evaded economic and ideological restrictions and produced unaudited goods and services, thereby making quite a fortune. This was especially common in the southern republics.

Dyeltsy began to merge with the elite of the party hierarchy and organized some sort of "mafiosi clans", in which "money was made" through corruption as well.

By the end of the communist era, the "shadow businessmen" controlled a good many of the formally State-owned industrial enterprises and their turnover was estimated to be the equivalent of 25 per cent of the GNP of Georgia (Tokmazishvili 1990). These people prefer "to play by their own rules" and may hinder the process of "just privatization", if such a thing is ever possible. They will appear as the new upper middle class in the new post-communist States. After the fall of communism, many former Communist Party functionaries openly joined the businessmen and have proved to be quite successful.

The major threat to the introduction of the "market economy" will be the bureaucrats, brought up in conditions of socialism, who still run the post-socialist State. But there are no other bureaucrats in the FSU as yet. Time is needed to replace the generations imbued with a long-established characteristic mentality. In independent Georgia, certain changes are happening at the top of the hierarchy. More successful new businessmen and bureaucracy are merging with the old *dyeltsy* and still active members of the former communist bureaucracy, and are sometimes already supplanting them.

Corruption of the bureaucracy in the post-Soviet realm is no secret. But it is not an inherent feature of the Georgians or any other nation, despite the suspicion that the southern republics are more exposed to this social malaise. Corruption is a result of over-concentrating decision-making in the hands of underpaid bureaucrats, of "bad" (illogical) legislation and regulations and of unrealistic State-imposed prices and incomes. Under centralized Soviet power, these preconditions reached absurd heights. For example, the price of cars increased without taking into account that the average Soviet citizen (including police officers) could never afford to buy one, relying on salary alone. Yet no-one asked how almost all police (militsia) officers could own cars, when their wages were barely enough to feed their families.

The "ethnic dimension of corruption" is changeable and it depends on the social structure of an ethnic group. Thus, in the nineteenth century, the negative stereotypes of a Georgian could have been as irresponsible, quarrelsome and heavy-drinking, but never as "bribe-taking", simply because there were hardly any Georgians at a high level of decision-making. Georgian generals and other high-ranking military officers in the Tsar's service mostly belonged to the nobility and knew at least that *noblesse oblige*. If anyone was considered to be corrupt in those days, it was civil servants from European Russia, who obviously arrived in the colonies to improve their financial wellbeing.

In the Soviet period, people from the southern republics rapidly adjusted to the "unwritten Soviet rules". The largest sums from republics such as Uzbekistan, Georgia, Azerbaijan and so on were going to the top-rank bureaucrats in Moscow.

As yet the middle class is very insignificant in number. Most of the white-collar workers and professionals possess nothing and are unlikely to acquire anything in the process of privatization. Small business is virtually ruined by bad government and crime. The aim of some political parties to create a large and rich enough middle class to be the guarantee of the stability of the State must be welcomed, but the aim looks unachievable in the immediate future. In a decade or so the realization of this aim will probably become more feasible.

In present conditions, polarization of wealth continues. The wealthiest will not increase so much in number but will become richer. Working class and white-collar workers, including the intelligentsia, will become poorer. The peasantry will benefit at first from the deficits in the consumer market, but will not be able to compete with foreign products once the market becomes more open. Property differentiation and the eviction of the majority of the rural population may be one result of the inevitable social change.

Migrations

The major flows of internal migration in Georgia are from rural to urban areas and within rural areas. Internal mobility has been apparent since the early 1930s, when industrialization acted as a pull-factor and collectivization in the rural areas as a push-factor. The movement towards urban places increased from the mid-1950s, when the rural population of the whole USSR underwent "the second emancipation of serfs" as the *kolkhozniki* (collective farmers) were given internal passports, which had been denied them under Stalin.

Up to 60 per cent of the natural increase of rural population, including almost everyone with secondary education, move to the cities and towns. Between 1959 and 1989, this type of mobility involved 517 000 people (Jaoshvili 1993). In consequence, rural population declined in absolute terms from 1973 to 1992, although not very fast. Migrants from rural areas and from small towns usually prefer larger cities. Over half of the rural migrants to urban areas are directed towards Tbilisi. The capital city was growing rapidly as a result of these migrants, in spite of the strict regulations in those years directed against in-migration to Tbilisi (Ch. 8). The other cities attracting the rural migrants were Rustavi, Kutaisi, Batumi and Sokhumi. To a lesser extent, Gori, Tskhinvali and Zugdidi acted as local poles of attraction. Most of those who migrate between rural areas move from the highlands of Georgia to lowland villages. This brought about the depopulation of some mountainous provinces (Racha and Lechkhumi). In the last years of the communist era, "planned resettlement" of rural population was carried out, from Mestia district in the province of Svaneti to the lowland areas of eastern Georgia. The adaptation of these migrants proved to be rather complicated and led to additional social problems. Until recently, migration from urban to rural areas was almost insignificant, but in the current economic crisis more urban dwellers tend to move, at least temporarily, to rural areas, especially if they have inherited or own some parcels of land. The absolute growth of rural population during the past few years is evidence of such a trend (Table 3.1).

External migrations up to the mid-1950s had a positive balance towards Georgia, in-migration from the other Soviet republics dominated. Migrational flows changed directions after 1957, which was a watershed when the rate of extensive industrial growth and the building of large new enterprises declined and instead intensive industrial growth commenced. Ethnic Russians started to move to the other Soviet republics; ethnic Armenians moved to Armenia, with some going to Russia. From the 1970s, true international migrations also became apparent and, for instance, Jews started to emigrate to Israel. The out-migration of ethnic Georgians also increased (Ch. 4). Altogether 178 000 more people left Georgia than entered for permanent residence over the period 1959–89 (Jaoshvili 1993).

However, these trends pale into insignificance compared with recent trends in migration. During the first half of the 1990s, the flows of emigrants have tended to grow immensely. In spite of the new "Law of Citizenship of the Republic of Georgia" (Law 1993), which is truly democratic and, unlike those of some Baltic republics, does not deny automatic citizenship of Georgia to any of its permanent residents, many of the ethnic population (so-called "Russian-speakers") preferred to leave. The major reason was the deterioration of the economic situation in Georgia. For example, until 1991 the number of persons who checked into Tbilisi always outnumbered those who checked out. Since then, the balance of migration has reversed. The absolute number of those who moved from Tbilisi out of Georgia was 5000 in 1989, increasing to about 15 000 in 1993.

Among recent emigrants, many are ethnic Georgians. During the communist era most belonged to the younger generations, seeking higher education in Russian universities and other institutes, especially medical schools. In the 1990s an increasing number are moving to the West for the same reasons. The skilled and highly skilled are starting to emigrate in large numbers, especially the younger businessmen and intellectuals. This trend of a negative brain-drain may possibly have disastrous results for the country.

Flows of less skilled, clandestine migrants from Georgia towards Turkey, Greece and Cyprus are seen already, prompted by the unemployment in Georgia and the possibility of earning some hard currency. This trend in international mobility is difficult to measure, for understandable reasons. These clandestine migrants at least gain some experience of a market economy, albeit a marginal one, which they had never had before. Usually these people return home, whereas the emigrants to Russia and western Europe are less likely to return very soon (if ever).

Way of life and types of dwelling

The ways of life of people in urban and rural areas of Georgia differ, as elsewhere in the former Soviet Union. Urban life is characterized by greater variability of labour and better social infrastructure, educational opportunities and entertainment. To no lesser extent, it is characterized by the direct preference given by the

State to urban settlements, notably to those with administrative functions, both under the communist government and equally under the independent one. Under Soviet administration, the urban population enjoyed individual apartments practically free of charge, if poor in quality. All this made the larger cities, especially the capitals of the Republic and its autonomous units, preferable places to live in.

The sociogeographical characteristic of Georgia is a rather greater closeness of the rural population to the urban. Many of the latter have their roots in rural areas, through direct kinship, or land allotments. This, incidentally, to a certain extent permits the country to survive somehow the economic crisis of the first half of the 1990s.

The way of life of the rural population in lowland parts of Georgia is characterized by close relations with the urban settlements. Multifunctional cities are located more evenly over the territory of Georgia than those in the neighbouring post-Soviet countries, and the relatively small distances to them and to industrial towns mean that a substantial proportion of the rural population can engage in non-agricultural spheres of labour without migrating to urban areas. Commuting has developed on a rather large scale, not only in the metropolitan regions but in smaller towns as well. For example, 80 per cent of the 10 000 employed at the large steel works in the small town of Zestafoni (26 000 inhabitants) reside in the rural area within a radius of 20 km, and are farmers as well.

The predominant housing type in large cities is the monotonous high-rise building. Only the central parts of Tbilisi, Kutaisi, Batumi and Sokhumi, built in the nineteenth and first half of the twentieth centuries, have an attractive appearance. Since the mid-1950s, the large-scale housing programme has meant the building of large tracts of uniform housing, first 5-storey, later 8–9, 12 and 16-storey. In spite of their low aesthetic quality and relatively poor construction, they were eagerly occupied by people who were on long waiting lists and received them practically free of charge, even if some subsequently spent large sums of money on adapting the apartments to their taste. Small towns, which constitute the majority of urban settlements in Georgia, generally do not differ in their appearance from rural areas. Only some of them have ugly boxes of high-rise houses on the outskirts, closer to industrial enterprises. The majority of houses in such towns are private, detached two-storey houses with gardens, very similar to those in the villages of Georgia. District centres have a more densely built-up area in the centre, where administrative buildings and limited number of the "compulsory variety" of shops and service enterprises are situated. In the Soviet period, they all belonged to the State. Now an unlimited number of small private shops have appeared as well, most of them now carrying the inscription in English "commercial shop", as if wishing not to be confused with State shops, but in practice meaning that everything there is expensive.

It is worthwhile mentioning that almost 80 per cent of the dwellings in rural areas (including small towns) have been built after the Second World War, especially in the 1950s and again in the late 1980s, when construction materials were relatively cheap. Almost all of them are private. Only in the remote mountain villages has the old housing changed to a lesser extent.

In rural areas of Georgia, overall housing space amounted to 51 700 000 m² in 1990, and in urban areas the figure was 50 100 000 (*National economy 1991*: 189, 193). At that time, the urban population exceeded the rural by 26 per cent. Thus, on average a villager had more housing space at his disposal than a city dweller. On the whole, housing facilities in rural areas and small towns were no worse, if no better, than in the large cities. Usually, rural houses were supplied with electricity and natural or condensed gas; many had piped water and quite a few had central heating. There is a problem with sewerage systems; in rural areas they are absent.

The type of rural dwelling in the western lowland of Georgia differs slightly from that in the eastern part. In the lowland parts of Samegrelo, Guria, Imereti, coastal Adjara and Abkhazia, the new dwellings have some similar features. These are two-storey redbrick or concrete block houses with four-pitch roofs covered with metal, preferably galvanized iron. Houses have wide, open verandas and open staircases in front. The staircase probably remains as a relic of the traditional wooden, one-storey houses that in this rather humid area were built on high stone piles and had a staircase on the outside. The open staircases made of concrete in the new houses maximize living space. Sometimes they are extravagant, wide, curved, with specially designed handrails, and serve as a status symbol, showing "the taste and wealth" of the owner – a kind of "keeping up with the Joneses". The ground floor of rural houses serves domestic needs; here are the kitchen, everyday dining room, workshop and wine cellar (*marani*). On the first floor are a large hall for traditional feasts, and several bedrooms. The yard in front of a rural house in the western lowland, easily observed from the street, with a lawn (kept green by the humid climate), flower beds, some subtropical trees (magnolia, pomegranate, persimmon) and vine alleys, gives a lovely appearance to the dwelling. At the rear of the house there is usually a personal plot with maize, vegetables, tea or other plants. The cow-shed and pigsty are also situated here, and chickens and turkeys are quite often left to wander in the yard. Fences are made of wooden planks or, in the subtropical part of the country, there are hedges.

The settlement type is more dispersed in west Georgia and villages here cover quite a large area.

The type of rural dwelling in the eastern lowland is more or less similar to that in the western part, but here the roof is more often covered with tiles or asbestos roofing slate; instead of the open veranda, there is usually a glazed gallery and the staircase to the first floor is inside the house; in this part of the country, the climate is harsher. Local stone is also used as a construction material, along with brick and concrete blocks. The yard is less green in the eastern part of the country, because of the semi-arid climate. Vineyards or fruit orchards occupy the greater part of the yard. The villages in East Georgia are more compact and the density of population is higher than that in the rural settlements of West Georgia. The yards in the former are smaller and personal allotments are usually situated farther away. In some villages, especially in Kakheti province, the houses are situated with their rear to the street, so that the entrance cannot be seen from the outside. Fences are made of wooden planks, iron net or from local stone. Gates to rural dwellings in Georgia used to be made of wood, but nowadays they are more often made of metal.

The type of dwelling in the mountainous regions in fact reflect property stratification; the same is true of the lowland area, but there the differences are not as striking. Wealthier people construct the same type of house as in the lowland, but taking into account the rigour of the climate. The poorer villagers, usually the elderly people, live in one-storey houses built of local construction materials. Cattle-sheds and sheep-cotes are characteristic outbuildings of homesteads in these areas. Distinctive in the mountain area of west Georgia are the tower-houses of Upper Svaneti historical province, beautiful medieval battle towers traditionally owned by separate households, surrounded by modern village houses. The towers are preserved as architectural monuments.

CHAPTER 4
Ethnicity and religion

Ethnic dynamics and structure

One of the most widely publicized characteristics of Georgia is its multi-ethnicity. This feature was advertised in the Soviet era as a very positive one, revealing the "efficiency of the nationalities policy of the CPSU". On the eve of independence and afterwards, this same fact was interpreted by local politicians and most foreign observers as a reason for the disaster in Georgia (Jones 1993a). A geographer, however, must take the situation as given. Georgia is a multi-ethnic country, and it has been so for centuries. Thus, the Jews claim that they have been present in Georgia since their Babylonian Captivity in the sixth century BC, Armenians have resided in Georgian towns since the Middle Ages, the Turkic tribes, the ancestors of the modern Azeris, settled here in the early seventeenth century, and so on. The estimated proportion of non-Georgians in the territory of present-day Georgia by the end of the eighteenth century was below 20 per cent (Jaoshvili 1984). Since then, it has grown substantially. Because politics were not involved, each ethnic group in earlier times had its own economic and social niche, and inter-ethnic peace was maintained. As a Georgian writer, Naira Gelasvili, remarked once: "The wise kings of Georgia knew how to manage so varied a population". Recent developments, however, have shown that, in this sphere at least, Georgia has not returned to the dark Middle Ages. It appears that the "management of the nationality problem" is a much harder task at the end of the twentieth century.

The data of every population census in turn were awaited in the USSR with the keenest political, rather than academic, interest. Demographic information became too serious an argument in ethnic tensions and eventually proved to be the cause of many tragedies at personal and community levels. Indeed, the start of the Nagorno–Karabakh conflict in 1988 shook the foundations of the Soviet State more than any other process or event. After – and if – democracy develops in Georgia and normal economic concerns prevail over political interests, the multi-ethnicity may serve as a positive factor. But nowadays the most serious problems of the emerging nation seem to be connected with this demographic characteristic.

Table 4.1 shows the ethnic dynamics of Georgia from 1926 to 1989, the years of the first and last Soviet censuses. We have had to use the only available demographic information, the data of the population censuses carried out in the Soviet

Table 4.1 Ethnic dynamics of Georgia 1926–1989 (population in thousands).

Nationalities	1926	%	1939	%	1959	%	1970	%	1979	%	1989	%	% change
Georgians	1788.2	67.6	2173.6	61.4	2600.6	64.3	3130.7	66.9	3433.0	68.8	3787.4	70.1	211.8
Armenians	307.0	11.6	414.2	11.7	442.9	11.0	452.3	9.7	448.0	8.9	437.2	8.1	142.4
Russians	96.1	3.6	308.0	8.7	407.9	10.1	396.7	8.7	371.5	7.5	341.2	6.3	355.1
Azeris	81.8	3.1	187.6	5.3	153.6	3.8	217.8	4.7	255.9	5.1	307.6	5.7	376.0
Ossetians	113.3	4.3	148.7	4.2	141.2	3.5	150.2	3.2	160.5	3.2	164.1	3.0	144.8
Greeks	54.1	2.1	85.0	2.4	72.9	1.8	89.2	1.9	95.1	1.9	100.3	1.9	185.6
Abkhaz	56.8	2.1	56.6	1.6	62.9	1.6	79.4	1.7	85.3	1.7	95.9	1.8	168.6
Ukrainians	14.4	0.5	46.0	1.3	52.2	1.3	49.6	1.1	45.0	0.9	52.4	1.0	365.3
Kurds	10.2	0.4	–	–	16.2	0.4	20.7	0.5	25.7	0.5	33.3	0.6	326.2
Jews*	30.4	1.2	42.5	1.2	51.6	1.2	55.4	1.2	28.3	0.6	24.8	0.5	–18.5
Others	91.9	3.5	77.6	2.2	36.6	0.9	27.1	0.6	44.8	0.9	56.6	1.0	–38.4
Total	2644.2	100.0	3540.0	100.0	4044.0	100.0	4686.4	100.0	4993.0	100.0	5400.8	100.0	204.2

* Including Georgian Jews.
Source: All-Union (1929), Population (1991).

period. All figures in this chapter, if not otherwise noted, are derived from the 1989 all-Union population census data, published by the Committee for Social–Economic Information of the Republic of Georgia, a body that has changed its official name at least three times from 1990 to 1992 (Population 1991, Nationality Structure 1991, Population of Tbilisi 1991, Number, Sex and Age 1990, Families 1992, Settlements 1990).

After the Georgians, who comprised more than two-thirds of the country's population, there are nine considerable minorities, the second most numerous being the Armenians and the third, since 1939, the Russians; in 1926, the Ossetians were in third place. In future decades the fastest growing minority, the Azeris, will probably become the most numerous nationality after the Georgians. However, the size of an ethnic group is not always proportional to its real significance in social and political life. As International Alert experts noted, "the Abkhaz remained the least numerous "major" minority in Georgia, but they provoked a level of confrontation which has escalated into open warfare" (Essaïed et al. 1993).

Probably one of the most important aspects in the case of a multi-ethnic country is the geographical dimension, in the first place the location and interlocation of ethnic groups. Since the present book, dedicated to Georgia, deals predominantly with the ethnic Georgians, in this chapter more attention will be paid to the location and dynamics of individual national minorities. But something must be told of the geography of the Georgians as well.

Georgians

The Georgians constitute an absolute majority in central-western, western and easternmost districts of the country (Fig. 4.1). In West Georgia as a whole, 81.4 per cent of the total population are Georgians, in East Georgia 61.6 per cent (Jaoshvili 1993). Cities are usually multi-ethnic; Sokhumi had 41.5 per cent Georgian population, Tbilisi, Batumi and Rustavi 65–66 per cent each. Only Kutaisi looked more mono-ethnic, with 90.8 per cent of its population Georgian.

The demographic dynamics of the Georgians in the twentieth century were generally upward, despite heavy losses in the 1930s–40s from purges and the Second World War. Their absolute number more than doubled from 1926 to 1989. In the USSR as a whole they numbered about four million, of whom 95.1 per cent lived within Georgia – the highest level of "attachment to the homeland" among the Soviet "titular nations". However, a tendency for out-migration was becoming apparent; in 1970 the same "index of attachment" had been even higher at 96.5 per cent. Most of the Georgian emigrants moved, and still move, towards Russia's largest cities and are engaged in science, medicine, industry and business. In Azerbaijan, there are rural communities of Muslim and Christian Georgians in the northern corner, the Zaqatala, Qakh and Balakan districts of the historical province of Saingilo. Christians from this area tend to emigrate to Georgia, but the Muslim Georgians gradually assimilate with the Azeris.

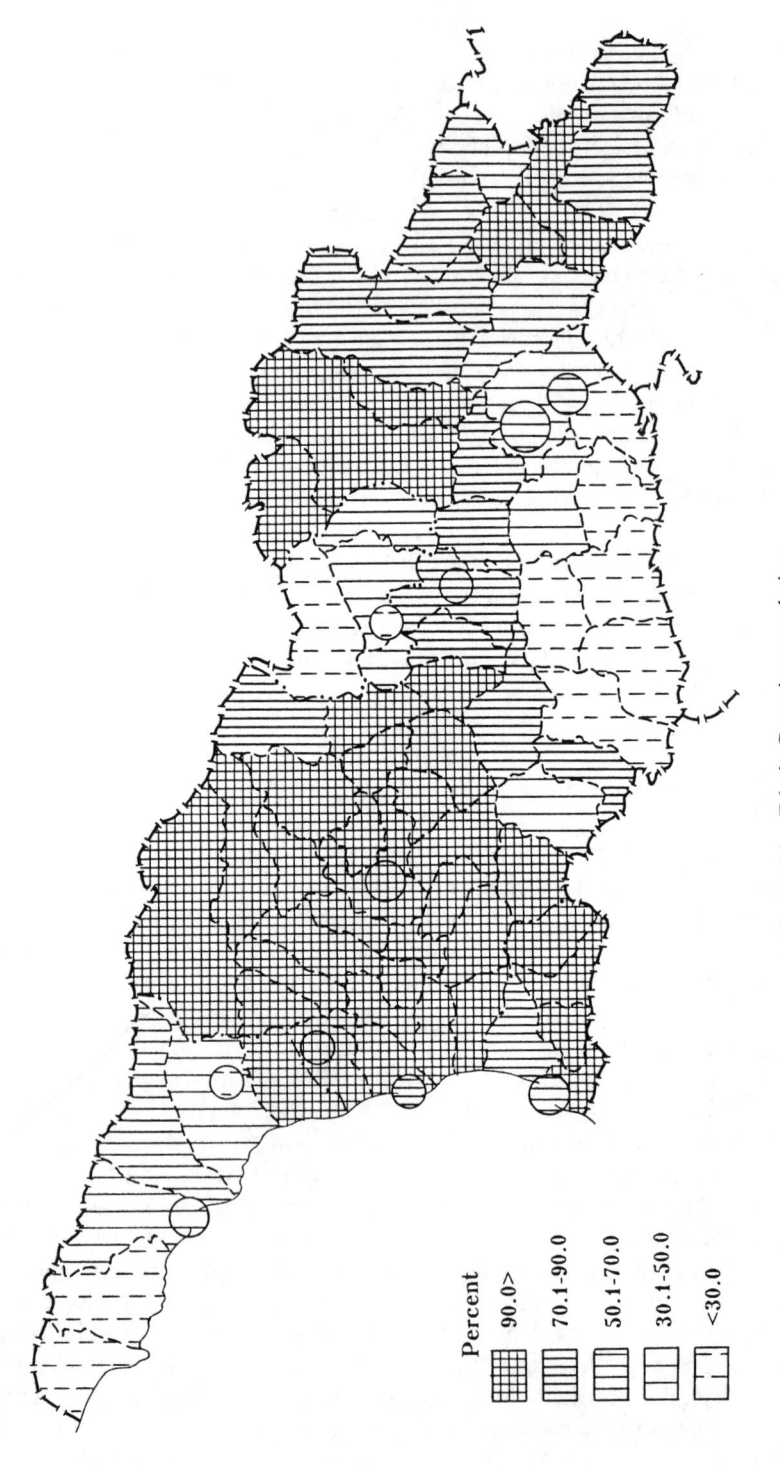

Figure 4.1 Ethnic Georgian population.

Outside the former USSR, the Georgians have no strong diasporas. According to the 1965 population census of Turkey (since when no data has been available and even that is not very reliable), Kartvelian languages (Georgian proper and lazuri) were the mother tongue or second language of 168000 people; those claiming to be gurji (Georgian) or lazi, but without fluency in these languages, might have exceeded these figures (Gachechiladze 1972). These Kartvelian-speaking Sunni Muslims think of themselves as true citizens of Turkey, which they consider their homeland. Strengthening ties with these people may play a positive role in Georgia's relations with Turkey and in Georgia's economic development.

In the Fereidan district of Iran there is a community of Georgian-speaking Shi'a Muslims, estimated as 30000–40000 strong, the descendants of a population deported to that country from Georgia's Kakheti province in the early seventeenth century and converted to Islam. Attempts to repatriate some of them in the 1970s and 1980s proved mostly to be unsuccessful. Even though maintaining Georgian as the vernacular, the majority had become culturally Persianized. They tend rather to emigrate to Isfahan and Teheran. In other countries, until recently Georgians did not form sizeable communities; there were only small ones in France and the USA.

The proportion of Georgians in the population of Georgia fell significantly in the pre-war period, from 68 to 61 per cent between 1926 and 1939. Over this period, their number increased by only 21.6 per cent, while the number of Armenians within Georgia rose by 35 per cent, and that of the Slavic peoples by 320 per cent (sic). The proportion at the time of the 1926 census was regained by the Georgians only in the mid-1970s, mostly as a result of the emigration of the same peoples. Since then, the proportion of ethnic Georgians in the total population has continued to grow. In the 1990s this is being caused by ever increasing emigration of the non-Georgians from a country in total crisis, and not by any high birthrate of ethnic Georgians. On the contrary, their birthrate has decreased dramatically and in some mountainous rural areas is much below the mortality rate (Ch. 3). The absolute number of Georgians in the country will probably fall during the coming decade, because of social problems, civil wars and emigration.

Sub-ethnic distinctions within this nation, as in many others, are revealed in dialects, even in local, unwritten languages (the *megruli* and *svanuri* languages, which differ from literary Georgian), religion and regional ways of life. Social regionalization is mostly founded on such sub-ethnic regional differences (Ch. 1). Some foreign observers, following scholars unsympathetic towards Georgia, have recently "discovered a new problem with Georgians": these sub-ethnic differences within the nation. They over-emphasize these differences as a cause of disintegration of Georgia. It is interesting that this phenomenon is especially exaggerated by Russian nationalists and contemporary communists, for example in the latter's newspaper *Pravda* (Zhidkov 1993) and by some Western scholars antipathetic towards the Georgians. The contributors to the *Guide to the peoples of Europe* (Fernandez-Armesto 1994) overestimate these differences and do not even consider the Georgians as one nation, as in Tsarist Russia.

The unified educational system since the nineteenth century, using literary Georgian, contributed to the consolidation of the nation. Thus, the school textbooks by Jacob Gogebashvili have been in use from 1876 to the present (with modifications, naturally). Consolidation was also assisted by urbanization, notably the concentration of representatives of all Georgian sub-ethnic groups in their "melting pot", the capital city of Tbilisi, where 21.7 per cent of the total Georgian population of the country lived in 1989, as against only 6.3 per cent in 1926. As foreign commentators have witnessed, the self-identity of the Georgians is strong. "Georgians, among whom there are regional distinctions, are nevertheless all highly conscious of Georgian traditions and culture" (Essaïed et al. 1993). Even in the recent Georgian civil war, sub-ethnic differences were not a serious issue. Georgians were killing Georgians on purely ideological grounds! Gamsakhurdia had his supporters among all sub-ethnic groups of Georgians and never considered himself as leader of a part of the country.

A notable feature of this nation is the very long persistence of surnames, many of which can be traced from the Middle Ages, with no change through the direct descendants. Almost every Georgian, on meeting another, can guess with high probability, just by his surname, the historical province from which the other comes and can try to detect at least an accent. Dialects have been disappearing, because of universal education and all-penetrating TV; moreover, a dialect or even a provincial accent may be an obstacle to promotion in Tbilisi. People will also adjust their behaviour to the stereotype ascribed to each sub-ethnic group, as usually revealed in popular anecdotes. For instance, the name of the present author indicates to many Georgians its derivation from the province of Imereti, although to his family's shame his is the third generation that, after settling in Tbilisi in the nineteenth century, has never visited the hill village of Tseva whence this surname can be traced from at least the seventeenth century and is still borne by all its remaining inhabitants.

Figure 4.2 shows the traditional distribution of surname endings in rural Georgia, by historical provinces; in urban areas there is a real mixture. The majority of endings are *dze*, meaning "son" in Georgian, or *shvili*, meaning "child". These two endings show no specific concentration and can be met everywhere, but in essence *shvili* is more characteristic of the eastern provinces. Some endings show origin in general (*ani, ia, ua, va, uri/uli*), or place of origin (*eli*, with no spatial concentration) (Topchisvili 1993).

The typical ending of Armenian names is *ian*, of Abkhaz names it is *ba*; *ov* and *ev* are Russianized endings used by the Ossetians and Azeris, although more Ossetians now turn to the original ending *ti*. Nevertheless, there are a few exceptions to these rules. For example, Anchaba-dze is an Abkhaz surname, Togo-shvili is Ossetian, whereas Ukle-ba or Kandel-aki (with typical Greek ending) are Georgian. There are also some other irregular Georgian names.

Location of the non-Georgian population

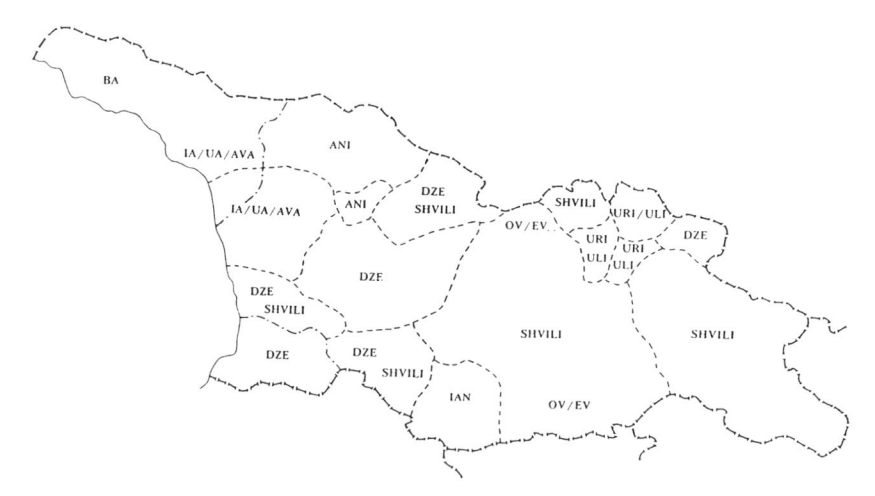

Figure 4.2 Traditional distribution of surname endings by historical provinces (rural areas).

Location of the non-Georgian population

From a geographical point of view, ethnic minorities in Georgia may be roughly divided into two groups: those predominantly territorially concentrated with a "core rural area" and those predominantly dispersed. Although none of those in the first group are wholly concentrated in one particular area, they are settled in some rural areas that have the appearance of a "core". Such groups are the Abkhaz, residing almost entirely in the northwest; Greeks, comprising the majority in Tsalka rural district in the central part of the country; Azeris, whose "core area" within Georgia has become Marneuli and adjacent districts in the central south; and the Armenians, comprising the majority in Javakheti historical province and a substantial community in rural Abkhazia. There are concentrations of smaller communities of Kistis (Chechens) and Avarians in some villages of the eastern historical province of Kakheti. The Kurds have a specific concentration in the capital city of Tbilisi. Jews, who earlier were more dispersed, after the huge emigration to Israel began in the 1970s, are now collected in the largest urban centres.

The dispersed minorities comprise mainly the Slavic peoples, Russians, Ukrainians and Byelorussians, who are spread all over Georgia, but live predominantly in the cities. Of the 71 nationalities, enumerated by the last census of 1989 as resident in Georgia, most form no communities at all and live dispersed among the major ethnic groups. Ossetians have a specific location; their major "core area" is the city of Tskhinvali and adjacent rural areas, but by 1989 the absolute majority of them (60%) were scattered all over Georgia, predominantly in the eastern part. The location of the principal minority groups is seen in Figure 4.3.

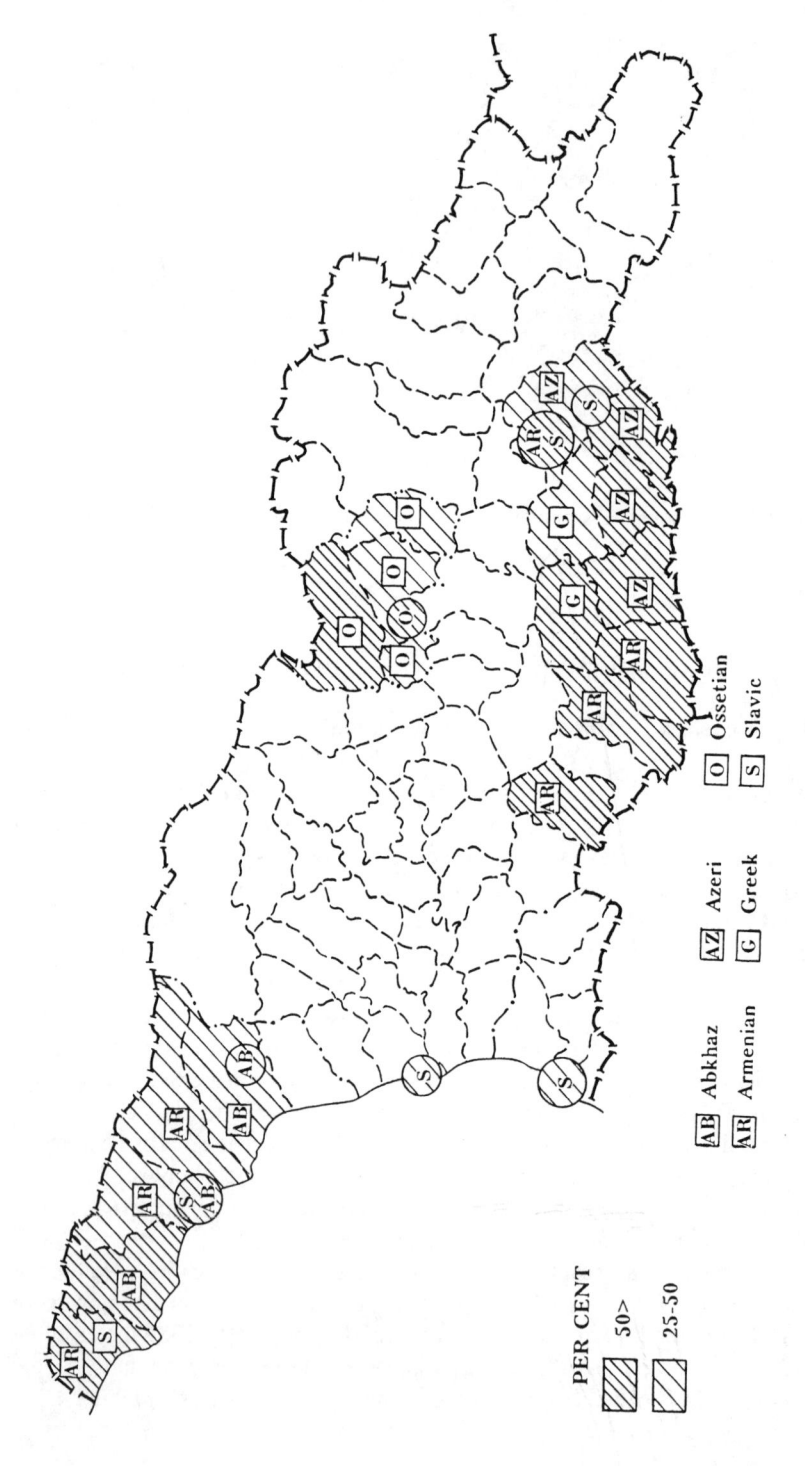

Figure 4.3 Ethnic non-Georgian populations, 1989.

Abkhaz

Recent tragic events in Georgia, notably the civil war in Abkhazia and international reaction to it, made known to the outer world a small group of people whose existence was previously familiar to only a handful of Western specialists.

The area of settlement of the Abkhaz has changed through time. Ancient historical geography is a matter for historians. However, it is a fact that in the nineteenth century, notably in 1867 and 1877–8, this not very numerous people suffered tragedies, when the Russian Empire, which blamed the Abkhaz as "guilty people" supporting the Ottomans, compelled them to emigrate to Turkey. As happened with their north Caucasian kindred, the Circassians and Ubykhs, most of the Muslim Abkhaz left while the Christians stayed.

The exodus occurred in waves. The numerical data on emigrants in the 1860s are obscure. The most reliable estimate of the number of *mahajirs* (emigrants), who left in 1877–8, is about 32000, while 13000 stayed (Statistical 1880: xi). Almost half of the emigrants soon returned back (Anchabadze 1976: 86). This can be proved by an accurate survey carried out in 1886 (Code 1893), when 28000 of the Abkhaz were listed in the area. The majority of the Abkhaz emigrants gradually assimilated with the Turks and the Arabs of Syria and Jordan, where smaller groups found themselves. A few of them preserved their ethnic identity (Abaza) and presumably still fewer kept even the language. According to the 1960 population census of Turkey, Abkhaz as the vernacular was claimed by 4700 people and 8000 knew it as the second language, after Turkish as the mother tongue (Republic of Turkey 1963). Abkhaz communities in Arab countries are smaller. The most optimistic estimate might be a doubling of the Abkhaz-speakers in Turkey since 1960. But the inevitable process of assimilation gives no ground for such optimism. The assertion that some 100000 Abkhaz left their homeland during the nineteenth century and that the number of those living abroad has since increased substantially (Inal-ipa 1990: 35) looks equally groundless.

> The land left by the *mahajirs* was distributed by the Tsarist government among the high-ranking military and civil officials, who used them for the colonization that took on a large scale in the 1880–90s. Colonists of different nationalities, Russians, Greeks, Armenians, Germans, Estonians, Bulgarians, etc., started to settle on "vacant" land. In the same period the resettlement of land-hungry peasants from the adjacent regions, predominantly from Samegrelo, increased. These peasants received no favour from the Tsarist officials, who even hindered their in-migration. Therefore, they usually became leaseholders of the big landlords.   (Anchabadze 1976: 86)

This trend created the spatial basis of a new pattern of population geography, which can be traced with more confidence.

In discussing the dynamics of the Abkhaz during the past hundred years, the major problem is the ethnic identity of the population of historical Samurzakano province, the modern Gali and part of Ochamchire districts between the rivers Galidzga in the north and Inguri in the south. Originally belonging to Samegrelo and settled by a Kartvelian people (Megrelians), it became a marchland area for the princes of Samegrelo and Abkhazia in the late Middle Ages. In those times the ethnic identity of the peasants paying duties meant nothing to the feudal lords. Eventually, in the early eighteenth century, the territory was gained by an Abkhaz prince, Murzakan Shervashidze, and his duchy within the Abkhaz Principality has since been called *sa-murzakan-o*, which means in Georgian "(the place) of Murzakan". It is worth mentioning that the place-name was created in Georgian proper, rather than in any other tongue, as this language served as the *lingua franca* over the whole territory of the ancient Georgian kingdom.

After this feudal acquisition, neither "Samurzakanian language", nor "Samurzakanian people" have appeared. The duchy became an area of active intermixing of population, with the Kartvelian element still prevailing. An Abkhaz historian witnesses that the Princes of Abkhazia started to settle ethnic Abkhaz in the territories that they gained from the Princes of Samegrelo, first northwest of Samurzakano, and later, from the eighteenth century, in the area between the Galidzga and Inguri. "But the number of Abkhaz settled, in all probability, was insignificant and the Abkhazianization of this region went at a slower pace" (Anchabadze 1976: 68); "the ruling class consisted predominantly of the Abkhaz, among the working people the Megrelians prevailed" (ibid.: 76f).

Many of the old place-names from the River Kodori to the River Inguri and most of those in Samurzakano can be interpreted only by means of the Kartvelian languages (Bgazhba 1974: 178–9). The name of the River Galidzga means in megruli "water's bank/edge". Even the name of the capital city of Abkhazia, Sokhumi, is a derivative from a Kartvelian (svanuri) word *tskhumi* meaning "hornbeam" (ibid.). The Abkhaz call the city "Aqwa".

Russian and Soviet statistics, the only ones that can show the number and ethnic composition of the population since the 1870s, are rather dubious, considering the inhabitants of Samurzakano variously as Georgian (Megrelian), or Abkhaz, or a separate ethnic group. Thus, a Russian source of 1880 gave a figure of 41 364 inhabitants for Sokhumi Region, out of whom 26 475 (64%) were listed as "Megrelians", all of them in Samurzakano, and 13 205 as "Abkhaz", outside Samurzakano (Statistical 1880).

Quite accurate statistics based on the "household lists" gathered in 1886, gave the figures shown in Table 4.2. It is useful to present the original table, as some scholars consider without argument that all the "Samurzakanians" were Abkhaz. Hewitt was probably misled by such sources when he cited a table where all the Samurzakanians were added to the Abkhaz and thus almost all the population of Sokhumi Region in 1886 (58 961) were shown as ethnic Abkhaz, while the "Kartvelian" population was less then 4000 (Hewitt 1993a). When 1886 is taken as the principal base-line for comparisons of ethnic change, such a miscalculation leads to overestimation of one ethnic group and underestimation of the other.

The most uncertain in Table 4.2 are the "Samurzakanians". Less than a decade

Table 4.2 Ethnic population of Sokhumi Region (1886).

Ethnic groups	Households	Persons	% (persons)
Russians	211	971	1.4
Megrelians	800	3474	5.1
Samurzakanians	6004	30640	45.2
Abkhazians	6231	28320	41.8
Greeks	515	2056	3.0
Estonians	198	637	0.9
Armenians	226	1037	1.5
Other	186	711	1.1
Total	14371	67846	100.0

Source: Code (1893).

earlier they had been enumerated as "Megrelians", according to the mother tongue, whereas now the Megrelians living outside Samurzakano were listed separately from those living within. Nevertheless, there was still no confusion of the "Samurzakanians" with the ethnic Abkhaz. Religion in this case could not play the role of "ethnic distinguisher", since all the "Samurzakanians", as well as the majority of Abkhaz, were Orthodox Christians. Therefore, the major factor of self-identity remained language, which cannot change over a short period of time. The mother tongue of most of the "Samurzakanians" without any doubt was Megrelian, a Kartvelian language. This has been established by the 1926 census.

The Questionnaire of the first population census of the Russian Empire in 1897 implied the registration of mother tongue only. The attribution of the population to the separate ethnic groups was carried out by the census organizers, who "in many cases while handling the census materials, considered it worthwhile to correct in a suitable manner the data of the given column (mother tongue)" (Troïnitsky 1905: 1). Hence, by the arbitrary decision of the editor of this part of the census (Patkanov), all the "Samurzakanians", including the Kartvelian-speaking majority, were listed as Abkhaz, artificially increasing the number of the latter to 59469 persons, a growth of 210 per cent in 11 years!. To the Abkhaz were added even the Abazins, who spoke a different (although kindred) language, residing in Kuban Oblast (Batalpashinsk district) in the north Caucasus (ibid.: xxviii).

According to the administrative statistics of 1914, in the population of Sokhumi Region the Abkhaz amounted to 27.3 per cent, whereas the Georgians formed 44.8 per cent (Project 1920: 89). It seems that these statistics were not very exact, as in only three years an agricultural and property census demonstrated that both ethnic groups were smaller in proportion (21.4% and 42.1% respectively). Samurzakanians were listed as Georgians. The proportion of Russians, Armenians and Greeks increased to 10–11 per cent each (Project 1920: 40). That the latter census was carried out during the First World War might have had some implications. However, a peculiarity is noticeable: Georgians ("Kartvelians") outnumbered the Abkhaz in the area already in the Romanov Empire. The same trend was evident in 1926. According to the population census, which gave every adult free choice to claim both his ethnic identity (even sub-ethnic identity in the case of the Georgians) and mother tongue, the Georgians were again the largest group with 36.3 per cent, whereas the Abkhaz, among whom 16 per cent claimed a Kartvelian language to be their vernacular, formed 27.8 per cent. This linguistic characteristic was the cause of later demographic change and it must be discussed in more detail.

Of the population of Gali district in historical Samurzakano, 73.4 per cent had Georgian self-identity in 1926. More than half indicated their mother tongue as Megrelian, the rest as Georgian proper. Meanwhile, 25.5 per cent considered themselves as Abkhaz, but for the majority of these the mother tongue was Megrelian. Only 10.5 per cent of the population of Gali district had fluent Abkhaz in 1926. According to this census, the number of ethnic Abkhaz in Abkhazia had decreased in comparison with 1897, demonstrating the obvious error in the data handling by the organizers of the earlier census. Among people with Abkhaz self-identity in 1926, numbering 55 918 persons in all, 8755 (16%) claimed a Kartvelian vernacular (All-Union 1929). This group was represented both by the ethnic Abkhaz, who had earlier migrated to Samurzakano from the northwest, as described in the quotation above from Anchabadze, and had assimilated linguistically in a Kartvelian milieu, and also by the ethnic Kartvelians who considered their national identity as belonging to the "titular nation" of the territory. Although the figure of 8755 might be considered insignificant for measuring ethnic dynamics, in this particular case it is large enough to explain the dynamics of the Abkhaz during the next two and a half decades. Most of the persons with a Kartvelian mother tongue started to consider themselves as Georgians. The growth of the literacy level affected the growth of national self-identity.

Recently the figures of the All-Union census of 6 January 1937, after being top secret for more than half a century, have been revealed (Polyakov et al. 1990). It appears that these figures were too exact to suit the Soviet leadership, and the scientific organizers were shot as "wreckers", in the manner peculiar to Stalinism. But the All-Union figures for the Abkhaz (55 561) appeared to be even smaller in early 1937 before the massive purges occurred, than in the 1939 census, which was carried out after the purges had raged over the whole country; by then the number of Abkhaz had increased by 1000, a 1.8 per cent increase in two years (quite plausible dynamics). It might be supposed that some of those "Samurzakanians", who had earlier considered themselves Abkhaz, by the mid-1930s had already changed their national self-identity.

During recent decades the increase of the Abkhaz population has been steady. From 1959 to 1989 their number within Georgia as a whole increased by 52.6 per cent, even faster than the Georgians, who increased by 45.6 per cent. It is supposed that assimilation also played a part, as belonging to the "titular nation", even in an autonomous republic, became beneficial. The proportion of Abkhaz in the autonomous republic increased from 15.1 per cent in 1959 to 17.8 per cent in 1989, although they were still outnumbered by ethnic Georgians, the proportion of whom by 1989 was 45.7 per cent. The Armenians formed 14.6 and the Russians 14.3 per cent in the same year.

The location of the Abkhaz reveals their concentration in two districts and one CRS of the autonomous republic. In Gudauta district they were the absolute majority with 53.1 per cent. This sub-ethnic group is called Bzyb Abkhaz and some of the community are closer to Islamic traditions. In Ochamchire District, Abkhaz amounted to 36.7 per cent of the population. Here the Abzhu Abkhaz sub-ethnic group is located, all belonging to Christian Orthodox traditions; their dialect became the basis of the literary Abkhaz language.

In the CRS of Tkvarcheli in Ochamchire District, the Abkhaz were 42.3 per cent of the population. Thirty years earlier this coalmining town had been populated mostly by Russians with 42.5 per cent. When the coalmines became exhausted, the town's population decreased. Half the Russians left, whereas the Abkhaz doubled. The proportion of the Georgians remained practically stable about 21 per cent, but in absolute figures they declined after 1970 by more than a thousand. Thus, the town became one of the "citadels" of Abkhaz nationalism, explaining the boycott of the all-Georgia multiparty elections of 1990 and 1992, which was imposed by the local authorities on the whole electorate of the town.

In these three administrative units lived 60.5 per cent of all the Abkhaz in 1989. In the other rural districts and towns of the Autonomous Republic, the titular nation was in an absolute minority. In the Gagra urban area the Abkhaz comprised 11.2 per cent; here the majority were the Russians, (30.5%), followed by the Georgians (28.1%) and the Armenians (19.4%). In Gali and Gulripshi rural districts, the Abkhaz accounted for 0.8 and 2.4 per cent respectively and in the capital city, Sokhumi, they numbered only 3647 in 1959 (5.6% of the city's population) and 14 922 in 1989 (12.5%) (Fig. 4.2). It must be stressed however that the number was not proportional to the real influence of the titular nationality.

The Abkhaz belong to the nationalities with a relatively recent literacy. The first Abkhaz alphabet was elaborated by a Russian linguist, K. Uslar, only in 1862 on the basis of Cyrillic, with some Georgian letters as well, but it was imperfect and at the end of the nineteenth century it had to be revised; the revision was accomplished by a Georgian and an Abkhaz. The birth date of Abkhaz literary fiction is attributed to 1912 (Anchabadze 1976: 101). In fact their culture in the twentieth century developed under the influence and mostly on the basis of Russian language.

Within the Georgian SSR, especially since the mid-1950s, the Abkhaz have had normal conditions to develop their culture. There were an Abkhaz university, theatre, television and radio services; books, magazines and newspapers were published in the vernacular. There were scientific institutions and 73 Abkhaz schools; that these schools were losing pupils was a different question, and attributable to the preference of parents to send their offspring to Russian schools. The major Party and administrative posts, very important in a one-party bureaucratic State, were held by ethnic Abkhaz in a proportion much above their number in the total population (Slider 1985). Moreover, they had an opportunity to complain to Moscow of "ill treatment by Tbilisi", whereas the "titular nationalities" of the autonomous republics in the Volga Basin or north Caucasus, since they were within the Russian Federation, could not complain in the same way of "ill treatment by Moscow".

Religion does not play a decisive role in the life of the modern Abkhaz and is not a factor in the conflict there. Most of the Abkhaz are at least nominal Orthodox Christians. Some of those from Gudauta District claim to be Muslim, a claim to some extent proved by the first names of the elderly people. According to the 1886 data, 14.6 per cent of the Abkhaz were listed as Sunni Muslim (Code 1893). Nowadays there is not a single mosque in Abkhazia, although there are active Orthodox churches. But in their relations with the north Caucasians and with the descendants of Abkhaz emigrants in the Middle East, most of whom are pious Muslims, the "Islamic card" is being used. That is displayed even in symbolism: the colour green, a sign of Islam, was used by the north Caucasian and the Abkhaz to distinguish themselves from the Georgians during the recent war (Rotar 1993b).

Ossetians

The Ossetians are another minority, who under the Soviet rule had territorial autonomy in Georgia as an autonomous oblast. The history of interaction between the Georgians and Ossetians covers at least two millennia. Most of what is known about the ancient ancestors of the modern Ossetians can be traced chiefly from Georgian historical sources. Written texts in Ossetian appeared only in the late eighteenth century, using Georgian script. Later the alphabet was changed to Cyrillic, but under the communists there were a series of "experiments", first changing to Latin script in 1924–37, then once again to Georgian in South Ossetia, and yet again to Cyrillic. This obviously led to resentment on the part of the Ossetian intellectuals. Similar frequent changes of alphabets (Arabic, Latin, Cyrillic) was imposed by Moscow upon all the other peoples originally without alphabets, notably those of Central Asia and the Caucasus.

The name by which this ethnic group is known to the outer world is derived from Georgian "o(v)s-i" (the name of the people) and "o(v)seti" (the name of their country in the north Caucasus). The Ossetians own name for themselves is "Iron", and the country is called "Iriston". The Ossetians are the only autochthonous people in the north Caucasus of Indo-European (Iranian group) linguistic roots.

The sporadic penetration of the Ossetians into Georgia, onto the southern slopes of the Caucasus, started in the Middle Ages. In the East Georgian foothills and plains they began arriving in the seventeenth and eighteenth centuries (Togoshvili 1981). As landless newcomers they were welcomed by the Georgian feudal lords, who were in permanent need of cheap labour. The Ossetians were baptized as Orthodox Christians. Within Georgia, until 1922 the Ossetians had no ethno-territorial unit. The term "South Ossetia" was used from the mid-nineteenth century to designate the mountainous area of the historical Georgian province of Kartli, settled by the ethnic Ossetians. For the most part it covered modern Java district, without Tskhinvali and its area (Gogebashvili 1912: 541). The fact that the natural border between Georgia and Ossetia follows the Great Caucasus Range and Daryal gorge was never disputed even by Ossetian scholars (Abayev 1992).

In 1922, an autonomous region was created for some 65 000 Ossetians in the north-central part of Georgia (Ch. 2). 53.3 per cent of all the Ossetians in Georgia lived within this Region in 1926. By 1989 this proportion had decreased to 39.2 per cent as the remainder spread all over Georgia. Tbilisi alone was the home of the largest community of Ossetians in the country. The 1989 population census revealed that there were hardly any rural or urban districts in Georgia without at least some Ossetians residing there. Indirectly, this indicates the absence of discrimination towards this ethnic group.

Intermarriages between the Ossetians and the Georgians are widespread (Gokadze 1992). In 1989, 32.5 per cent of the Ossetians were fluent in Georgian and 20.5 per cent even considered Georgian their mother tongue. That was the highest rate of inter-ethnic integration in Georgia (Table 4.3). Even a hundred

Table 4.3 Distribution of the ethnic population of Georgia according to vernacular and fluency in Georgian and Russian, 1989 (%).

Nationality	Claims vernacular			Masters fluently as second language	
	Language of its own nationality	Georgian	Russian	Georgian	Russian
Georgians	99.7	–	0.2	0.1	31.8
Abkhaz	96.7	1.2	2.3	2.4	80.5
Ossetians	76.7	20.5	2.6	32.6	36.6
Russians	98.7	1.2	–	22.5	0.7
Ukrainians	53.4	2.4	44.0	14.2	41.6
Byelorussians	54.2	2.0	43.2	11.0	37.4
Azeris	97.7	0.9	1.3	9.3	34.2
Armenians	85.0	5.7	9.2	20.3	42.9
Jews	13.3	29.4	56.5	27.8	24.0
Georgian Jews	95.1*	–	4.6	3.1	49.5
Greeks	57.0	5.0	35.0	15.4	44.7
Kurds	74.7	11.5	12.3	43.8	26.2
Total	95.7	1.5	2.6	5.7	32.3

*The mother tongue of the Georgian Jews is Georgian
Source: [Ethnic Structure, 1991]

years ago, 30.5 per cent of the Ossetians residing in Tbilisi gave Georgian as their mother tongue (Kobyakov 1880: 135). The demographic behaviour and way of life of the Ossetians, especially of those living outside the autonomous region, resembled that of the Georgians. This probably explains to some extent the low rate of increase of Ossetians in the country; some of them assimilated with the Georgians and the Russians. A further process also deserves attention. That is emigration from the industrially less developed autonomous region towards

Vladikavkaz in North Ossetia and beyond to the large Russian cities. In contrast to the Georgians (at least until recently), the Russian-speaking Ossetians easily adapted to non-familiar environments in new areas. Moreover, the acquisition of higher education by many Ossetians permitted them to obtain better positions in the major Georgian and other Soviet cities. In Georgia Ossetians are predominantly city dwellers, with 78.4 per cent living in urban areas; by this index they equal the British. This urbanization led to an almost complete change in the ethnic population of Tskhinvali, the centre of the former autonomous region. In 1886, not a single Ossetian resided in this township (Code 1893); by 1926, the 1152 Ossetians comprised 19.8 per cent of the population (All-Union 1929) and in 1989 they were 74.5 per cent or 31 500. Urbanization created better conditions for the development of the Ossetian culture within Georgia, with the support of the Soviet Republic's government.

In North Ossetia, part of the Russian Federation, intensive Russification was in progress and until 1988 there was not a single Ossetian school in that autonomous republic. In contrast, by September 1990 in the South Ossetian Autonomous Region there were 90 schools teaching in the native language; in addition, there were Ossetian schools in every area in Georgia outside the autonomous region where they formed a more or less significant ethnic community. There were in Tskhinvali a teacher's training college, a scientific Institute of the Academy of Sciences of Georgia, carrying out research in local history, linguistics and literature, a State theatre, State library, State museum, State Ensemble of Folk Song and Dance, and so on. Papers, magazines and books were published in Ossetian. It has been calculated that for every 10 000 persons in South Ossetia there five times as many titles and three and a half times as many copies of books and brochures were published in the native language as in its northern "sister autonomous republic" (Zhorzholiani et al. 1992). Almost all the highly skilled scientific and cultural workers of South Ossetia were trained in Tbilisi. All this, although resembling the "propaganda of the nationality policy of CPSU", does no more than point to the higher national self-identity of the Ossetians living in the autonomous area within Georgia.

In 1991, when ethnic conflict in the area broke out (Ch. 9), many Ossetians had to leave Georgia, mostly for North Ossetia. Some irresponsible persons considered this a retaliation for the Georgians banished from the city of Tskhinvali and the villages in the vicinity. Inter-ethnic relations were dramatically worsened. From 1990 to the middle of 1993, in Tbilisi alone 4200 more Ossetians left than entered (Gachechiladze & Bradshaw 1994). That represented about 20 per cent of the ethnic Ossetians residing in the city up to 1989. Since 1993, relations have started to improve, some of the Ossetians are returning and it is possible to think that normal relations will be restored.

Armenians

The Armenians settled in Georgia in waves. In the eighteenth century they settled in eastern Georgian towns, many arriving from Karabakh (Jaoshvili 1968); in 1829–30 about 30000 settled in Javakheti province. A large influx of Armenians from the Ottoman Empire arrived in 1897–1902, when 55000 of them settled in Georgia. In Tbilisi alone, immigration increased the Armenian population from 46700 in 1897 to 124900 in 1910 (Jaoshvili 1984: 228). During the First World War there was an additional large influx into Georgia of Armenians fleeing from the Ottoman Empire; most settled in Tbilisi and Abkhazia.

During the Soviet era, the numbers of Armenians in Georgia increased until the 1970s, especially in the pre-war period. Thereafter, their number started to decrease even in absolute figures. This was attributable to their migration to Armenia, especially to vigorously growing Yerevan, where for a while the most widespread foreign language after Russian was Georgian, and to the Russian Federation. In part too, this decrease was attributable to assimilation of the Armenians by ethnic Georgians (Gujabidze 1983). There are three major areas where the Armenians are concentrated in Georgia: Tbilisi, Javakheti and Abkhazia. In 1989 these three areas contained 34.3, 22.3 and 17.5 per cent respectively of all Armenians in Georgia.

Since the Middle Ages, Armenian communities have existed in Georgian towns, especially Tbilisi, occupying a distinct economic niche as tradesmen and artisans. In nineteenth century Tbilisi, quite a large Armenian intelligentsia emerged, which mostly moved to Yerevan after the independent Armenian Republic (1918–20) was established, to be later succeeded by Soviet Armenia. An Armenian community 150000 strong lived in Tbilisi in 1989, making up 12.1 per cent of the city's population.

After the Russo–Turkish war of 1828–9, the Armenians of the Erzurum province of the Ottoman Empire, who supported the Russian side in that war, preferred to settle within a Christian State. The Russian government allocated them space in the ancient Georgian province of Javakheti, at that time recently annexed to Russia and sparsely populated as the majority of the Muslim Georgians had left. Thus, a refuge was given to the new ethnic group in Akhalkalaki (an eleventh-century name meaning "new town" in Georgian), which comprised Javakheti province. Today Armenians make up more than 90 per cent of the population of that province. Genuine cultural autonomy is enjoyed by the Armenians of Javakheti; the native language alone is used in both everyday and official life (Lebanidze 1993).

Until recently, on both sides in Georgia and Armenia there were "buffer settlements" of Russians, descendants of *dukhobortsy*, a religious minority deported in the nineteenth century by the Imperial government. Now the majority of these have returned to Russia, and there is direct contiguity of Armenian settlements on both sides of the border.

The third large concentration of the Armenians is in Abkhazia, where they have been present since the 1860s. From 1926 to 1989 their number tripled to become the third largest (14.6%) after the Georgians and the Abkhaz. The Armenians are specially strongly represented in the rural population of Sokhumi and Gulripshi districts, at 29.4 per cent and 25.3 per cent respectively.

In Georgia the Armenians have 200 secondary schools, newspapers, State radio programmes, and a State theatre in Tbilisi. In communist Georgia, they enjoyed an unofficial quota in the Supreme Council and government. Being enterprising and hard-working, the Armenians managed to achieve high material standards, even under a Soviet rule that tried to equalize personal incomes. Many Armenians became integrated into Georgian society. However, as the Armenian Republic lay next door, the best conditions for promotion always lay abroad. This engendered a trend for the most energetic of the Armenian intellectuals to emigrate from Georgia.

Slavic peoples

Russians, and Slavs as a whole, were present in Georgia from the beginning of the nineteenth century. In that century, the most significant Slavic group apart from the Russians, especially in the cultural and social life of Tbilisi, were the Poles. These were participants in the Polish uprising of 1863, who were deported to the Caucasus. The majority being young males, they naturally intermarried with the local women. The descendants of those who married Georgian girls gradually Georgianized and there are a few Georgians with Polish surnames; the remainder Russified. After the independence of Georgia was restored, there were attempts to revive the Polish community through the newly legalized Catholic Church.

In 1989 the Slavs were represented in Georgia by Russians (341 000), Ukrainians (52 000) and Byelorussians (8600). They can be considered together as having an identical settlement pattern, being predominantly urban dwellers, and a very similar demographic behaviour, with low birthrate and small families. In 1989 the average Russian family had 3.1 members, a Ukrainian family 2.8. This small family size is explained by the presence of a high proportion of Soviet (now Russian) Army officers in these ethnic groups, who have to change their location quite often and are therefore reluctant to create large families. Intermarriages between the Slavs are frequent, in essence leading to the Russification of all the Slavs outside their own republics. Almost half the Ukrainian and Byelorussians in Georgia claim Russian as their mother tongue (Table 4.3).

The Slavic population in Georgia increased especially in the 1930s, as the result of industrialization, which required many skilled workers. In addition, many escaped to Transcaucasia from the terrible famine imposed on the Ukraine and southern Russia by the forced collectivization policy in 1932–3. During the Second World War, Georgia gave refuge to many Slavic evacuees from the territories occupied by the Nazis. Although the majority of these later returned to their homeland, a substantial number remained in the cities of Georgia.

At its highest level in the mid-1950s, the population of Slavic origin in Georgia reached 500 000, or 13 per cent of the total; thereafter it decreased. The reason for the out-migration was the slow-down in the rate of industrial development, which could be met by the rapid increase of the local working class, deriving from ethnic Georgians migrating to urban areas. The decrease in the number of Slavs is also affected by the very low birthrate and by intermarriages with the local population, especially the Georgians; that usually meant at least the formal adherence of the children to Georgian nationality. Linguistic assimilation with the Russians was more likely in the larger cities, but in smaller towns and rural areas the process was vice versa. Thus, to some extent ethnicity was dependent on the situation.

The largest Slavic communities are in Tbilisi and Abkhazia. In Tbilisi in 1989 there were 125 000 Russians, 16 000 Ukrainians and 2000 Byelorussians. Together they represented 11.5 per cent of the capital's population, down from 19.8 per cent in 1959. In Abkhazia from 1926 to 1970 the Slavic population has increased six times and reached 93 000 Russians, 12 000 Ukrainians and 2000 Byelorussians. By 1989 the number of Russians in that Autonomous Republic had decreased to 75 000, while that of the other Slavs remained stable.

After Georgian independence was restored, the process of out-migration of the Slavic peoples steadily increased. From Tbilisi alone, 29 000 Russians were officially registered as out-migrants ("checked-out") in 1989 and up to mid-1993 (Gachechiladze & Bradshaw 1994). The majority were the military and their families. Nevertheless, a complete exodus of Russian population from Georgia is improbable. First, because most of them are members of Georgian families. A survey has shown that the proportion of inter-ethnic marriages among married Russian women in Tbilisi increased from 36 per cent in 1959 to 54 per cent in 1988. Most frequently the spouse was Georgian (Gokadze 1992). The other factor discouraging Russian emigration is the real absence of any hatred towards them in Georgia.

A public opinion poll carried out in April 1993 under the direction of the present author, showed that the migrational tendencies of Russians in Georgia were substantial, but not overwhelming; more than half planned to stay. The major motives for moving out of Georgia were the economic crisis and inadequate social maintenance in this country and they expected better conditions in Russia. It must be added that emigration to Russia needs large sums of money; housing there at the moment is more expensive than in Georgia. Political reasons for emigration played a distinctly secondary role. One of the reasons, indicated by 35 per cent of the respondents, was ignorance of the State language of Georgia (Gachechiladze 1993). Really, the Russians had no necessity to learn the language of any union republic, as Russian served as a real *lingua franca* everywhere. Even so, many Russians – 22.5 per cent in Georgia as a whole and 34.5 per cent in Tbilisi alone – claimed knowledge of Georgian as the second language. That obviously eased relations between the Slavic groups and the ethnic majority in the area, relations that had become very close during the essentially friendly coexistence of the past two centuries.

Azeris

The first ancestors of the modern Azeris of Georgia, the nomadic Turkic tribe of Borchalu, settled on the plains of lower Kartli in the early seventeenth century. The area was devastated and almost depopulated of Georgians during the long wars with Persia, whence the Shi'a Muslim Borchalu migrated. Later other Turkic tribes, some of them Sunni Muslim, also entered and settled in Eastern Georgia.

Until the 1930s, the Turkic peoples in Georgia named themselves "Mussulman" or sometimes "Turk", although they were called "Tatar" by the local Christian population. In 1937 all the Turkic peoples in the Transcaucasus were given official recognition as "Azerbaijanis" by order of the all-Union Soviet leadership – in those days synonymous with Stalin. Even the bilingual Turkish and Georgian-speaking Meskhetian Muslims, no longer present in Georgia (see Ch. 9), were considered as Azerbaijanis in the 1939 census. This explains the sudden growth in the number of Azerbaijanis in Georgia in 1939 and their decrease in 1959 (Table 4.1).

The Azeris are by far the fastest growing community inside Georgia. In 63 years, from 1926 to 1989, their number almost quadrupled, when the national average doubled. The only other ethnic group close to the Azeris in the pace of increase are the Kurds. In part the increase in Azeris was the result of in-migration from Azerbaijan, which still persists, especially in Sagarejo, Dedoplistskaro and Marneuli Districts. Mostly, however, it was attributable to the high birthrate, reaching 28.8 per thousand in 1989, giving a rate of natural increase of 22.8 per thousand (Totadze 1993: 193). This exceeded the natural growth rate of ethnic Georgians by three times. In all districts where Azeris reside, their growth as a proportion has progressed. For example, during 1959–89 in Marneuli District their share in the population increased from 72 to 83.8 per cent, in Bolnisi district from 63.4 to 66.0 per cent, and in Sagarejo district from 15.3 to 26.3 per cent. The Azeris are predominantly (75%) rural dwellers. That, together with their religious traditions, probably best explains their high birthrates. They usually form large mono-ethnic rural communities. Out of 21 villages in Georgia with more than 5000 inhabitants, 7 villages are populated almost exclusively by Azeris.

A high proportion (49%) of Azeris are engaged in agriculture. A typical sight in the kolkhoz bazaars, especially in Eastern Georgia, are Azeri women selling vegetables; they are, incidentally, preferred by Georgian urban consumers as being easier to bargain with. There are 159 Azeri schools in Georgia, and Azeri newspapers are published. In a State Teachers' Training College in Tbilisi there is an Azeri Language and Literature Department. But the majority of young Azeris have a better chance to enter higher education and subsequently to rise in their careers in Baku or Gyanja in Azerbaijan, simply because they do not know the State language of Georgia (Table 4.3). The majority do not know even Russian. They do not mix with any other ethnic group within Georgia. All this means only very loose cultural contacts between the Azeris and Georgians as a whole. In general, this ethnic group is more integrated in the economic life of Georgia than it is in cultural and political life.

Greeks

The history of relations between the Georgians and the Greeks goes back into the distant past. The Milesian towns of Phasis, Dioskuria, Gyenos and Pitius were established on the Black Sea coast, more than two millennia ago. But the Greeks who reside in modern Georgia are relative newcomers. The first wave of Greeks, 800 households, arrived from Gumushane district in Turkey in the eighteenth century, invited by the Georgian King Erekle II to develop silver and lead mining. Their descendants live to the present in Marneuli district. In the nineteenth century, Greeks again migrated from Anatolia; the largest influx came in 1829–30, when Christians, who spoke only Turkish and who were termed *urum* (a reminiscence of Rome/Byzantium), arrived from Erzurum pashalik. They settled in modern Tsalka District villages, which had earlier been abandoned by the Georgians, with only the old churches to witness their historical presence. In coastal areas of the Russian Empire the so-called Pontic Greeks from the Anatolian shore began settling in the eighteenth century, and preferred to live in the expanding Christian State to the north. By the end of the nineteenth century, the Greeks comprised substantial communities in all Georgian Black Sea towns.

In 1989, Greeks made up 61 per cent of the population in Tsalka District, but the relative importance of this "core area" was diminishing; 38.6 per cent of all Georgian Greeks were residing here in 1959, but only 27 per cent 30 years later. That was the result of the Greeks moving to urban areas, especially to Tbilisi, where their number over the same period tripled 22 000 (21.6% of all Georgian Greeks). The third area of concentration is Abkhazia, with 14.6 per cent of all Greeks.

Although the Greeks are of the same religion as the Georgians, their cultural integration was mostly with the Russians; 96.3 per cent of Greek pupils attended Russian schools. Although 57 per cent of them claimed their mother tongue was Greek (Table 4.3), the Greeks did not in fact give precise answers; at least half of them spoke Turkish at home. More than a third of them considered their vernacular to be Russian. They actively assimilated with Russians, even changing their surnames into the Russian style, such as Popov, or Gavrilov. Some changed their nationality as well, which was one of the reasons for their low rate of increase in Georgia.

In spite of this, the Greeks have not entirely lost their self-identity. When in the 1970s the Georgian Government offered them the opportunity to study Greek at primary schools, with an eventual conversion to entirely Greek schools, the innovation was welcomed, although the majority still preferred Russian schools for their children as giving better career chances in the USSR. When, after the dissolution of the USSR and the emergence of the NIS, the possibility of emigrating to Greece arose, many Greeks were reminded of their origins. As a result of emigration, not many Greeks remain in Abkhazia and their community in Tsalka is seriously diminished.

Jews

There are two Jewish communities (in fact, linguistic groups) in Georgia: the Georgian Jews with Georgian mother tongue, and the European Jews, theoretically Yiddish but in practice Russian-speaking. The latter are predominantly concentrated in Tbilisi, where they arrived mostly in the twentieth century together with the Russians.

The Georgian Jewish community claims to be one of the oldest elements of the diaspora in the world. There is some evidence of their presence in Mtskheta, the ancient capital of Eastern Georgia, since the sixth century BC. Modern Georgian Jews do not differ very much from Georgians proper, either linguistically or even anthropologically. Before the Jewish emigration to Israel started in the 1970s, they constituted a large proportion in some Georgian towns. Thus, in 1926, the Jews of both linguistic groups constituted 3 per cent of the population in Tbilisi, 10 per cent in Kutaisi and in some smaller market towns and townships formed an even more significant ethnic group, 25–26 per cent in Surami and Kulashi, 30 per cent in Tskhinvali, and 36–40 per cent in Sachkhere and Oni. By 1989 their communities in these towns had diminished dramatically and Jews had become concentrated in Tbilisi (55% of the total Jewish population) and Kutaisi (16%).

The Soviet government was more tolerant of the emigration of the Georgian Jews than of those from Russia and other western Soviet republics, mostly because the Georgian authorities had more liberal attitudes and also because the Georgian Jews, in contrast to their Russian kindred, were much less engaged in the scientific–technological and cultural activities that were potentially important to the Soviet military and cultural authorities. The Georgian Jews are mostly engaged in retail trade and other services and have quite a high level of welfare. They are not represented in Georgian literature, art or science in such overwhelming proportion as, say, in Russia. Maybe because of such a "division of labour", the attitude of the Georgians towards the Jews was tolerant, even friendly, as both ethnic groups had their own economic niches. Anti-semitism had no social basis in this country. On the contrary, a recent public opinion survey carried out by the USIA Office of Research revealed that the Georgians had the most positive feelings towards the Jews, the second most positive group for the Georgians being the Russians.

Kurds

The Kurds' name for their own ethnic group is Yezid, as the Kurds of Georgia are represented mostly by the followers of Yezidism, a religious minority of this people. In fact, they were persecuted by the Muslim Kurds and found themselves stranded in Georgia after taking refuge from Eastern Anatolia during the First World War and shortly after. Nowadays there is also an influx of Sunni Muslim-

Kurds, migrating from Armenia, which is becoming strongly mono-ethnic. However, these recent immigrants do not as yet constitute a significantly large community in Georgia.

The first wave of immigrating Yezid-Kurds, being rural dwellers and almost entirely illiterate, became the least privileged ethnic group in the city of Tbilisi, where they settled, occupying cellars and engaged in unprestigious jobs such as street-cleaning and manual loading operations. Their demographic behaviour maintained the attitudinal inertia of rural dwellers. They had, and still have, the largest households in Georgia, on average 5.1 members in 1989. A closed community with strong clan organization and kinship relations, they practically never mixed with other ethnic groups.

It took the Yezid-Kurds two generations for full adaptation to urban life. After the mid-1970s, Tbilisi city authorities granted them free flats in high-rise houses. Practically all had at least primary education and many of them secondary. Special quotas were allocated by the Georgian Government to the Yezid-Kurds for access to higher education.

The ethnic group began to resettle in Georgia. Communities of Yezid-Kurds sprang up in the towns of Rustavi and Telavi, although 90 per cent of them still are concentrated in Tbilisi. Gradually the activities of the Yezid-Kurds changed to retail commerce in State shops and to the unofficial but tolerated control of warehouse operations. Both these occupations gave the best opportunities at that time for profitable "second economy" activities under conditions of constant deficit of consumer goods on the Soviet market. This improved the material welfare of quite a few members of this small community. Not involved in any ethnic tensions (as city-dwellers they have not so far claimed territory from Georgia!) the Yezid-Kurds are becoming a thriving community within this country.

Geography of religions

Multi-ethnic Georgia is also a multi-religious country. Under communist rule, when the State claimed to be not only secular but also "militantly atheistic", the role of religion in everyday life diminished dramatically. But although most of the churches, mosques and synagogues were closed and converted to warehouses, or at best to libraries or clubs, and the clergy were mostly dispersed, the people still professed adherence to particular religions. Children were baptized, often in clandestine manner; equally clandestinely, boys born to traditional Muslim or Jewish families underwent circumcision. The different funeral rituals best revealed the geographical manifestations of the influence of the different religions.

Orthodox Christianity was in the worst position at the beginning of the communist era. As the State religion in the Russian Empire, it had to be suppressed first. But during the Second World War, Stalin needed the support of the Russian Orthodox Church, and State policy towards this confession to some extent liberalized its attitudes. Similarly, the Georgian Orthodox Church, independent of the Russian one, also gained some relief, but on the whole it could not restore its social role, which was not strong even in the nineteenth century (Velichko 1904: 37). In contrast, the Gregorian Church in practice retained its influence over the majority of the Armenians. Other religions were kept in the background. This was especially the case with regard to religions with their "centres abroad" and out of reach of Soviet power, such as the Protestant Churches, which were labelled "sectarian" and "dangerous for the people". In the 1980s, with the growth of Muslim fundamentalism and the war in Afghanistan, the Kremlin's attitudes towards Islam became very hostile and "atheistic work" in Islamic areas was stepped up, but without real results; some rituals simply went underground.

The situation changed in the last years of the communist era. In most of the Soviet republics, the Churches started to become more efficient. In Georgia, the national liberation movement, or in practice some of its influential leaders, attempted to use Orthodox Christianity as a banner and to attach it to the national idea. These people were not concerned that Orthodoxy was not only a Georgian phenomenon, nor that at least 10 per cent of the Georgians do not belong to this faith, being Muslim, Catholic or Protestant. Moreover, there were and are many who in reality are atheists, not of course "militant", but indifferent towards any religion, albeit considering themselves as belonging to the "World of Orthodoxy, or of Islam, or of Catholicism" and simply following their family traditions. They would not wish a single faith to be given a political role. Fortunately, the Georgian Orthodox Church itself did not follow this "political mission", which was obviously leading to cultural and political isolationism.

Figure 4.4 demonstrates the spatial variation of religions in this country. In reality it shows rural areas, where different religions may most influence the way of life of the population. It was impossible to attribute most of the large cities to a single faith, since they were multi-religious and housed the majority of religious minorities. Some of these, like the Krishnaites, are quite exotic to Georgia.

A majority of the population, estimated at 75–78 per cent, belong at least nominally to the world of Orthodox Christianity. Theoretically, these are all the flock of the Catholicos-Patriarch of the Autocephalous Georgian Orthodox Church, residing in Tbilisi. Services are conducted in Georgian or Russian. As well as the majority of Georgians, adherence to this same faith is professed by most believers of the Russian, Ukrainian, Byelorussian, Greek, Ossetian and Abkhaz nationalities. Not a few Orthodox Christians, if not very pious in attending public services, at least celebrate such Church festivals as Easter (the most widely observed in this country), Christmas, St George's Day and Our Lady's Day. In several areas some specific saints' days are traditionally celebrated. In certain mountainous areas of Kavkasioni, some types of syncretic faiths have survived to the present, Christian in appearance, but pagan in essence.

Of the other Christian faiths, the most widespread is the Armenian Apostolic (Gregorian) Church, with 7–7.5 per cent of the total population. Its centre is Yejmiadzin in Armenia. Most Armenians are considered to belong to it. The city

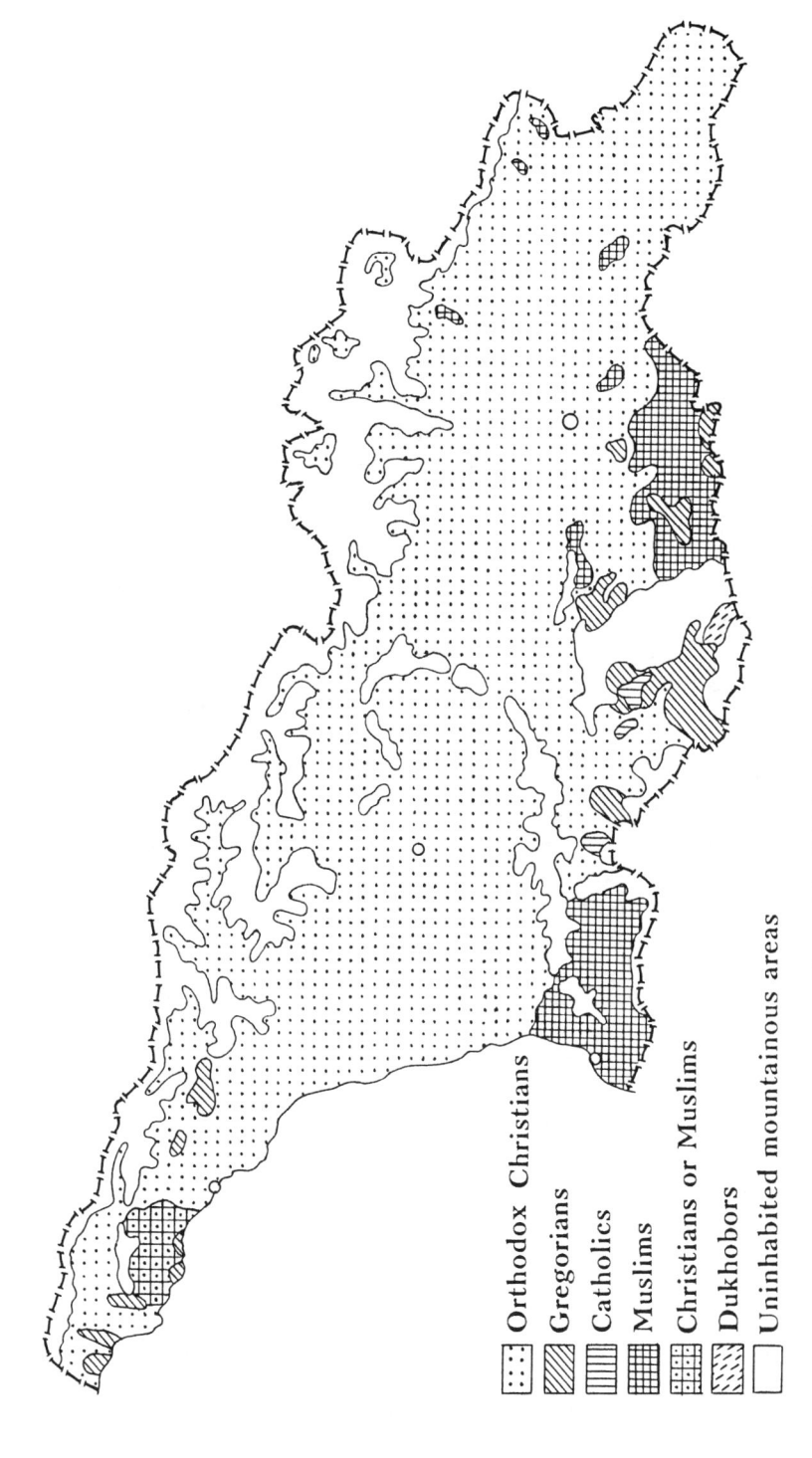

Figure 4.4 Religions in rural areas, early 1990s.

of Tbilisi, the province of Javakheti and rural Abkhazia are home to the majority of followers of this faith. There are also some villages in Eastern Georgia, whose Georgian-speaking inhabitants claim to be Georgian, but to belong to the Gregorian Church. Some Armenians and some Georgians belong to the Catholic faith, an estimated 1–2 per cent mostly in southern Georgia. In the cities are Catholics of Polish and German descent. Since the 1960s, Protestant Churches have become more active, especially the Baptists. In most of the larger cities there are growing communities of Protestants, with about 2 per cent of the total population, but among active worshippers they may amount to at least twice as many.

Islam occupies the second largest area in rural Georgia. An estimated 12 per cent of the total population live in the *Dar-ul-Islam* ("the Land of Islam") and this proportion is tending to grow. In the southwest in the Adjara Autonomous Republic, there are Sunni Muslim Georgians and in the centre-south are mostly Shi'a Muslim Azeris. The enclaves of Islam throughout eastern Georgia are rapidly expanding, thanks to the high birthrate in Azeri villages. In Kakheti province there are two small Sunni Muslim communities of Kistis or Chechens in Akhmeta District and of Avarians in Kvareli District. Georgian Muslims, the Adjarans, easily intermix with the Christian Georgians, even allowing their women to marry "the non-faithful", as they realize they belong to the same nation. The same happens with the Christian and Muslim Abkhaz. In Abkhazia, notably in the Gudauta area, the population since the seventeenth and eighteenth centuries has undergone Islamization, but the only operating religious organizations in this area nowadays are the Orthodox Churches, and Islam seems to be at least temporarily in the background. For this reason the area is cross-shaded on the map.

There are communities of the Judaists (Jews) in urban areas of Georgia, representing 0.5 per cent of the total population. The majority of the Kurds residing in Tbilisi belong to the Yezid religion, also with 0.5 per cent. Small communities of Russian *raskol'niki* (heretics), notably Dukhobortsy, Molokane and Old Believers were part of the spectrum of Georgian religions from the mid-nineteenth century, but now some of them have returned to Russia and some of the dwindling communities have dissolved into other communities. In all, less than 0.5 per cent of the total population belongs to these faiths.

Inter-ethnic relations: sociolinguistic patterns

Since Chapter 9 of this book is dedicated to politicogeographical aspects of ethnic relations, some consideration is given here to sociolinguistic patterns. The natural process of linguistic and cultural assimilation is going on everywhere. As noted above, as a rule Georgian emigrants settle in the large cities abroad, mostly in Russia but nowadays starting also to move to western Europe and North America. Being usually urbanized and well educated (including foreign languages, at least Russian), they easily adapt to the new situation and actively integrate into the local economic and cultural life. If close contacts with their ancient homeland cease and especially if they enter ethnically mixed marriages (which is very probable as the migrants are predominantly young and single) it is likely that within two, or at most three, generations the descendants of these Georgian immigrants will almost entirely assimilate with the leading ethnic groups of their new homelands. In fact, the largest Georgian diaspora in Russia consists of first-generation immigrants from Georgia, who still have affection for the latter. One may strongly doubt whether this will persist in their offspring by the mid-twenty-first century.

The same process of linguistic and cultural assimilation has proceeded in Georgia, especially since the Republic of Georgia was proclaimed in 1918, to be later succeeded by a Union republic within the USSR. However, as the Georgian SSR was a "sovereign State" mostly on paper and Georgian was only formally declared as the State language, no distinct linguistic policy could have been carried out. Russian remained the most important *lingua franca* in communication with the minorities.

Figures 4.5–4.7 reveal geographical patterns of the linguistic situation, if indirectly, in 1987. It can be seen that Georgian schools were situated in the areas where the Georgians dominated in absolute numbers (Fig. 4.5). Georgian schools were attended by 65 per cent of the pupils, which was less than the actual ratio of Georgians in the population. Two to three years later the situation changed somewhat; with the greater success of the national liberation movement, the proportion of pupils at Georgian schools increased to 68 per cent.

In areas with ethnic minorities, Russian schools were the most attended (Fig. 4.6). In addition, in areas with dominant ethnic Armenian and Azeri populations, there are secondary schools teaching in their native languages, whereas in Ossetian and Abkhaz schools most of the subjects are taught in Russian, apart from the native language and literature of the respective nationalities.

Thus, any linguistic assimilation that was going on in Soviet Georgia was in favour of the Russian language. Moreover, some of the Georgian pupils (40 000 or 6.9% of all pupils), also attended Russian schools in 1987, especially in Abkhazia, where the share rose to 22.9 per cent of the Georgian pupils in the area, and also in districts and cities where the Georgians were not numerically dominant (Totadze 1993: 192; Fig. 4.7).

The probability of full ethnic assimilation is higher after linguistic assimilation has occurred. But there is a political aspect to be taken into account as well. For example, in the 1876 One Day Population Census of Tbilisi, then a provincial city of the Russian Empire, it appeared that Georgian was the mother tongue of many more persons than the total of ethnic Georgians. The local Armenians claimed Georgian as their vernacular (Kobyakov 1880: 133). But this phenomenon did not lead to the Georgianization of the local Armenians, as they preserved their monophysite faith. In any case, the Georgians themselves did not belong to the ruling nation. Moreover, the Armenians of Tbilisi tended to give their children a Russian education.

The situation changed once Georgia became, albeit nominally, a "sovereign

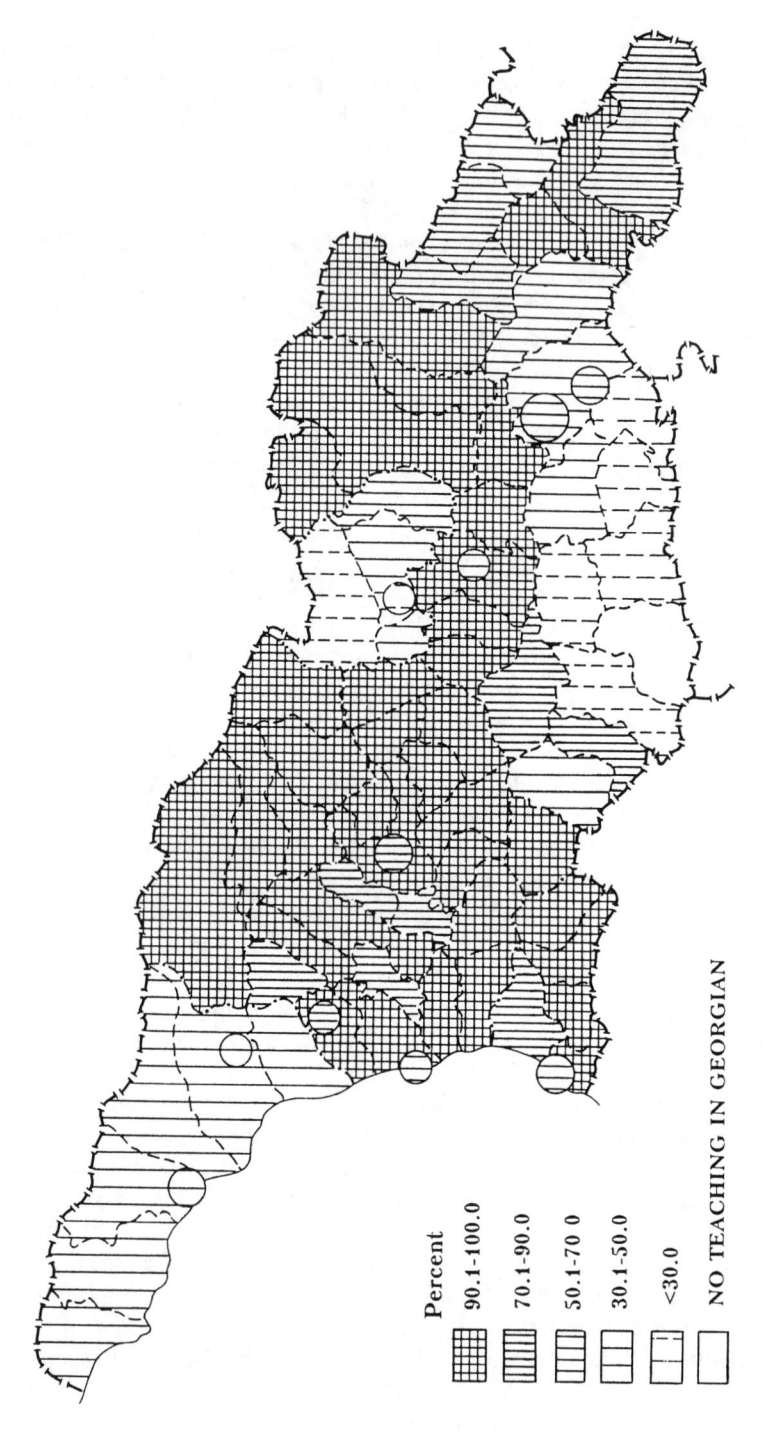

Figure 4.5 Pupils enrolled in Georgian schools, 1987.

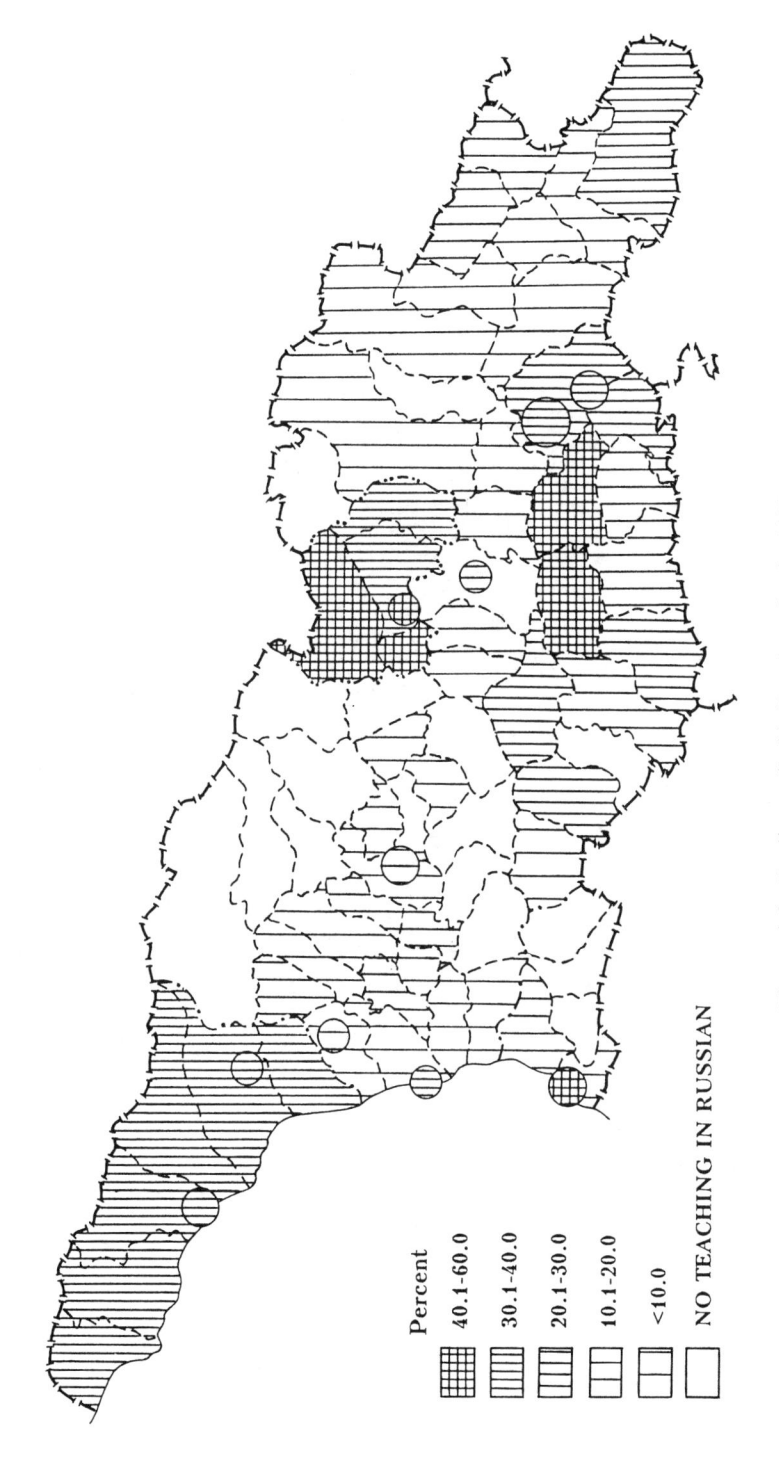

Figure 4.6 Pupils enrolled in Russian schools, 1987.

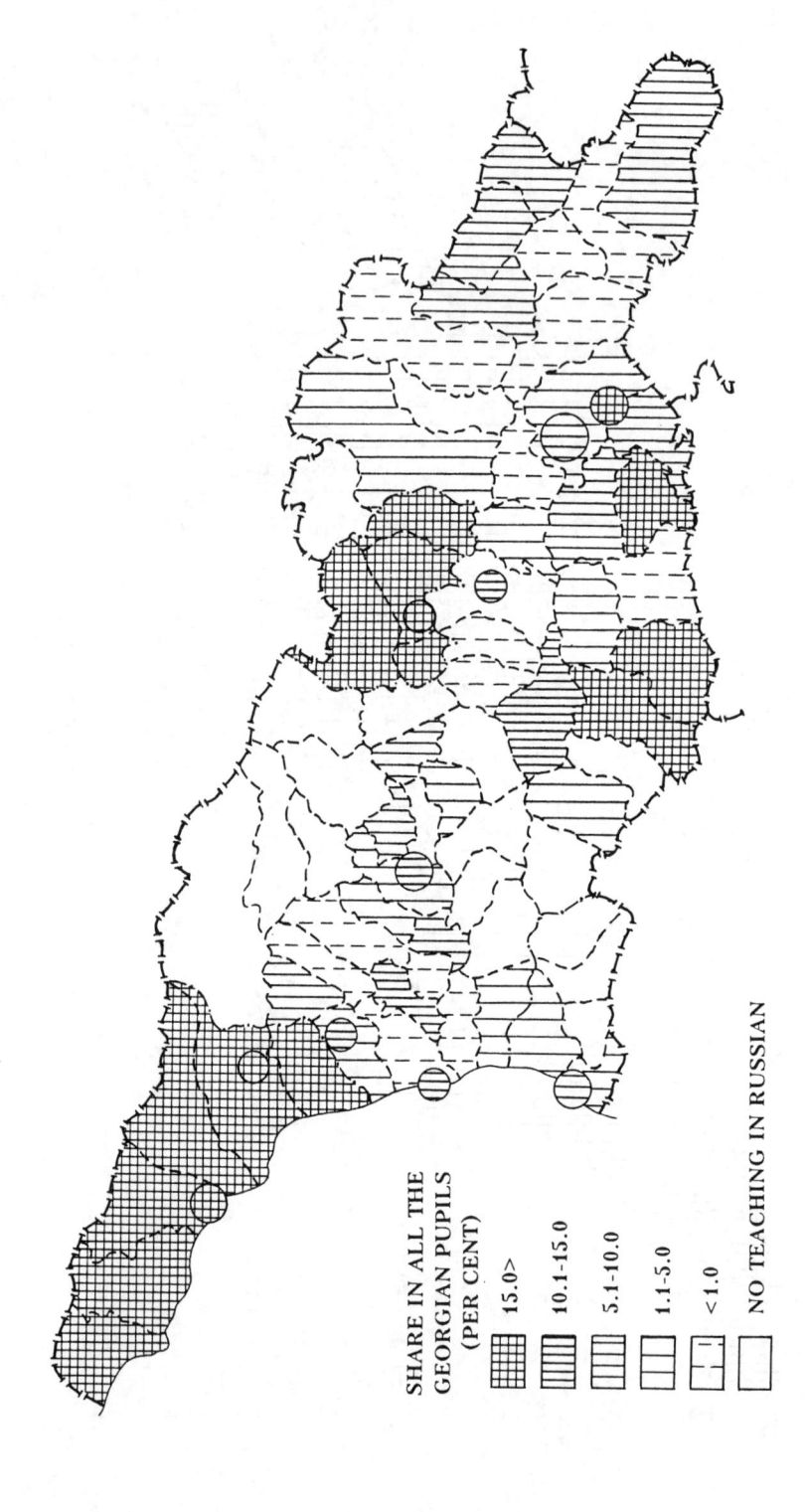

Figure 4.7 Ethnic Georgian pupils enrolled in Russian schools, 1987.

State" within the USSR. Belonging to a "titular nation" under the State-administrative, one-party dominated system was always more profitable than remaining a member of a minority group. In particular, if one had strong linguistic and close kinship ties with the leading group, it was considered senseless not to join the majority formally by "changing the nationality" in the internal passport. Nationality recorded in the internal passport was often changed by many Georgian-speaking Armenians, including those monophysite Georgians previously reckoned as being Armenian, by some of the Georgian-speaking Ossetians, even by representatives of the Slavic peoples such as Poles and Russians living in a Georgian milieu, and many in kinship relations with the Georgians and culturally assimilated with them. So there can be Georgian Ivanovs, Smirnoffs or Sikorskis too. In the case of the monophysite Georgians, there is much archive material of the nineteenth century proving the prevalence of religious adherence over ethnicity (Topchishvili 1990). According to the 1897 census, 2.23 per cent of the "Kartvelian peoples" (i.e. the Georgians) belonged to the Gregorian monophysite faith (Troinitsky 1905: xxxii).

In some autonomous republics of the USSR, notably in Abkhazia especially after the mid-1950s, belonging to the local "titular nation" also gave a better chance for promotion. This normally led to the assimilation of some Georgians with the Abkhaz. The reverse process in the autonomous area in recent decades practically never occurred. So there are Abkhaz with typical Georgian surnames.

Table 4.3 demonstrates the level of ethnic interaction as measured by mother-tongue and knowledge of other languages in Georgia, according to 1989 census data. The Slavic peoples, Greeks, Kurds and Armenians considered Russian their vernacular to a high degree, but only 0.2 per cent of the Georgians did so. Among the titular nationalities of the Soviet Union republics, Georgians had the highest proportion who considered the language of their nationality to be their mother tongue. An expert in demography (Totadze 1993: 193) doubts that the high figures for those claiming the language of their nationality as vernacular are very precise. The Russian language became the actual mother tongue to many more people. For example, 96 per cent of the Greeks, 81 per cent of the Kurds, 61 per cent of the Ossetians, 40 per cent of the Armenians, 30 per cent of the Abkhaz (with the rest studying in Abkhaz schools where most subjects were taught in Russian) and 7 per cent of the Georgians studied at Russian schools, and many of these were practically illiterate in their mother tongues. Nevertheless, the figures from the table give comparable material.

In 1989 the closest linguistic relations of the Georgians were with the Ossetians (and, in spite of the tragic ethnic conflict, these relations are likely to be restored, if perhaps not to the same high level), with the European Jews, Kurds and Armenians. Georgian Jews do not differ linguistically from the ethnic Georgians. It is clear that assimilation with the Georgians was relatively easy for those belonging to the Greek Orthodox tradition and for people belonging to the other Christian faiths, but it was extremely hard for the Azeris, Jews and Kurds, principally because of the restrictions imposed by their respective religions.

It is interesting to contrast the knowledge of Georgian and Russian by the Abkhaz. Almost all the adult Abkhaz population (80.5%) in 1989 mastered Russian, and only 2.4 per cent Georgian; within Abkhazia proper it was 1.6 per cent. In 1970, knowledge of Russian by the Abkhaz had been significantly less at 59.3 per cent because most of the rural population was ignorant of it, but the knowledge of Georgian had been at the same low level, 2.0 per cent. This can be explained on the one hand by the efficiency of the special policy carried out from the nineteenth century, described in Chapter 2. Russian, used almost exclusively in all official establishments of the area, left no room for the other official State languages. On the other hand, in everyday contacts in a multi-ethnic society composed of many Russian-speakers and in addition, accommodating annually millions of tourists from Russia, Russian was needed more than Georgian.

Without wishing to exaggerate the significance of this situation, it does indirectly display the cultural alienation of the Abkhaz from the Georgians. Yet at the personal level, there were many close links; for example, the highest proportion of inter-ethnic marriages by the Abkhaz was with Georgians, the most frequent language of communication within the family being Russian or one of the Kartvelian languages.

PART II
SPECIFIC ISSUES

CHAPTER 5
The changing problems of society

Problems of transition to a market economy

By the end of the USSR, the Georgian SSR was not the lowest of its component Union Republics in its level of development. The Georgians were considered by the other Soviet nationalities as one of the wealthiest peoples; hospitality and love of the good life were among the most widespread stereotypes of the Georgians. If the Human Development Index (as propounded in *Human development* 1994) had been measured for the Soviet republics, which were theoretically "sovereign States", Georgia might have been in the leading group, ranking quite high in the world and especially so among developing countries. It enjoyed high life expectancy, a very high educational attainment (Ch. 3) and a high standard of living (Ch. 6). The adult literacy rate was close to 100 per cent and female participation in higher education was almost equal to that of the males. Regional differences in the standard of living, although substantial, were not striking; disparities in income distribution between social groups and genders, if by no means egalitarian, in spite of communist propaganda, were more or less tolerable. The continually falling birthrate, especially among ethnic Georgians, made per capita income sounder, even if the economic growth rate was not very high. Employment structure was gradually changing towards the type characteristic of more developed countries, where secondary and tertiary activities become more and more important, although the mass media were constantly lamenting "the depopulation of rural areas", "the loss of traditional [i.e. rural] values" and "the young people abandoning land and moving to the cities and towns".

True, from a distance in time and especially from a period when the country is in a catastrophic plight, the situation in the late 1980s looks much rosier than it was in reality. It is equally true that it would have been incorrect to measure HDI for a part of the much larger country and then to compare that index with those for really sovereign States. Nevertheless, raw statistical data and also empirical observations made the Georgia of those days resemble more developed than underdeveloped countries. This gave greater confidence to the first political leaders of the New Georgia, who considered such a situation as everlasting.

Now, however, this Newly Independent State is in total economic disarray, to say nothing of political failures. It is happy with its official status as a developing country, and mass hunger is prevented only by the good will of the international community, especially by the munificent humanitarian aid of the USA and European Union. Poverty and deprivation have become apparent. Even worse, a society that was relatively rich is becoming relatively poor. The problems of poverty in rich countries (Townsend 1993: 37) are quite abruptly changing into the problems of poverty in poor countries. Such a situation is hardly bearable for society and the accompanying problems of crime and moral crisis are becoming even more grave. The transitional period, into which Georgia and most of the post-Soviet States entered, did not bring the best life and happiness for everyone and everywhere. On the contrary, a common feature of the first half of the 1990s was disappointment. The naïve hopes expressed by most of the new political parties that the simple act of turning towards a market economy would resolve all the social problems that the Communist Party had been unable to solve, proved to be unfulfilled, at least for time being.

What is the reason for such a situation? Was it caused entirely by subjective factors, as it now appears to the majority of Georgian citizens, who are willing to blame all their misfortunes on the greediness of successive governments, or on the imperial attitude of the strongest neighbour, or on the radicalism and incompetence of the leaders of the national-liberation movement, or on all of them together? Or was such a situation perhaps inevitable, caused by such objective realities as geographical factors and universal laws of historical development, which could have been foreseen?

The true answer lies somewhere between these two views, with a slightly greater leaning towards the second one. It might be very difficult for public opinion, developed during decades of totalitarian rule and corresponding ways of thinking, to realize that not everything was the result of the ill will of "enemies of the people and the nation" and that it is merely necessary to find the scapegoats. Of course, the pace of the country's advance to liberty and democracy, declared as the major objectives by most of the political parties and all of the governments of the past five years, was affected by some subjective factors characteristic of the different leaders, revealed in impatience, intolerance, unjustified presumption and self-consciousness, and eagerness to resort to arms when negotiations could have given better results. These characteristics have been so skilfully exploited by internal and external opponents of Georgian statehood and territorial integrity.

But I make bold to say that objective factors are more important in explaining the serious situation that was encountered by Georgia on its path towards market economy and political and economic independence. Without going into great depth in a matter that is more the concern of political science than of social geography, I would simply stress some geographical factors that could easily have been envisaged as certain snags. Wise leadership might have taken them into account to avoid complications.

Location should never have allowed Georgia to feel itself situated safely, as if on an isolated island. The geopolitical location needed to be put across more strongly. The country occupies a very important area, especially from the point of view of the giant neighbour to the north. The vulnerability in this context should have been envisaged and a more flexible strategy of international relations could have been chosen right from the first steps towards independence.

The country lacks significant mineral resources, especially fuel. At the moment this is the most important factor blocking economic revival. The necessity to pay very substantial sums at world prices after independence had been achieved was easily predictable. Another geographical factor, very much intermingled with history, is that the territory is not settled by a single people, but by several ethnic groups, consequently hampering the building of a nation-State. This ought to have affected internal policy and orientated it towards real, rather than professed, tolerance and co-operation.

There might be some other explanations for the difficulties of transition to the market economy. Most of the economic space of the ex-USSR, including Georgia, had not passed through true capitalism before the "socialist revolution" occurred in Russia. In rural areas after collectivization, some sort of "feudalism" returned. Private enterprise was heavily restricted, administrative dictat ruled the economy instead of market relations. In such circumstances, it was next to impossible for a "national bourgeoisie" to emerge and without it no market economy could develop. In reality, market relations did not die out entirely, revealing themselves in agricultural production on private plots and sometimes in odd forms such as the "second economy", which flourished in the Soviet period because of deficit and not because of competition. But tight restrictions did not allow earners of "non-labour profits", which in practice exceeded the maximum that the socialist State allowed its ordinary citizens to earn, to reinvest capital legally, and therefore most of it was used for immediate consumption.

There are some speculations that the transition to a market economy may be hindered by inherent "ethnic characteristics". A quite objective Georgian psychologist, analyzing Max Weber, denies the existence of the prerequisites of the "capitalist spirit" in the Georgian nationality (Nizharadze 1994). That is true of historical Georgia. We really were unfortunate not to have converted to Calvinism in the late Middle Ages! Or even to Catholicism, the ethics of which are in essence antipathetic to all capitalist tendencies (Weber 1923), but which in our circumstances, when the Georgians remained faithful to the most conservative faith in Christianity, would have meant some sort of Westernization. Catholics, incidentally, were represented among the rare Georgian bourgeoisie before Sovietization in a much higher proportion than among the total population. In the Middle Ages, Georgians were not engaged in commerce, which was one of the reasons for the nation's backwardness (Ch. 2).

However, for contemporary Georgia this is only partly true. Examples of personal adherence to commerce and industry were manifest in this country even under the communists and I do not mean only the "second economy". As soon as the possibility appeared of producing something outside the State sector through the co-operatives that were encouraged during *perestroyka* after 1987, Georgia soon became one of the leaders in the number of co-operatives and in their volume of production (Gachechiladze & Gagua 1990). The practical needs of hungry people and the impossibility of driving personal cars or tractors without fuel accelerated the speed of transition towards some kind of "market economy", albeit sometimes taking odd, if not criminal, forms. Thus, in spite of an overall decrease in agricultural production, there was an increase in sales of local grain, chiefly maize, beans and vegetable oil produced on the farmers' personal plots and on the "half-privatized" tracts, which had not yet been legally registered and which therefore still belonged formally to the State through the *kolkhoz/sovkhoz* system.

Another example is the emergence of hundreds of small "home-made oil-refineries", some of them "miracles of technology" according to the police reports, that used as their raw material crude oil extracted from the small oilfields in east Georgia or even from holes drilled in the oil pipelines. In 1994, most of these illegal enterprises were demolished by police. These examples of "market economy", although in fact criminal and liable of course to prosecution and capable of undermining a legal transition to true market relations, nevertheless indirectly show a potential of entrepreneurship in the nation, which if channelled legally could be used fruitfully for the whole of society.

Actually, if an effective legal basis had existed, if order in the country had been maintained and if such a "subjective factor" as "mafia running the country" were extinguished or at least strictly contained, then the capitalist spirit might have been revealed among the Georgians to a much higher degree. Nizharadze (op. cit.) already cited considers the possibility of the emergence of new social groups, bringing new ethics and a new style of life. All this, however, will not happen overnight.

The move towards a market economy will by no means lead to greater equity. On the contrary, it is obvious that the distribution of wealth will become even more polarized. Social injustice will grow (Smith 1994). Many employees of enterprises still officially State-owned and of State offices receive their wages from an impoverished budget in Georgian coupons, which are dramatically falling in purchasing power. Such people, together with pensioners, are the major victims of the turn to "uncivilized" capitalism. Yet it is equally clear that there is no alternative to the market economy. At all events, a socialist economy cannot be restored. As David Smith has written:

> ... that the Eastern European version of socialism has failed is beyond doubt. It failed, literally, to deliver the goods, efficiently, reliably and in quantities consistent with the expectation of people aware of rapidly rising living standards in the capitalist world. Its governments failed to establish legitimacy, and ultimately lost the support and eventually the grudging acquiescence of the mass of people. One system of injustice was replaced by another. Whether or not these defects were intrinsic to the versions of socialism adopted, or capable of eradication within a reformed structure dedicated to "true socialism", the alternative of a "market economy" was virtually inevitable. (Smith 1992: 135)

The point is that the capacity of a market economy to deliver efficiency in production and particularly to achieve equity in distribution depends on the market "working perfectly". In the case of the post-Soviet space, notably in Georgia, major distortions include the existing and post-privatization distribution of property. This distribution was frequently done in an unfair and often clandestine manner, and restraints on competition were imposed by the "mafia" and the "kleptocracy" in economic management; this was the legacy of "real socialism". The majority of the population, incidentally, do not understand what they are entitled to claim from the "national pie" during privatization (see below).

It seems as if the people largely understood the inevitability of turning to a market economy and the problems that might follow such a turn, even in the Soviet period. In a poll, carried out by the Centre of Sociological Studies (CSS), Academy of Sciences of the Georgian SSR, under the present author in June 1990, 59 per cent of 1500 respondents surveyed in 15 districts and CRSs of Georgia indicated a belief that real economic welfare for the country would be achieved by a free market economy and the legalization of private property. A centrally planned socialist economy as a guarantee of welfare was still supported by 25 per cent; the rest considered it hard to answer. At the same time, only 10 per cent of the respondents anticipated Georgia being a pure capitalist country in ten years time, whereas 49 per cent believed that it will still be in the transitional stage from socialism to capitalism and 15 per cent were sure that Georgia would persist as a socialist country even at the end of the twentieth century. In addition, 62 per cent of respondents envisaged the deterioration of the economic situation during the next year (Gachechiladze 1990e). It is obvious that, despite such a "rational public" in this country, an absolute majority (except, no doubt, among the best experts in economics) were not anticipating the terrible economic and social plight that awaited the country and almost all of its inhabitants in the following years. It is understandable that a fast and complete change to a market economy is not easy, even though it is inevitable.

The situation has become paradoxical. On the one hand, the people's very life is maintained by the State. In 1993–4, bread was rationed to the population at a price 30–40 times cheaper than its real cost; electricity supply depended on centrally imported fuel. All this had to be paid for from public sector enterprises because private concerns were too few to pay enough taxes. This provided a good excuse for the still influential Ministries to justify restraint on their privatization. Indeed, privatization began with many complications by mid-1994, when most industry stopped production through lack of fuel and raw materials. On the other hand, moving towards the free-market economy means overwhelming rejection of State ownership of enterprises and, above all, of land. This will lead to positive results for society as a whole only in the distant future, although in the immediate future the beneficiary will be only a small part of society. This dilemma is not easily resolved.

The problems that face Georgia are virtually twice as grave as those of the other NIS, as none of them has all the problems of civil wars, ethnic tensions, hyperinflation and collapse of economy, at the same time and in the same place. Even neighbouring Azerbaijan, much resembling Georgia in its own misfortunes, at least owns immense reserves of oil that give the country hope of economic recovery in the future. And Armenia, although in severe economic difficulty, at least has no ethnic problems.

Yet despite everything, Georgia still exists. Future observers will probably discuss "the miracle of Georgian survival", while contemporaries watch economic dislocation, indiscipline and human frustration. The crisis might be very lengthy, but it cannot last forever. At least as new generations grow up, generations that will be more accustomed to the values of a market economy, they will change the country's fortunes in different way. The questions are, how long will it take the country to come out of crisis, and will there be enough Georgians, if any, by that time? At all events, it seems a suitable time to discuss what the people think about the social problems of the country.

Social problems as perceived by public opinion

Several surveys carried out by the CSS in the late 1980s and 1991 and by its successor, the Institute of Demography and Sociological Studies in 1992–4, provide an opportunity to monitor changes in the attitudes of the population towards social problems. During the late 1980s, the major problems were connected with the poor supply and quality of consumer goods, the sanitary conditions of settlements, inadequate housing, especially in urban areas, and, predominantly in rural areas, poor transport infrastructure (Gachechiladze 1990c,d).

In the first half of the 1990s, the character of the problems changed so dramatically that to use the same list of problems was futile. After the economic crisis became overwhelming, the composition and the sequence of social problems became very different from what they were only a few years ago. The most serious problems appeared to be price rises, increase of crime, the crisis of morality, the risk of famine and the threat of unemployment. Moreover, these are likely to preserve their places as priority problems in public opinion in the immediate future. In 1992–4, several public opinion polls put the same question to respondents about the problems most worrying society in Georgia. At least 1000 adults were interviewed in a nationwide sample, covering most of the social regions of Georgia and representative of all the major demographic groups of the population. The surveys were carried out by the Department of Sociological Study of Sociopolitical Change under Ms D. Karaulashvili of the Institute of Demography and Sociological Studies, Georgian Academy of Sciences. The question under discussion was included at the request of the present author (Gachechiladze 1994a). In Table 5.1 the results of three polls are given. The respondents were invited to name from a list handed to them five problems that personally worried them the most; thus, total percentages exceed 100. In fact, not all these problems could be described as

The changing problems of society

Table 5.1 Major societal problems of Georgia 1992–4 (July; per cent of the total interviewed).

Problems	1992	1993	1994
Price rise	75	77	72
Crime level	74	60	66
Situation in Abkhazia	16	55	57
Threat of famine	36	39	49
Threat of unemployment	32	24	46
Deficit of consumer goods	35	31	35
Crisis of morality	33	36	31
Wide spreading of firearms	48	33	30
Threat of civil war	32	27	24
Situation in Tskhinvali region	41	22	22
Ecological problems	10	8	11
Problems of privatization	9	5	4

purely "social" ones. Civil war and ethnic conflicts are rather political issues, but as they all concern society as a whole, they can be referred to as "societal problems".

The first two problems, with others a long way behind, are price rises and the crime level. Earlier, under the communists, the people also worried about price rises, which occurred "in waves", sometimes twice a year, especially after the mid-1970s. Central TV in Moscow would announce in the evening news the doubling from the next morning of the price of, say, petrol, coffee, carpets, beverages, and almost always, of gold. This inevitably made those who already owned gold even richer, and the rest relatively poorer. But the price of staple products such as bread, milk, sugar, urban transport, communal services, electricity, housing rent and so on remained unchanged for decades, subsidized by the State.

Meanwhile, on the free market after such TV announcements, prices leapt up, especially for the best quality products. This free market was represented by the *kolkhoz* bazaar, where private producers and retail traders, so-called *spekulyanti*, the latter illegal under socialism, sold predominantly agricultural products. Regional differences in welfare were also becoming more apparent (Ch. 6), but the average material welfare of the population, in spite of common grumbling and dissatisfaction, was in general increasing, albeit slowly.

From 1991 the rise in prices became an overwhelming process, both in the then still-existent USSR and its successor NIS. After Georgia was compelled to introduce its coupon as a provisional currency in April 1993, inflation soon turned into hyperinflation. In the early days of the introduction of the Georgian coupon, a US dollar was worth 670 coupons; by August 1993 US$1 was worth 13 000 coupons, and at the end of August 1994, 1 900 000 coupons (sic!). The prices have grown almost proportionately, although by Western standards the price of such things as food and housing may seem not high at all, but the nominal wages, paid in coupons, increased less than 30 times. It is understandable that wages can never catch up with prices in a country where production has almost stopped, but the comprehensive commentaries in the mass media do not satisfy the hungry stomachs of the citizens.

The crime rate in the Soviet cities also worried public opinion, but among the 25 problems enumerated in the surveys of 1987–9, in no social region of Georgia did the crime level reach a higher place than 15th (Gachechiladze 1990c,d). From 1990 the upward trend of crime has become more apparent and in and after 1992 the civil wars gave a sense of impunity to the criminal element, some of whom joined the armed forces, mostly under the command of non-professionals; in consequence, the crime problem became of paramount importance, if not indeed the major menace to State-building and economic revival.

The problem embraced the whole country, but nevertheless there were some geographical areas, notably the major roads in the west and south of the country and large cities, where the chance of becoming a victim was much higher than elsewhere (the geography of crime is discussed in Ch. 7). Since 1994 a certain stabilization can be seen; the police have become more effective and the crime rate seems likely to stop growing.

The problem of the spread of firearms is closely related to the crime rate. In 1990, 383 crimes were committed using firearms and in 1993 3796 such crimes were registered, an almost tenfold increase, to say nothing of those unregistered! The first large dispersal of firearms happened at the end of 1991 and beginning of 1992 as the result of the "Tbilisi War" in the capital city (see Ch. 2). The civil wars that followed contributed to this phenomenon as well. Successive Ministers of Defence subsequently spoke of "something like 25000 automatic submachine guns dispersed among the population", as if they were not responsible for the indiscipline that caused this kind of dispersal! The large gulf in opinion about this problem between different surveys is explained by the extreme nervousness of the public in July 1992, when the rating of this problem attained the highest percentage. The public could scarcely tolerate the view of civilians, officially belonging to several paramilitary groups, openly carrying arms in the streets. The polls carried out when the civil wars (notably that in Abkhazia) were raging at full force, showed that society had almost got used to the everyday sound of firing. Since 1994 stricter laws have been introduced against the misuse of military armaments and they have begun to be implemented more rigorously. To some extent this has affected public opinion, although the problem is by no means solved as yet.

The widest differences between the polls in the proportion of answers related to the problem connected with the situation in Abkhazia. The smallest percentage of answers, 16 per cent, was obtained in July 1992, when a bloody war in the "Tskhinvali Region" (former "South Ossetia") was just coming to an end and people did not want even to imagine the appearance of this new tension area in the country. Georgia had just been accepted as a member of the United Nations, and the common desire was for peace to be maintained. Thus, the majority did not want to think that the situation in Abkhazia would soon become the gravest problem to Georgia and its population. Although by that time the separatist movement in Abkhazia was already reaching its most active stage, the Georgian mass media were playing it down. By the next survey in September 1992, the problem of the Abkhaz conflict, which had turned into a prolonged civil war, already occupied third place in its relative importance to public opinion in Georgia as a whole, whereas in Abkhazia itself and in Tbilisi it moved firmly into first place.

The civil war in Abkhazia was in actuality the major problem of Georgia in 1992–3. It took almost all the rather scarce resources of the country, influenced the deterioration of the economic situation and affected the country's foreign political relations, above all with Russia. From the social point of view, this war had many negative results, such as growth in the illegal dissemination of firearms among the population, influencing the overall crisis of society by the growth of aggressiveness, crime and social apathy. The war caused the appearance of hundreds of thousands of IDPs. It is understandable, therefore, that public opinion gave the situation in Abkhazia a high position on the scale of contemporary problems of Georgia, especially in areas with an ethnic Georgian population, where the problem was usually given as the most important.

In contrast, the relative significance of the situation in Tskhinvali Region, the area of another ethnic conflict, was gradually diminishing. Its ranking fell from 41 per cent in July 1992, when the war there had just ended in a cease-fire, to 22 per cent two years later. The role of mass media is apparent; as Georgian TV, radio and press curtailed their information about the region, so interest in it decreased, although the conflict is by no means finally solved. The geographical dimension of attitudes to this problem is noteworthy. The closer respondents were to the region, the more they were aware of it. The respondents of Gori district, next to Tskhinvali, cited the problem three times more often than respondents from Batumi, some 200km away.

In effect, ethnic relations did not worry the people of Soviet Georgia; in the surveys of the 1980s, this answer consistently holds the lowest position. It was considered up to the Communist Party to solve global inter-ethnic problems, although on a personal level it seemed that there were no ethnic problems at all. Nowadays, however, these relations have become a problem of utmost urgency. In a survey carried out by the USIA in early 1993, 22 per cent of ethnic Georgians and 30 per cent of non-Georgian respondents considered relations among the nationalities in Georgia to be "essentially good", 33 and 47 per cent "not exactly good", 20 and 14 per cent "rather bad", whereas 24 and 7 per cent insisted that "the situation is very serious". Ethnic tensions in Georgia are examined more fully in Chapter 9.

The danger of famine worried at least a third of the population. It was more stressed in the cities, whereas in rural areas people could to some extent rely on self-sufficiency. The considerable aid from Western countries allowed Georgia to have a bread supply, although rationed. But naturally, such aid cannot last for ever, hence public opinion stressed the threat of famine.

The threat of unemployment is perceived by that part of the population engaged in the civil service and manufacturing. Females cited it more frequently than males. Among those who were aware of future unemployment, urban blue- and white-collar workers dominated over farmers. On the whole, however, since the real market economy has not yet directly impinged upon the interests of the majority of the population, many were unable to see a distinction between a symbolic salary and an unemployment allowance. It seems inevitable that this social problem will become even more acute in the immediate future.

The deficit of consumer goods, which some years ago was the major complaint of the population, has now moved to a lower place in the table. Against the background of much more urgent problems, there seems no sense in mentioning the absence or inaccessibility through high price of clothes, footwear, furniture and the like. The people hoped that merely turning away from economically ineffective "true Socialism" would have quickly brought them these very goods, but alas!

The crisis of morality is probably the worst result of the chaotic development in the path to radical social change. Immorality, first seen in the weakening of the rules of conduct that maintain social solidarity, became characteristic of an increasing segment of society. The supplanting of those moral values which had already become "traditional" under socialism, by "new ones", which sometimes are older ones simply long forgotten, is proceeding too fast. Many things, earlier legally and morally forbidden, now became permissible. Thus, if just a couple of years ago the "*spekulyanti*" referred to earlier were prosecuted and most people looked upon them as criminals, now their activities in buying goods cheaper and reselling them at a profit is simply "trade" under a market economy and, if taxes are paid, naturally is considered to be a legal action. It was not safe for high-ranking officials to demonstrate their wealth under the Soviet regime, as inquiry could have followed, but now many of the increased number of bureaucrats have profitable private businesses. Crime or drug-abuse for an increasing number of young people does not seem to be morally intolerable nowadays. Juvenile misbehaviour in the streets and classrooms cannot be tolerated by the older generations, whose answers predominantly stressed "the moral degradation of society and individuals".

Although it is obvious that Georgia is not the only country where lawlessness and related problems occur, the answers of the respondents are understandable; they see what is all around them. Legislation cannot keep pace with the social processes. Moreover, a long time is needed for social change, for a real transformation of society in a democratic manner.

The threat of intra-Georgian civil war loomed over the country from the autumn of 1991. Its first outbreak was the "Tbilisi war" and subsequently it smouldered, especially in western provinces, where in the polls this answer was mentioned by respondents to a degree much above the national average. In spite of everything, the civil war did not develop into heavy bloodshed, although it ruined many households and even whole communities. By November 1993, the intra-Georgian civil war had in effect come to an end. But public opinion is still anxious, as some radical party leaders periodically assert their readiness to resort to arms "in search of justice", in reality of power.

Two problems, connected with environment and privatization, have proved at the present to be less important to the population, but both of them will become quite weighty societal problems later. The ecological situation is paradoxical. Since most factories have halved or even stopped their activities and traffic has diminished because of the fuel shortage, the air and water pollution rates have dropped substantially. But a new threat has appeared: cutting the forests for firewood and lumber. Rural dwellers, who are compelled to collect firewood, do not consider this problem more important than any of the others mentioned above, whereas the urban population have scanty information from the mass media, which concentrate on the other problems.

Seemingly, the problem of privatization concerns only businessmen. Because privatization of urban apartments, previously rented from the city councils, was carried out very fast and practically free of charge in 1992–3, most of the urban population, especially white-collar workers, simply do not understand what else they are entitled to get from the "national pie".

Privatization even of smaller enterprises implies the availability of large sums of money, which most of the population do not possess. Thus, a relatively small part of the population will benefit from the partition of the estate left by the late Soviet Georgia. This will undoubtedly promote an intensification of property stratification and will cause an inequality in society that will inevitably become a more apparent social problem once the shock linked to the overall crisis subsides. There is also a moral problem in the transition; the cost is borne by the masses while the few get rich. For how long is the public ready to accept this as justified?

Most of the problems discussed are characteristic of modern Georgia as a whole and sometimes no specific spatial distinctions can be detected. For example, prices can be spatially different, but the problem of their rise worries everyone, everywhere. To some extent the same can be said of such social malaises as the crisis of morality and the problems of privatization, and so on. However, several problems are more evident in urban or rural areas. The crime rate, ethnic tensions and threat of famine have a clear geographical dimension. Basic material welfare is not evenly distributed spatially. In the following chapters, spatial aspects of some of these problems will be discussed.

CHAPTER 6
Regional differences in welfare

Changing trends of welfare

In the 1990s there is a clear trend to a dramatic fall in welfare in the post-Soviet space as a whole. In Georgia, where this trend is probably most prominently seen, it is the result of macroeconomic instability, aggravated by the relations with former economic partners and the internal political turmoil. The level of welfare in Georgia, which was one of the most flourishing Union republics under Soviet power, has fallen very low. It was apparent even earlier that the country was living beyond its means, but it is now seeming to be an extremely painful process to adapt to a situation where the world market dictates its conditions, instead of a closed economic system where any rubbish could be produced "according to the plan".

The decline in the standard of living in Georgia was seen most clearly in the decay of overall consumption and the deterioration of its structure. In 1985 the expenditures of an average household on foodstuffs amounted to 36 per cent of its budget; they reached 49 per cent by 1991, 62 per cent by 1992 and 79 per cent by 1993 (Consumption 1993, Report 1994). Hence, consumption of other goods and services is almost entirely out of the picture. The absolute volume of foodstuffs consumed decreased dramatically, especially of meat, from 41 kg per capita in 1989 to 18 kg in 1992, of milk and milk products from 332 kg to 110 kg, and even of bread and flour products, which had always been over-consumed in Georgia and which fell from 188 to 131 kg per capita (Consumption 1993). In the following years, the situation became even worse. According to a poll carried out by the newspaper *Svobodnaya Gruziya* (1993) at the end of 1993, the daily food of an inhabitant of Tbilisi mostly consisted of tea (mentioned by 97.4% of the respondents), bread (95.8%), potatoes (94.0%) and vegetables, mostly cabbage (80.3%); less than one third said that their family consumed meat, milk or milk products.

Georgia had a more or less balanced structure of incomes and expenditures in the 1980s. Table 6.1 shows that incomes were then growing and so were savings. This does not mean that everyone in the country lived well, but not everyone lived badly. On the spatial level, there were regions where the population in general was better off and also regions with a poorer population. This spatial structure of welfare is also changing. In Soviet times the urban areas always were better off.

Table 6.1 Money incomes and expenditures of the population of Georgia 1980, 1985, 1989 (millions of current rubles).

Type of income and expenditure	1980 Rubles	%	1985 Rubles	%	1989 Rubles	%
Income						
Labour	5005	83.2	6398	81.8	8124	79.9
Regular wages	3706	61.6	4859	62.1	6561	64.5
Wages paid by co-operatives	–	–	575	5.6		
Other wages and compensation	121	2.0	162	2.1	208	2.1
Income paid by collective farms	393	6.5	505	6.5	509	5.0
Income from sale of farm products	786	13.1	873	11.1	846	8.3
Transfer receipts	1013	16.8	1427	18.2	2044	20.1
Pensions & allowances	672	11.2	878	11.2	1117	11.0
Scholarships	41	0.7	40	0.5	40	0.4
Income from the financial system (insurance, interest, etc.)	186	3.1	318	4.1	426	4.2
Other income	114	1.9	190	2.4	461	4.5
Total income	6014	100.0	7825	100.0	10168	100.0
Expenditure						
Purchases	4723	84.3	5703	79.8	6712	75.3
Retail goods	4114	73.4	5006	70.1	5855	65.7
Services	609	10.9	698	9.7	857	9.6
Transfer & savings	878	15.7	1443	20.2	2196	24.7
Taxes, fees, dues, etc.	547	9.7	757	10.6	1006	11.3
Savings	313	5.5	619	8.7	1156	13.0
Other	17	0.3	67	0.9	34	0.4
Total expenditure	5600	100.0	7146	100.0	8908	100.0
Income less expenditure	480		679		1260	

Source: Statistical (1993: 263).

Even nowadays, the major urbanized area of Tbilisi Metropolitan Region theoretically must be the best placed, as the government tries to supply its population (almost a quarter of the total) with electricity, gas and bread; other areas lack even these minimum facilities. This is to say nothing of spiritual welfare (i.e. the possibilities of education and training, access to information, and so forth) which have always been concentrated in the capital cities of the Soviet republics and remain there to the present day. But on the other hand, the inhabitants of rural areas and small towns have some reserves of agricultural products of their own, although the high prices mean that the majority of the urban population cannot afford even to buy locally produced fruit, which had always been in abundance in Georgia.

It is evident that this situation cannot last for ever. The way out of the crisis may be very long, but it will at least lead somewhere. The regional disparities in welfare distribution will acquire new patterns. Some regions will exchange places on the scale of welfare. Thus, the initial situation before the beginning of the dramatic changes is of scientific interest. A country in crisis is one thing; spatial differences in welfare are better compared in a country where there is economic stability.

Spatial patterns of welfare in the late 1980s

Several indicators of material welfare in Georgia in the 1980s have been analyzed by the present author. They revealed the existence of quite remarkable inequalities in the distribution of wealth (Gachechiladze 1987, 1989, 1990a). The data under consideration were collected for 1989, the last year of political and economic stability, although the trends towards crisis could already have been foreseen at that point. Comparison of the various indicators was still easy, because prices were still under State control and most official incomes passed through the State–controlled banking system, where savings were also accumulated. Inequalities on the level of the individual household were already apparent, but they were not as striking as they are becoming at the present day. In addition, spatially detailed data were available relating to the autonomous units of South Ossetia and Abkhazia. Since then, the conflicts in these areas have prevented the collection of reliable information.

Material wealth in the 1980s was distributed mainly according to work opportunities, that is, it was found for the most part at those locations where goods were processed and services rendered. This is also true of the modern situation to a certain extent. However, wealth also depends upon specific natural conditions, resources, and so on. This applies not only to the individuals in society, but to the communities as well. Spatial organization in this case becomes an even more important factor. The place and its functions, space, geographical location and distance all affect to a considerable extent the volume of wealth acquired by communities. In addition, and possibly even more important, much depends upon administrative decisions, particularly those taken at a level higher than that of a particular community. In the final analysis, economic, natural, political, historical, social and ethnocultural factors determine a spatial distribution of wealth, which is used by communities in different ways.

Under socialism, deliberate efforts were made to equalize spatial levels of social development. Regional policy was used to achieve this. Inequality in the distribution of wealth was alleviated somewhat by social consumption funds, comprising education, medical care, assistance to younger and elderly generations and the disabled, and so on. However, it was not possible to eliminate inequality completely with such funds. The distribution of the social consumption funds was guided by planning norms, which quickly became outdated, and often resulted from inertia, that is they reflected the level already achieved. Thus, they could not bring about any dramatic equalization of spatial levels of social development (Gachechiladze 1982). The mountainous rural districts of Georgia, for example, possessed a definite advantage in the receipt of social consumption funds. For practical purposes, however, this failed to reduce the intensity of out-migration by young people, which naturally caused a deformation in the sex and age structure of the population and, in the end, created complications for human development. Young people with secondary education had, and have, increased expectations and, if there were insufficient employment opportunities, in terms of quantity and quality (and most of the highland area did indeed lack such opportunities), then such migration was inevitable. People vote with their feet for social justice, moving to places where there is a better standard of living.

Thus, even when there is a general increase in expenditures of social consumption funds – and in Georgia they grew from 1.0 to 6.2 billion roubles between 1970 and 1985 (National Economy 1986) – spatial inequality was maintained. Often that was seen in the quality of social services. For example, the State paid more per capita for pupils in secondary education in rural schools than for those in urban ones, but not enough to persuade the best teachers to come, or to stay, in the villages. As a result, many school subjects were taught by non-specialists. Most Georgian rural schools lacked teachers of foreign languages, including Russian. On the other hand, in areas with ethnic minorities, it was a problem to find a teacher of the Georgian language. Such teachers could have been "outsiders" from the cities, in need of a flat and a normal salary, enough for self-support, but these conditions were lacking under the "planned economy". This last example, incidentally, is not connected only with social consumption funds or material welfare, but has a wider social context. The lower the actual level of education, which is not always revealed through certificates and diplomas, the lower the level of general culture. The absence of teachers of non-native languages has left the younger generation unaware of the culture of other nations. Thus, the seeds of primitive nationalism find a more fertile soil in such social environments.

Criteria for analysis

The so-called "real income of the population", calculated in Soviet statistics on the basis of the difference between income and expenditure in comparable prices, reflected in a very generalized way the level and dynamics of people's standard of living. "Real income" was growing in the Georgian SSR; the rise in incomes from 1980 to 1989 can be seen in Table 6.1. Unfortunately, it was not calculated by region within the republic. Hence, other data had to be collected and measured to compare regional discrepancies in the level of material welfare of the population within the republic.

Several measures of income and expenditure were adopted as indicators of material welfare, in particular: monetary income, retail trade turnover, the provision of everyday services, total deposits in saving accounts, and the number of motor vehicles. All data were calculated on a per capita basis. They refer to 1989, but comparisons were made with 1980, 1985 and 1987 for which dates also these indicators were measured. These indicators by no means encompass the entire scope and structure of material wealth that, along with social and spiritual well-being, characterize the population's standard of living. But other data were either missing or contributed little to the establishment of the pattern of material welfare. Some of these were mapped and analyzed in *The social atlas of Georgia*

(Gachechiladze 1989a). For example, the number of telephones per 1000 persons (69 in 1988) had a rather odd spatial structure, as their distribution to a large extent depended on subjective administrative decisions. Since market forces were very weak under socialism, they could not influence at all the installation of a telephone station; that was entirely a matter for decision by the planning bodies, influenced in turn by bureaucratic considerations. The highest level of telephone provision in 1988 was in the cities of Tbilisi (137), Poti (106) and Sokhumi (98), followed by some mountain districts, and the lowest level was in the area surrounding Tbilisi. Rank correlation of the material welfare rating and the level of telephone provision was very low, at 0.14 (Gachechiladze 1989a: 225–6). The five indicators listed above, with certain reservations, were considered to be representative of the material wealth of the population.

Evaluation by individual indicators

Monetary income is an important component of the population's real income. In Georgia as a whole, wages comprised more than 70 per cent of this income, whereas in several rural districts a considerable portion (more than half) was made up of income from the sale of agricultural products. The monthly wages of blue- and white-collar workers have shown smaller discrepancies than those of overall monetary incomes, since the latter were much affected by the real structure of agriculture.

The average wage in Georgia in 1989 was 197.7 roubles, as against 240.4 in the USSR as a whole and even 270.1 roubles in Estonia. By this indicator, Georgia exceeded only the Central Asian republics and Azerbaijan (National Economy 1991: 38). Within Georgia, maximum wages were recorded in Tbilisi (267.7), followed by Gali District in Abkhazia, Tetritskaro District in the Kvemo Kartli social region, and the CRS of Poti (201–220). Wages were in general higher in the cities than in rural areas. The lowest wages were in Dmanisi, Vani and Akhaltsikhe Rural Districts (123–5 roubles).

The average monthly salary of collective farmers was 169.9 roubles in 1989, compared with 200.8 in the USSR as a whole, with the maximum, 317.7, once again in Estonia (National Economy 1991). The average monthly pension in Georgia was 54.8 roubles per pensioner, including those disabled from childhood, and the maximum pension was 132 rubles.

The US dollar in those days was officially worth 0.67 Soviet roubles, although the unofficial black market price per $US was 3–4 roubles. Taking into account the relatively low prices of communal services and staple products, the average salaries and wages quoted above provided a subsistence minimum for the employed population. Clearly, however, the situation described does not give any basis to talk about a "Welfare State" in Soviet Georgia.

The highest per capita figures of total monetary incomes in Georgia were recorded in large cities and in lowland rural regions with intensive agriculture (Fig. 6.1). These comprised the coastal areas of the rural social regions of Samegrelo, Guria, Adjara and Abkhazia, the area within the Tbilisi Metropolitan Region and the city of Tskhinvali. This pattern remained fairly stable throughout the 1980s. Some mountainous and sparsely populated districts in the East Kavkasioni social region benefited from an advantageous agricultural structure and also from a less dense population. They demonstrated substantial per capita monetary income; for example, Kazbegi and Dusheti Districts by this index were among the leading communities of Georgia. This was solely dependent on transhumance sheep breeding, the products of which had a high purchase price. However, political realities will inevitably affect the living standards of these districts. The winter pastures for their large flocks of sheep traditionally served certain lowland areas in the north Caucasus rented by the government of the Georgian SSR from the Dagestan Autonomous Republic within the Russian Federation. Now that the border between Russia and Georgia has become an international border and the rent has to be paid in hard currency, the winter pastures can no longer be used by these communities in Georgia. Moreover, the transhumance routes went through villages settled by North Ossetians, who became hostile towards the Georgian shepherds after the conflict in South Ossetia broke out in late 1990.

The majority of mountain areas in the 1980s, however, showed far fewer possibilities for a high income than those in the lowlands. A notable example was the Adjara Autonomous Republic, where all five rural districts cover a relatively small land area in strict accordance with vertical zonality, from the coastal Kobuleti District, with highly profitable tea and citrus cultivation and developed resort services, through Khelvachauri, Keda and Shuakhevi Districts, to the mountainous and densely populated Khulo District, with cattle-breeding of low productivity. Per capita monetary income declined nearly uniformly as the elevation of the territory increased. Kobuleti District in the 1980s exceeded Khulo by 2.6 times. Discrepancies in monetary income per capita throughout Georgia were quite considerable. For example, Kazbegi District, in first place in 1980, exceeded by 4.5 times last-placed Sachkhere District, a hilly area in the rural social region of Imereti. By 1985, the gulf between the districts had widened to seven times.

The volume of income officially accounted for was apparently less than the amount that actually reached the hands of the population. Many rural residents managed to avoid selling at the relatively low prices paid by the State for agricultural production from the private plots, but instead sold it in the *kolkhoz* bazaars at free prices. Account should also be taken of the "second (shadow) economy" and various criminal activities, which created substantial unofficial income. However, these all had a rather insignificant effect on the overall geographical distribution of monetary income.

Total deposits in saving accounts were constantly increasing in the USSR as a whole and in Soviet Georgia in particular, reaching 8.1 billion roubles in Georgia in 1989 (i.e. 2.1% of the all-Soviet total). The average figure for current deposits in the USSR was 1734 roubles in 1989. Against this background, average savings

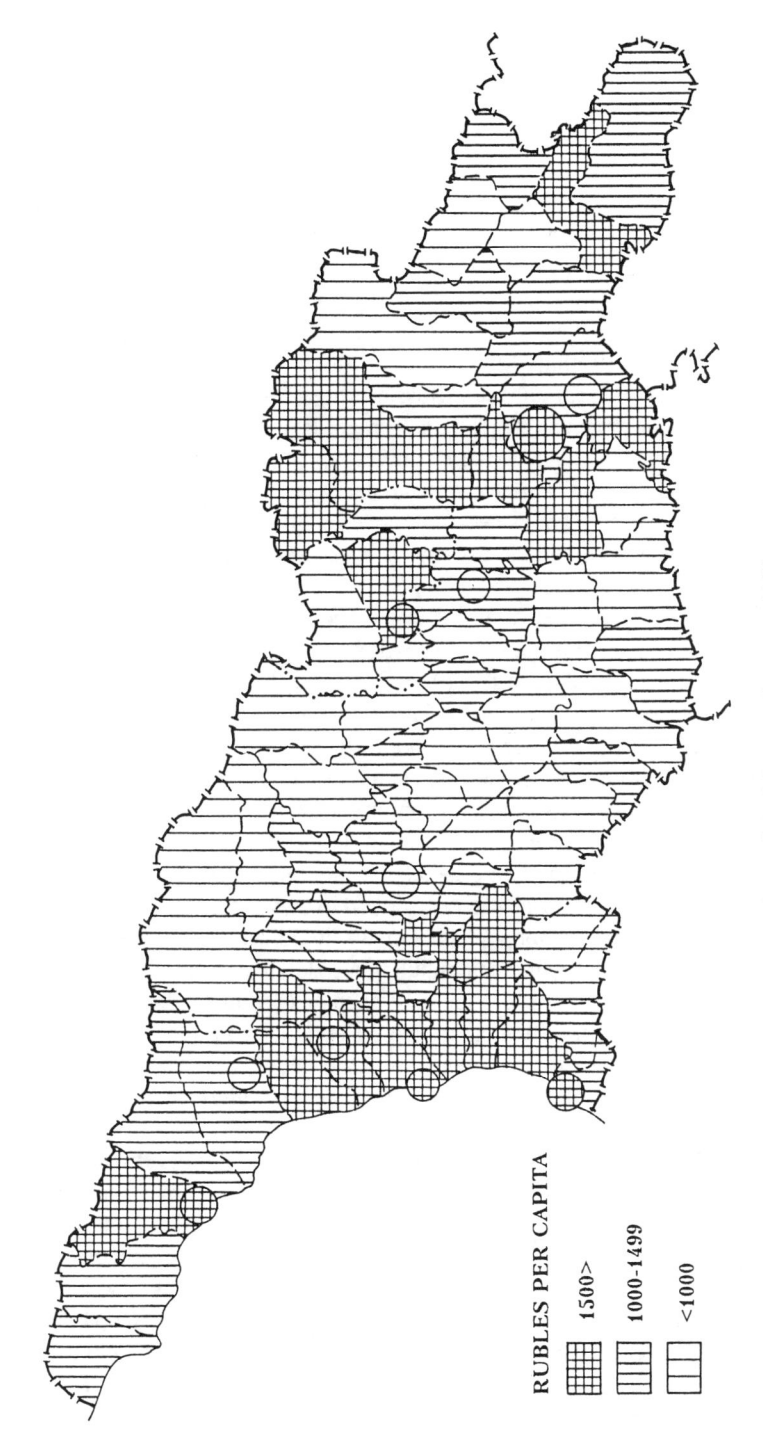

Figure 6.1 Monetary incomes, 1989.

in Georgia were among the highest, at 2459 roubles. Only Armenia was higher with 2794 roubles (National Economy 1991: 48). This, indirectly, shows that substantial savings here were owned by a better-off minority of the population. Even so, these figures were to some extent understated. The so-called "non-labour incomes", which were mostly acquired through "second economy" activities, could not be entirely hidden in the one and only Savings Bank of the USSR; despite the officially proclaimed privacy of deposits, everyone knew that the Bank was controlled by State organizations. Therefore, large monetary incomes were usually split up into smaller deposit accounts by their owners.

Contrary to the widespread belief in the USSR, Georgia was not the leader in savings per capita. With its 1279 rubles in 1989, it was surpassed by Armenia, the Ukraine, the Baltic republics and Russia proper. In some areas of Georgia, per capita deposits were much larger than average. That could be explained on the one hand by more substantial monetary incomes, but also on the other by the deficit of purchasable goods and services, which meant that money had to be deposited for quite long time before goods became available. In the specific conditions of "real socialism", when demand almost always exceeded supply, the latter explanation is not to be ruled out.

Figure 6.2 reveals the pattern of distribution of per capita deposits in saving accounts. The difference between the highest and lowest on a per capita basis was at least six times throughout the 1980s. The highest figures in 1989, more than 2000 roubles per capita, were found in the CRSs of Tskhinvali, Gori, Sokhumi and Gagra, and in the rural districts of Dedoplitskaro and Signagi in Kakheti, and Oni and Akhalkalaki districts in the mountains. On the whole, large cities displayed higher figures for savings than rural communities. The geographical pattern of per capita deposits did not depend entirely on the economic factors of incomes and wages, but to some extent on the social–psychological attitudes of the population, which with some reservation can be ascribed to ethnic or even sub-ethnic characteristics. For example, among leading areas with highest per capita deposits were those with a dominant Armenian population (Akhalkalaki and Ninotsminda) and those with a substantial proportion of Armenians (Akhaltsikhe and Tsalka rural districts, and CRS Gagra). Armenians were distinguished for their thrift and, probably, greater credit-worthiness in the Savings Bank of the USSR! It is worth noting as well that the Armenian SSR in those days had the highest per capita deposits in the USSR.

People in the southern republics of the USSR, especially in rural areas, did not fully trust the Savings Bank, the only bank where Soviet roubles could be deposited, a fact that eased the collection of the data under analysis! In some areas it was more common to keep money "under the pillow" at home, or to convert it into gold. The Azeri population of Kvemo Kartli social region had this habit; hence, one of the lowest per capita deposits was recorded in Marneuli and Bolnisi rural districts with predominantly Azeri populations. Most of the rural areas, especially in western Georgia, also had low indices of savings. All the districts forming the rural social region of Samegrelo had low per capita figures (336–554 rubles).

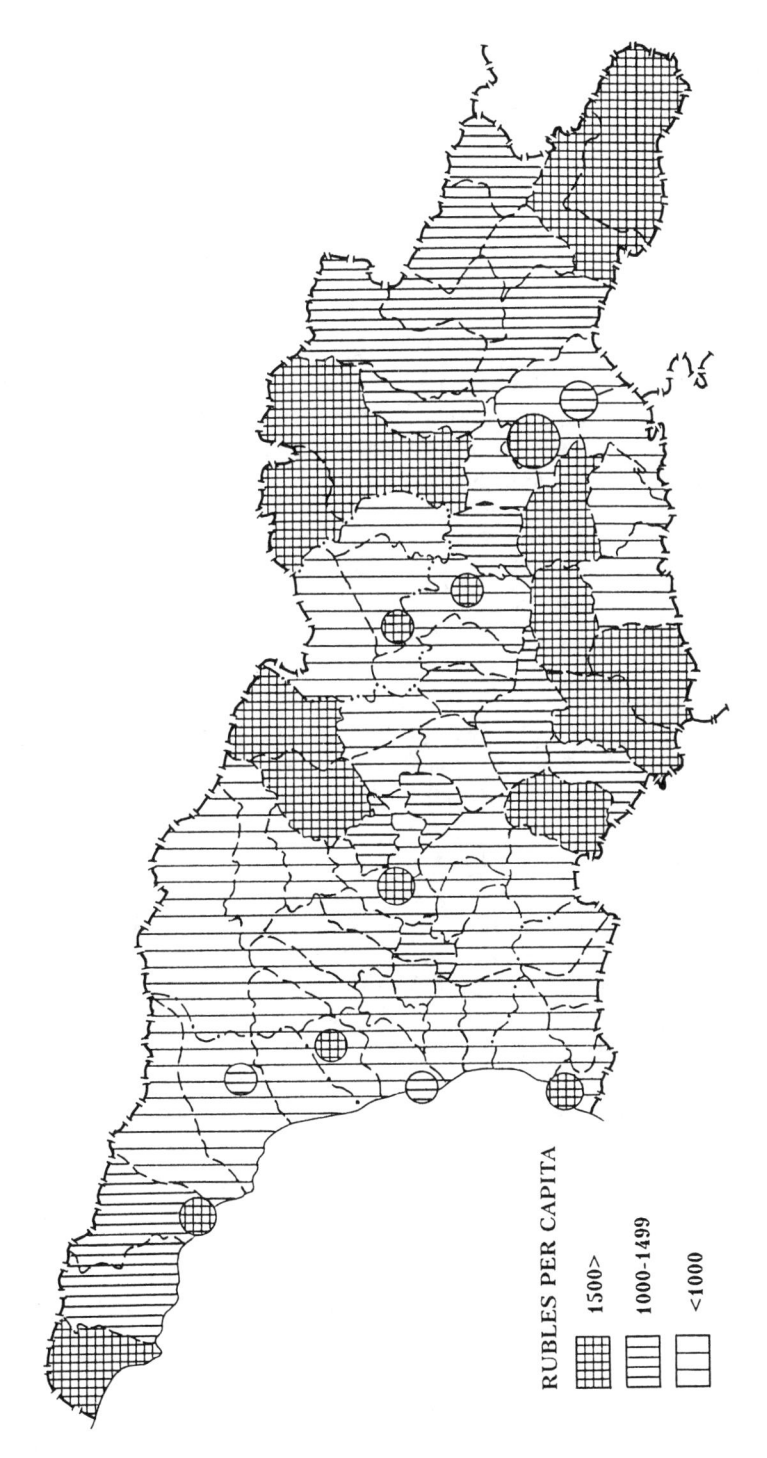

Figure 6.2 Deposits in savings accounts, 1989.

Similar figures applied in the adjoining districts of Gali and Ochamchire in Abkhazia, where the same sub-ethnic group is dominant. This type of economic behaviour in this area with high monetary incomes can be explained by the tradition of keeping money at home or by investment in real property, and spending to acquire expensive goods.

Data on retail trade turnover, it would seem, provide the most distorted picture in terms of geographic comparisons, because purchases are not always made in the place of residence. But trade turnover per capita is probably the best indicator of spatial differences in welfare distribution. It is estimated that the inhabitants of Georgia in the 1980s spent 0.5–1.0 billion roubles annually outside their republic, predominantly in Russia. However, this invisible import was to some extent compensated by invisible exports, the money spent in Georgia by many tourists from Russia and on purchases by the population of other neighbouring republics. For the inhabitants of the northern districts of Azerbaijan, the city of Tbilisi served as the central place where they purchased a large part of the industrial goods they required.

Actually, in the USSR a certain equilibrium of the State and private market was eventually created, the latter represented by the *kolkhoz* bazaar, where prices were determined according to supply and demand. An increasing number of people shopped in these bazaars, principally for fruit, vegetables, meat and milk products (especially cheese), and flowers. According to a research project carried out by the Department of Human Geography, Tbilisi State University in 1979, the seven *kolkhoz* bazaars in Tbilisi were visited daily by at least 60 000 customers and almost 40 per cent of the total expenditure for foodstuffs were spent there. Annual turnover of the 175 bazaars throughout Georgia was officially estimated as 350 million roubles in 1989 (Trade 1990: 5). This figure looks to be a serious underestimation; turnover might have well exceeded one billion roubles, in effect not taxed. A substantial part returned not to the farmers but to the middlemen and professional (albeit "criminal") traders, the so-called *spekulyanti*. By number of trading places per 1000 of population, Georgia occupied first place in the USSR (National Economy 1991: 151). By the mid-1990s these bazaars were practically the only place where some of the population – those able to pay – could obtain food, as the disordered change to market relations left the still State-owned and only gradually privatized shops absolutely empty.

Turnover in the State-owned shopping enterprises (including public catering) in 1989 amounted to almost six billion roubles. Trade, even in State shops, gave substantial side benefits to those engaged in this sector of economy. The government always had to keep eye on the management of the State shops. In practice these were becoming more and more independent. The spontaneous location of State-owned shops was increasingly resembling that in capitalist countries, seeking a site where the highest profit could be achieved.

Figure 6.3 shows the distribution of trade turnover on a per capita basis in 1989. This social indicator correlates best with the overall material welfare of the communities. The highest figures, over 2000 roubles, were for Mtskheta rural district

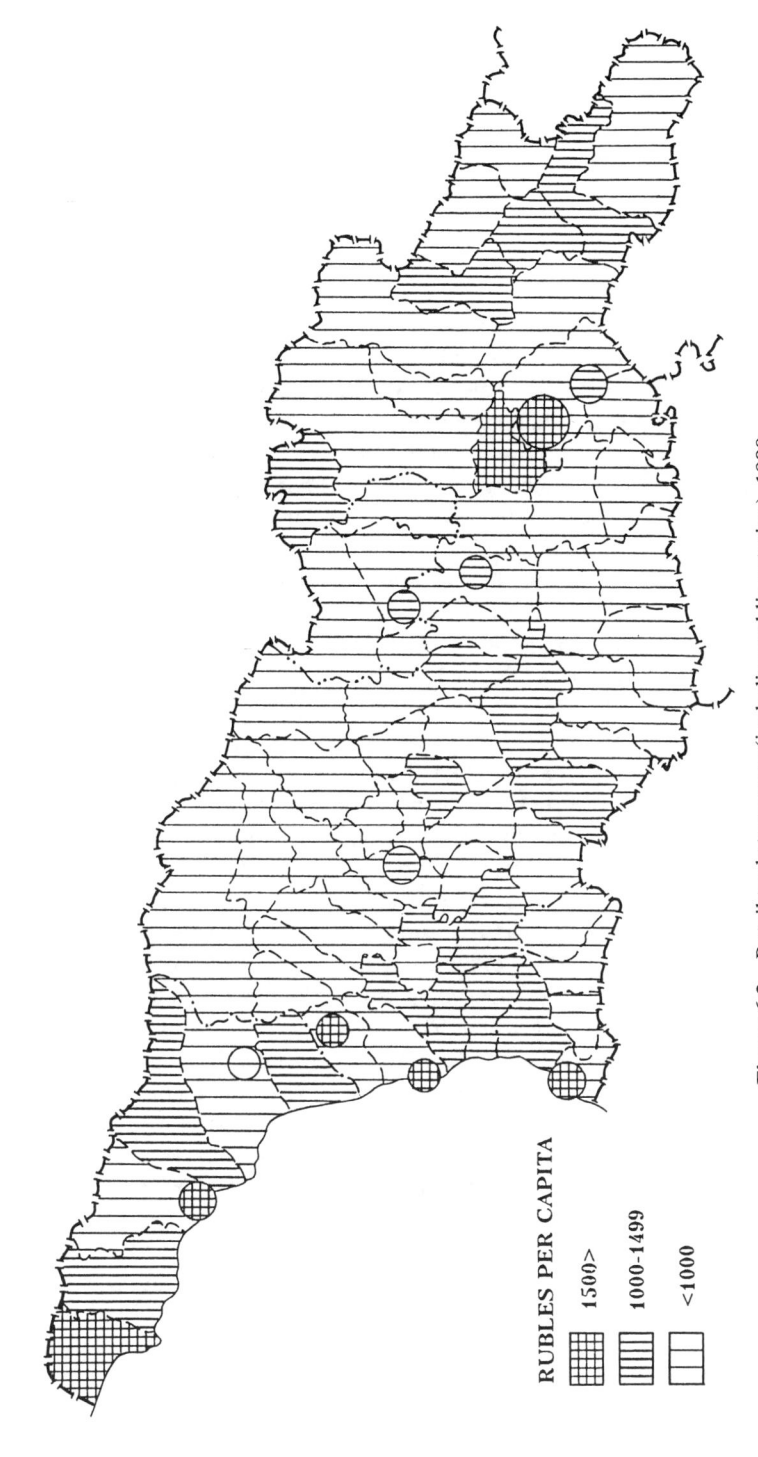

Figure 6.3 Retail trade turnovers (including public catering), 1989.

within the Tbilisi Metropolitan Region, where major fairs were located, and in CRS of Zugdidi, where a large amount of material wealth was accumulated. There was a high turnover in all large cities, major transport nodes (Samtredia, Poti), and in the well developed resort areas (Gagra, Tskaltubo, Borjomi). In Georgia, the distance to large cities is not very great and they served as the major central places. Most of the rural districts had low per capita figures of trade turnover.

The provision of everyday services more or less parallels the pattern of trade turnover, but the figures are much smaller. The average per capita turnover of these services in 1989 was 238 roubles; the maximum of 416 roubles was reached in the resort area of Borjomi, and the minimum, 50–60 roubles, in the mountain districts of West Kavkasioni and the Southern Upland.

A more important component of material welfare seemed to be the possession of private motor cars. The automobilization of the USSR started in effect in 1969, when the huge VAZ automobile factory located in Toliatti on the Volga started to produce ever-increasing numbers of cars, modelled initially on the Fiat 124, but later with an extended range of models. The automobile stock in Georgia increased by nearly seven times between 1970 and 1985. With 63 private motorcars per 1000 people in 1984, Georgia was in fourth place among the Soviet republics, after the Baltic republics – Estonia with 111 per thousand persons, Lithuania 91 and Latvia 78 (Analysis 1985). By 1989 the indicator for Georgia had increased to 74 and it maintained its fourth place among the 15 Soviet republics.

Possession of a car in the USSR was a symbol of wealth. Apart from the numerically few, highly paid, elite intelligentsia, most of the white-collar and blue-collar workers could not afford to buy a car, although this disadvantage was offset by quite effective public transport. In some rural areas of Georgia, where people had higher legal incomes, it was easier to acquire a car than in urban centres. To a certain extent the figures of car possession indicate spatial differences in the benefits from the "second economy". Figure 6.4 displays the spatial contrasts in the distribution of private cars per thousand persons. The highest values were in Kakheti social region, Tbilisi and its metropolitan Region, the CRSs of Zugdidi and Gagra. The lowest figures were observed in the northern districts, mountain Adjara and the hill districts of Sachkhere and Kharagauli in the Imereti rural social region.

For a time, the spatial differentiation in the per capita supply of cars seemed to decrease, although it was nevertheless considerable. In 1980 the value for the highest-ranking Signagi District in Kakheti exceeded last-placed Tsageri District in poor West Kavkasioni by 5.1 times; these two districts maintained their ranking in 1985, but the gulf between them narrowed to 4.6 times. By 1989 the gulf had again widened. The wine-growing Gurjaani district ranked first with 169 motorcars per 1000 persons; its neighbour Signagi District was second. This figure exceeded by more than six times the 27 cars of Mestia in West Kavkasioni. The relative figure for Tbilisi was 107 motorcars per 1000 persons.

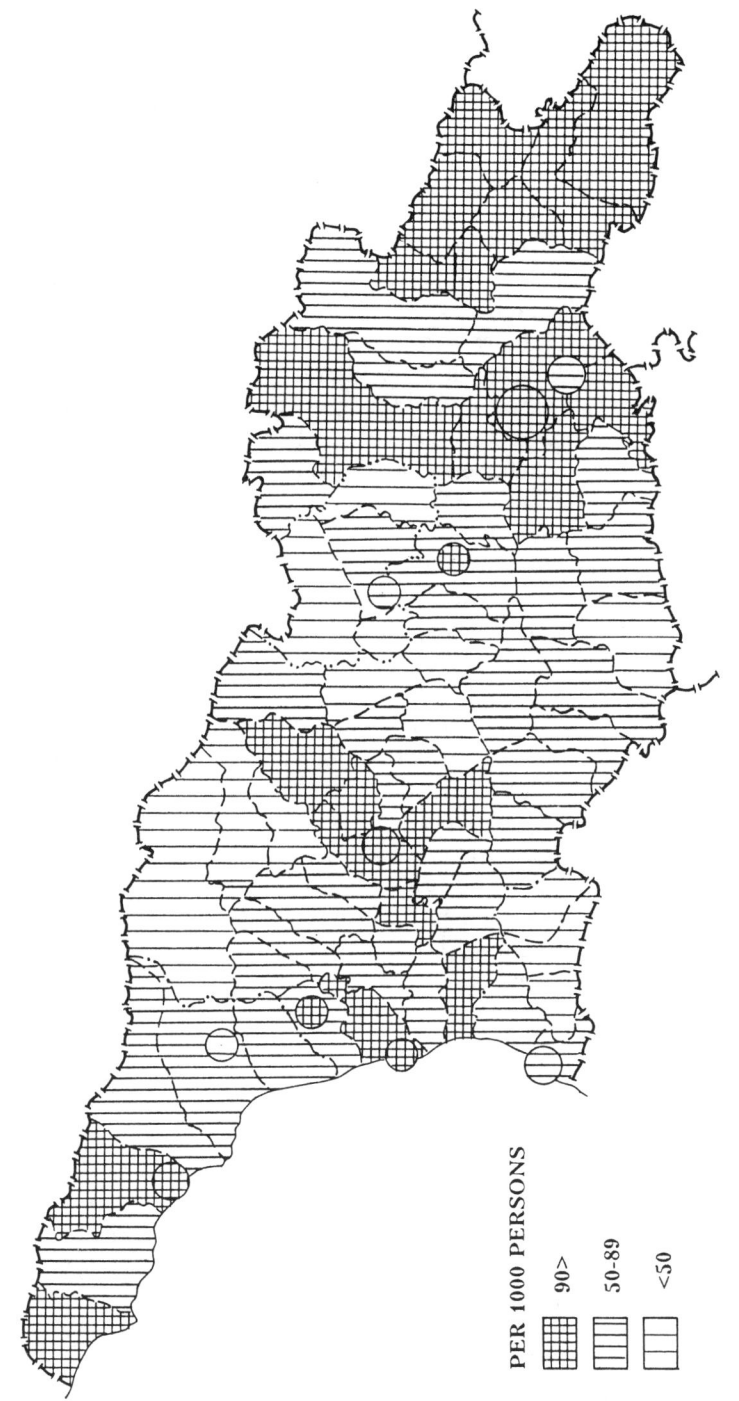

Figure 6.4 Registered private cars, 1989.

Summary rankings

Different indicators thus gave diverse geographic patterns of people's material welfare. Because the average per capita indicators reflect expenditures as well as income, the localities need to be summarized in terms of their overall ranking, in order to obtain a generalized picture. This gives the specific "inverted rating" of the material welfare of the communities, that is to say, the lower the sum of individual rankings, the higher the overall rating. In the period 1980–9, the majority of the CRS and rural districts of Georgia maintained their relative rankings.

In first place was the capital city of Tbilisi. Although by none of the social indicators was it the first, it was always among the first ten and therefore its sum of rankings was the lowest, at about 40 points throughout the 1980s. The runners-up over the whole period under study were Signagi rural district and the CRS of Zugdidi. In general, the large cities had the higher ratings. The lowest places were held by the rural districts within the social regions of West Kavkasioni, rural Adjara, Kvemo Kartli, with over 280 points (Fig. 6.5). A significant number of the least well off communities are located at elevations exceeding 1500m above sea level. Local climatic characteristics and the land surface of too steep slopes have an effect on the structure of agriculture and ultimately on the low level of welfare of the rural communities, including all of West Kavkasioni, Sachkhere and Kharagauli Districts of Imereti rural social region. Lower welfare indicators are characteristic of rural districts with a high natural population increase as well, Bolnisi and Dmanisi Districts in Kvemo Kartli social region with a dominant Azeri population. In mountain Adjara, both physical-geographical and demographic negative factors were present, which influenced the low per capita welfare.

A generalized pattern of welfare distribution by the 21 social regions is shown in Figure 6.6. It is intentionally given for 1987, although in practice that did not differ from the 1989 pattern, because in 1987 two sociological surveys were carried out to evaluate public opinion on the material welfare of the population by the social regions of Georgia. The terms "high", "medium" and "low" level of material welfare are relative, applying to the Georgian realities of the late 1980s; they cannot be used for comparison on an international basis.

A high level of material welfare per capita in the setting of Georgia as a whole was characteristic of the urban social regions of Tbilisi, Zugdidi, Sokhumi and Gori. A medium level was observed in the urban social regions of Kutaisi, Tskhinvali, Poti, Batumi and Rustavi and in the rural social regions of Abkhazia, Kakheti, Guria and East Kavkasioni. All the other rural social regions had a low level of welfare. Among the districts in this last category, there were doubtless some that had a definitely higher material welfare, but other districts pulled down the whole region. For example, Kobuleti District within the social region of rural Adjara had a very high individual rating, but the other rural districts of that social region, with an underdeveloped economy and high birthrate, affected the overall low level of the region. The same is true of Samegrelo rural social region, where poorer mountain districts affect the average welfare figures.

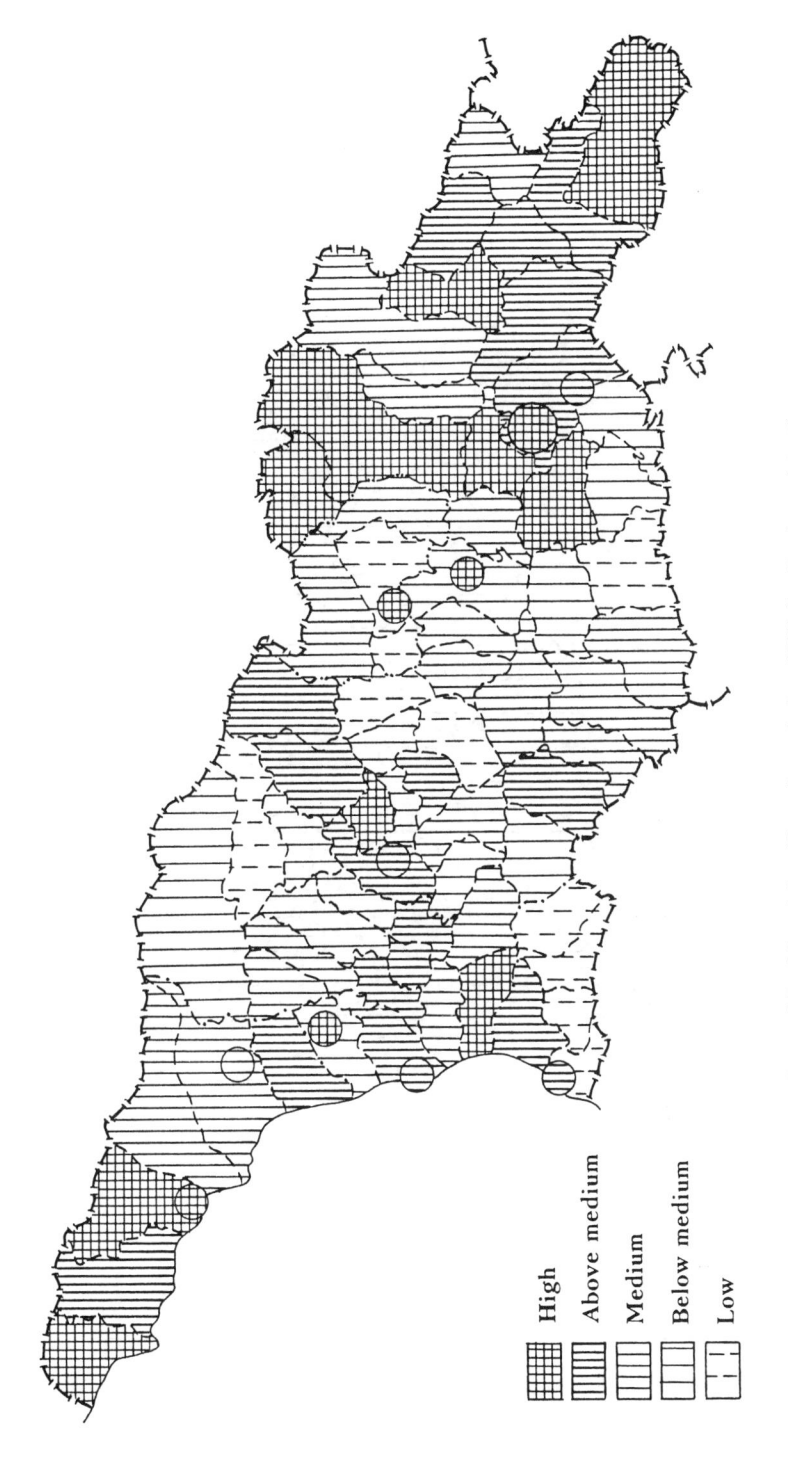

Figure 6.5 Material welfare of population, 1989 (by district and CRS).

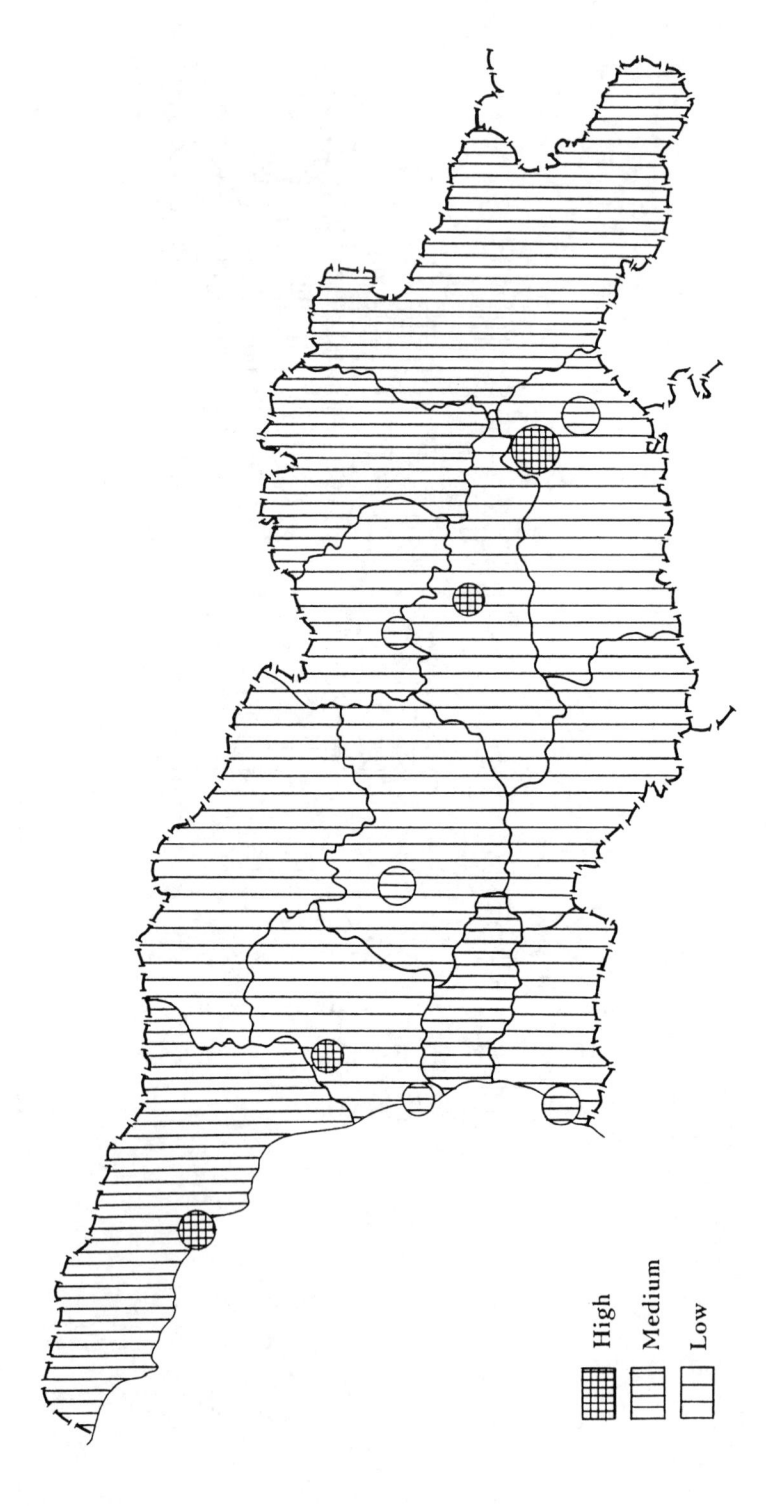

Figure 6.6 Relative material welfare of the population of Georgia, 1987 (by social regions).

Public opinion of the welfare of social regions

The pattern observed in Figure 6.6 is very much the same as that in Figure 6.7, where the welfare of the social regions of Georgia according to public opinion is depicted. There are, however, several differences that can be explained by the stereotypes of public opinion as revealed in people's mental maps.

Before commenting on these differences, something must be said about the survey materials on the basis of which the map has been drawn. In November and December 1987, the two surveys were carried out on the basis of nationwide samples, polling 2244 and 2470 respondents respectively, by the Department for the Study of Public Opinion. The Department was part of the Georgian Academy of Sciences sector on social science information, a predecessor of the CSS; the sector in those days worked for the Central Committee of the Communist Party of Georgia (Slider 1985). In the surveys a specific question was posed: "In which three social regions of Georgia is there the highest level of material welfare?"

The respondents were allowed to use their own perception of the meaning of the term "material welfare level" or to be guided by the stereotypes of their normal thinking. A majority of the respondents (77%) understood the question and gave definite answers. The results of the two surveys were very much alike, although different sampling techniques were used and the primary sampling units did not coincide. The coefficient of rank correlation of the results of the two surveys was 0.930.

It is obvious that public opinion in this country possesses some kind of empirical, although scientifically indifferent, "geographical way of thinking", at least in comparing regional levels of welfare. This can be explained by, first, the relatively small but variegated territory of Georgia, secondly the well developed transport network and accessibility of the most of the territory, and thirdly the contacts of the urban population, which has strong roots in the rural areas and kinship ties all over the country and which visits different regions quite often. Besides, the social regions very much coincide with the historical provinces of Georgia and its major cities, which are familiar to the majority of the population. At least public opinion has revealed a knowledge of the real wealth of the social regions. The rank correlation with the "inverted rating" achieved by the techniques described above was 0.623 (Gachechiladze 1990: 144). Deviations are easily explicable by the general perception of social space. In both surveys, the first four social regions in terms of material welfare and even their sequence were identical; public opinion considered these to be Tbilisi, Kutaisi, Zugdidi and Sokhumi. The four poorest social regions were equally uniformly considered to be the rural social regions located in the highland areas: Meskheti–Javakheti, East Kavkasioni, "Rural Tskhinvali" (at that time, South Ossetia excluding the CRS of Tskhinvali) and West Kavkasioni.

The "inverted rating" and public opinion both considered Tbilisi to be in first place by material welfare. It should be noted that public opinion to some extent overestimated this level; over 70 per cent mentioned the capital among the three best off regions. This was explicable, as the respondents relied on their perception,

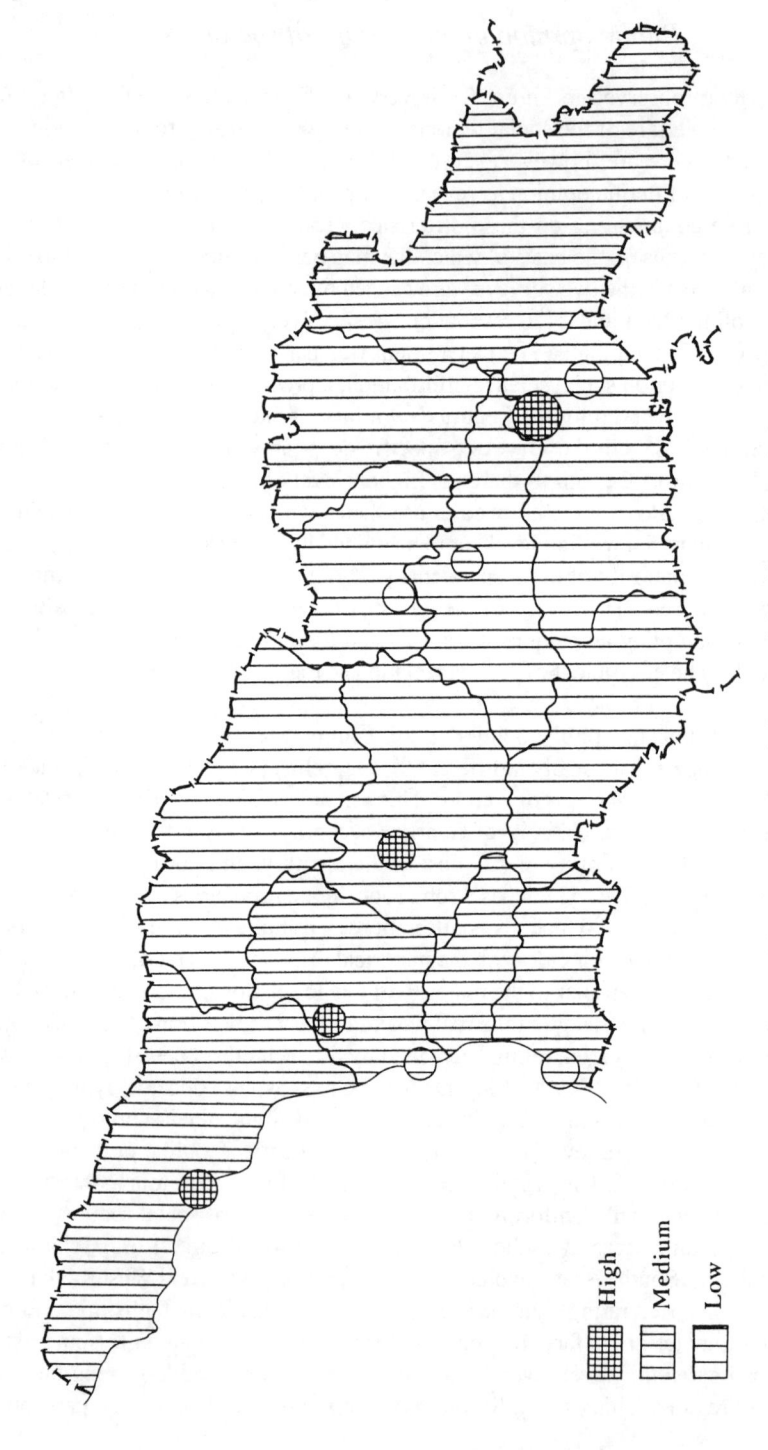

Figure 6.7 Public opinion on the relative material welfare of population, 1987.

which was affected at least by the large numbers of cars in the streets. Hyperurbanization of the capital city, caused by overconcentration of administrative, industrial, cultural and service functions in a trend similar to that in the other Soviet republics of the time, gave an image of Tbilisi as the most thriving and wealthiest centre, where everyone wanted to live. Public opinion is a barometer of the subjective factors in internal migrations. Tbilisi, incidentally, was twice as often mentioned as "the wealthiest" by respondents outside the city; the residents of the city itself were more modest in their evaluation.

Among the three other leading social regions on the public opinion scale of material welfare, the urban regions of Zugdidi and Sokhumi definitely coincide with the "inverted rating", whereas the CRS of Kutaisi was surpassed by the CRS of Gori. I wish that I could say that public opinion might be more correct. The hospitable city of Kutaisi was probably remembered by most respondents from other regions, who gave it a high place on the scale, by dint of its bountiful feasts! The actual indicators, however, gave Gori the preference on a per capita basis.

Among the "backward" social regions, according to public opinion, the three again coincided with those of the "inverted rating". Only the wealth of East Kavkasioni was underestimated. This highland area was empirically very well known to respondents, as the major road from the Transcaucasus to Russia passes through it. With its ever-decreasing population, it does not give an impression of the accumulated wealth. But as sheep-breeding was a very profitable branch of agriculture, this affected the upward shift of the region on the rating scale. With the economic crisis in Georgia, which will affect this region severely, the opinion of our "rational public" will probably become more plausible. Conversely, public opinion gave a rather high place to the rural Adjara social region, which is one of the poorest by the "inverted rating" on a per capita basis. This again can be explained by spatially limited perception. The mountainous Adjara districts with their high birthrate, limited land resources and virtually without any industrial development, were situated along the State border of the USSR, and in Soviet times they were a closed area and less visited by people from outside. Meanwhile, Kobuleti District, with its beautiful seaside resorts and groves of tangerines, was much more familiar to the public, whose impression of Rural Adjara as of one of the wealthiest regions was formed in this very area.

It can be assumed that public opinion tends usually to overestimate the wealth of other regions and to underestimate that of its own area of residence. Thus, respondents in the CRS of Tskhinvali, centre of the then South Ossetian Autonomous Region, held a rather low opinion of the material welfare of their own city, whereas by most indicators Tskhinvali was one of the leading places on the all-Georgia scale. Public opinion on the whole gave a quite sensible evaluation of the material welfare of the population. Perhaps sometimes it was even more reliable than the "inverted rating", which was not able to evaluate fully the wealth acquired through the "shadow economy", which was a very important factor of material welfare in Soviet Georgia, as elsewhere in the former USSR. May it even be that Kutaisi was given a more precise place by public opinion than by my calculations?

CHAPTER 7
Spatial aspects of deviance

General trends

Susan Smith begins her chapter "The challenge of urban crime" in an outstanding book by British geographers with the words, "The streets of Britain are getting meaner" (Herbert & Smith 1989: 271). As everything is understood in comparison, it seems to me that in the case of the streets of modern Georgia something stronger needs to be said, such as, "Tbilisi in 1992–93 very much resembled Paris of the times of Henry III" (in order to keep some readers from turning to the encyclopedia, I should remind them that Henry III of the House of Valois reigned in the sixteenth century). Hopefully this comparison may be a temporary one and is not likely to become a trend, but the streets here are meaner than in Britain!

Crime, which always accompanies the weakening of State structures and the inevitable chaos in societies undergoing dramatic social change, strongly increased over the whole territory of the former USSR. Since 1989 when the first information on crime appeared openly in the Soviet press (Dyatlov 1989), it became apparent that there had been a substantial increase in crime in the country even before then and that the figures were growing annually. In 1988, 1 867 000 criminal offences were registered in the USSR as a whole, an increase of 3.8 per cent over the previous year. In the following year, 1989, the number of crimes increased by 32 per cent to 2 500 000. In this period, the fastest growth of crime was in Estonia (57% increase), Lithuania (46%) and Byelorussia (36%) (SocioEconomic 1990). In 1990 the number of crimes in the USSR increased by 13 per cent and reached 2 800 000. The number of murders and attempted murders has grown dramatically from 14 700 in 1987 to 24 900 in 1990 (National Economy 1991: 278).

The next year the USSR collapsed and statistics are now collected individually in each Newly Independent State. Naturally, there were regions within the USSR with a level of crime higher than average. Soviet Georgia until 1990 was not a republic at the head of this list; of crimes registered in the USSR, 0.7 per cent were committed in Georgia, although 2 per cent of the total population resided here. On the whole, Georgia had rather modest per capita crime figures and one can be assured that the streets of Tbilisi were safer than those of New York and probably even some British cities of those times.

Times have changed since. In an English magazine recently was written:

Certainly, the crime wave is connected to the failures of reform. Rules, where they exist, are vague. Public servants are underpaid, demoralized and hungry for bribes. Weapons are sold by disillusioned and unpaid soldiers and ex-soldiers. New frontiers, badly policed, tempt smugglers of drugs and merchandise. Hundreds of government regulations and licences remain in place, providing opportunities for corruption and crime . . . In the rush to privatize, the authorities rarely have time to check bidders' documents, or the source of their cash . . . Street-market mafias impose monopoly prices, which in turn have helped spin the wheel of inflation . . . The interior ministry says it cannot offer special protection to the rich. Hiring more police would not work anyway; their pay is so wretched that bribes are tempting, and they accept recruits without proper screening . . . So entrepreneurs wanting protection recruit their own gangs, which come in useful for debt collection too. And lawlessness spreads". (Crime 1994: 29).

This lengthy quotation concerns crime in Russia, but with little variation it is true of any of the post-Soviet States, including of course Georgia.

Changes in the dynamics and structure of crime and conviction

Because Georgia found itself, for reasons analyzed elsewhere, in one of the worst political and economic situations among the post-Soviet States, one of the worst outbreaks of criminal deviance occurred as well. Between 1988 and 1992, recorded crime totals rose by 46 per cent, including crimes prosecuted by criminal police, which more than tripled. Serious criminal offences in the same period increased by about 5.6 times. Under the Soviet criminal code, serious crimes were considered to be premeditated murder and murder attempts, causing serious bodily injury, rape, robbery, burglary, malicious hooliganism, theft of arms, theft of a large amount of State (not private!) property, arson, and so on.

A notorious feature became the well armed highway gangs, who took advantage of the nation being engaged in civil wars and the consequent weakening of State structures and instituted their almost entire "control" over the major roads. This made traffic unsafe and virtually blocked economic relations between provinces. Only in early 1994 were harsh measures, using tanks and armoured cars, taken against the gangsters, and the roads were cleansed of them. Table 7.1 demonstrates dynamics and structural changes in registered crime statistics between 1985 and 1994. Only selected, specific categories of crime are included in the Table.

Until 1988, the total number of registered crimes had tended to decrease and the structure had been more or less stable. It is hard to say to what extent this decrease and structural stability depended on the "planned economy"; in the USSR as a whole the same tendency was apparent (National Economy 1991: 278). In the

Table 7.1 Dynamics of registered crime (1985–92).

	1985	1986	1987	1988	1989	1990	1991	1992	1993	1994
Total	18573	18395	17634	16582	17646	19711	21982	24142	22066	17643
Prosecuted by criminal police	–	–	–	7017	8409	11675	16649	21705	19865	15071
Serious crime	–	–	–	1387	1958	2609	4046	7726	8735	5683
Crime committed (% of total)										
Against personal property:										
by theft	9.6	10.5	11.1	12.6	15.2	22.1	24.5	23.0	21.1	22.4
by robbery & burglary	1.5	1.2	1.2	1.5	1.9	3.7	6.2	11.1	13.0	11.1
Against public property:										
by theft	3.9	3.3	3.3	3.4	4.8	7.0	11.6	20.5	16.7	11.6
by robbery & burglary	–	–	–	–	–	0.7	1.6	3.5	4.6	2.3
Against the person:										
premediated murder & its attempt	0.8	0.7	0.8	0.9	1.2	2.0	2.4	3.9	4.7	3.9
serious bodily injury	1.1	1.0	1.2	1.4	1.8	1.7	1.7	1.5	1.3	1.7
sexual offence	0.5	0.5	0.5	0.4	0.4	0.5	0.5	0.3	0.3	0.4
Against public security & order:										
malicious hooliganism	5.8	5.1	4.5	4.0	4.0	3.2	3.0	1.5	1.7	2.1
drug-related crime	4.7	4.7	3.9	2.3	2.1	2.4	–	2.5	3.9	6.3
driving violations leading to grave results	10.9	10.4	10.7	11.7	13.3	7.4	–	2.2	1.5	1.9
Other	61.2	62.3	62.8	61.8	55.3	49.3	48.5	30.0	31.2	36.3

Source: Data of the Committee of Social–Economic Information of the Republic of Georgia and the Ministry of Internal Affairs.

USSR, the lowest level of crime was recorded in 1987 and since then the curve has gone upwards. In Georgia, which was always lagging behind during *perestroyka*, the same trend appeared after 1988. Clearly, not all crime was registered in the Soviet period, especially small offences, and it is impossible to consider latent crime, which presumably might be quite large. Serious criminal offences such as premeditated murder and attempted murder, grievous bodily harm, crimes against the State or personal property (especially if a large amount is involved) could not avoid registration.

Up to 55 per cent of criminal offences were cleared up in the late 1980s. In 1992 this index dropped to 40 per cent, including only 45 per cent of murders, 29 per cent of thefts of personal property and 19 per cent of robberies.

The most notable structural change is the sharp increase after 1989 in the proportion of crimes against private property, especially by robbery and burglary, which increased almost tenfold from 1987 to 1992. There were also increases in theft of public property and in violence against the person, especially premeditated murder and attempted murder.

In the nineteenth century, murders were probably the only well registered crime and on a per capita basis, the Transcaucasus in that century almost equalled the situation in the 1980s. According to data for 1877 in Tbilisi and Kutaisi Provinces, all registered crime totalled a mere 273, or 0.22 per 10000 persons, and of these, 82 were murders. *En passant*, the crime rate in Yerevan Province, largely coincident with today's Armenia, was the same as in the Georgian provinces, but in Yelisavetpol (Gyanja) and Baku Provinces and Zaqatala Region covering today's Azerbaijan, the crime rate was six times higher at 1.29 per 10000 persons and totalling 1547 in all, among them 371 murders (Segal 1880).

From 1985–8 the number of murders alone increased from 140–160 annually to 770 in 1992 and to 875 in 1993; in these last two years there were also respectively 167 and 152 attempted murders. An absolute majority of murders are registered and these are thus among the most reliable figures. The major factor affecting this tragic development was explained earlier in Chapter 5, when the wide spread of firearms was mentioned as being one of the major societal problems. The disastrous results of the "Kalashnikovization" of a sector of society is evident. It must be added that despite the peremptory declarations of some journalists that, "for every three Georgians there are four automatic submachine guns" (e.g. Leskov 1993), actually not more than 2–3 per cent of the population were in possession of firearms. But even this number was quite enough to be a real block to the normal economic and social development of the nation. From 1994 with the beginning of a certain stabilization in the country, the police at last became active; hundreds of illegal firearms have been withdrawn and their owners arrested. This presumably will have results on the level and structure of crime, which will appear in the statistics of coming years.

Traditionally, sexual crime was not a widespread offence in Georgia, probably because of a continuing respect towards women that has not yet vanished completely. Thus, its low rate is no surprise. However, the decrease in drug-related crime can be explained only by negligence on the part of the police towards this really dangerous and ever expanding type of deviance.

Some decrease in crime connected with violations of traffic rules and driving regulations leading to fatalities is more understandable, as the fuel shortage has led to a sharp reduction in the use of personal and public motor-cars. Highways, once jammed with traffic, became almost empty. Nevertheless, in 1993, 528 people died, as compared with 850–900 annually during the 1980s. In Tbilisi, 23 per cent of the deaths and 39 per cent of injuries occurred. The peripheral areas of the capital were especially notorious for traffic crime (Kvirikashvili 1994).

Among other crimes, not mentioned in Table 7.1, some are simply becoming obsolete because of the changes in the ideological paradigms. For example, among economic crimes, *spekulyatsia* (nothing more sinful than reselling the goods for profit) was the leading offence. In 1988 every tenth convicted person received a prison sentence of some years for the resale of goods (Table 7.2). Nowadays the streets of cities and villages are full of petty traders, who openly do the same thing; instead of legal prosecution from the police, they are illegally "taxed" by racketeers and by the very same police. But they are welcomed by the mass media as the "first swallows of the spring of the market economy", the last a term diffidently covering what was earlier called "capitalism".

Another example is crime connected with the "anti-alcohol campaign" of 1985–7, initiated by Mr Gorbachev and aimed mostly at uprooting the hard-drinking habit among the population of Russia proper. Georgia, with its long tradition of wine-drinking and the marvellous home-produced wine spirit called

Table 7.2 Dynamics of conviction (1985–90).

	1985	1986	1987	1988	1989	1990
Total convicts	14087	14626	11240	9396	8442	7481
Among them for the criminal offences committed (% of total):						
Against personal property (all):	19.5	17.7	20.1	22.3	21.5	15.7
by theft	10.5	8.3	9.2	10.3	9.9	11.8
by robbery & burglary	2.2	1.8	1.7	1.9	2.0	3.5
Against public property (all)	11.9	11.1	11.3	12.3	11.1	11.6
Against the person:						
premeditated murder & its attempts	1.9	1.6	1.9	1.8	1.9	2.3
serious bodily injury	0.9	0.8	1.2	1.7	1.7	1.8
sexual offences	1.4	1.0	1.0	0.9	0.8	0.6
Against public security & order:						
malicious hooliganism	7.5	6.5	6.5	4.8	5.5	4.4
drug-related crime	5.2	4.9	4.9	3.9	3.1	4.3
traffic regulation and driving violations leading to grave results	7.1	6.8	7.8	7.6	8.5	8.6
Economic crimes (all):	12.4	15.8	16.4	17.2	16.2	16.8
speculation	6.9	7.9	9.1	10.0	9.6	10.7
deception of consumers	4.6	5.0	6.0	6.2	6.3	6.0
spirit-making for sale	0.9	2.9	1.3	1.0	0.3	0.1

Source: Data of the Committee of Social–Economic Information of the Republic of Georgia.

"chacha", mostly for rather moderate domestic consumption, became an incidental victim of this campaign. In 1986, 422 persons were imprisoned for producing spirit at home, representing 2.9 per cent of all convictions in that year.

In spite of this anti-alcohol campaign, the habit of hard-drinking among the Russians was not uprooted; instead of buying vodka in the State food stores, they started to produce it at home, without paying any taxes to the government. This contributed to the shortage of sugar in the country. The campaign, that began with good intentions (paving the road to hell?), proved to be deficient in common sense and virtually failed, causing the USSR losses of tens of billions of roubles. With its collapse, the number of convictions for this type of offence in Georgia came down to practically zero by the 1990s (Table 7.2).

From another point of view, the anti-alcohol campaign itself permitted many producers and traders of the fraudulent spirits to make real fortunes. It is naive to think that there were only 422 bootleggers illegally processing "chacha" for sale in Georgia.

The number of convictions was fairly stable until past the middle of the 1980s, at about 14000–15000 annually. From 1987 it began to drop, in the same general trend as in the USSR as a whole and in all the other Union republics. This can be explained by a certain liberalization of the regime and, correspondingly, of legal practice. After 1989 with the dramatic growth of crime, the number of convictions in the Russian Federation started to grow again, but in all the Transcaucasian republics it continued to fall, not least because of the decrease in the rate of clearing up crime.

The pattern of convictions in Georgia remained more or less the same during *perestroyka* and the preceding period (Gabiani & Gachechiladze 1982, Gachechiladze 1989). The most widespread crimes, of which almost one third of convicted persons were found guilty (Table 7.2), were those committed against public security and public order. These were disturbing the peace (called hooliganism in the USSR) and violations of traffic regulations and driving rules leading to death or serious injury. Second numerically used to be economic crimes; almost 15 per cent were convicted for speculation and the deception of the consumers. In the 1980s, convictions for crimes against personal property increased and by 1992 had already became the most numerous. Of some 6000 persons arrested by the police for various crimes (not yet legally convicted by courts) more than 30 per cent were suspected of crimes against personal property. Thus, the structure of convictions is going to change.

The criminal code of Georgia was modelled on that of the RSFSR, as in the other former Soviet republics, and is not yet changed. It retains some discrepancies with common sense and the new economic realities, such as the articles referred to above concerning speculation and home distilling, that give opportunities for violations of the law both by ordinary criminals and the police. Because legislation has not been brought into line with reality, some crime figures could not be analyzed in a scholarly way. This especially concerns up-to date information on crime, which before 1990 more or less adequately described the realities of the then-existing State. The use here of information for the late 1980s was considered better for spatial comparisons, as it covered all the districts and towns of the country, where civil wars were not yet raging.

Spatial patterns of crime and conviction

Geographical differences in crime were mostly neglected by Soviet criminologists, whereas Soviet geographers did not consider it their job to interfere in such a delicate (and dangerous) sphere. The major problem was the top secrecy of data concerning crime in a totalitarian State. The rare figures occasionally published allowed no comparison at all. It was by great luck that Anzor Gabiani managed to obtain detailed information on convictions in Georgia for the years 1975–7. This made it possible to process 42 000 "lists of convictions" pertaining to individuals, linked in each case to the place where the crime was committed. With the collaboration of the present author, the results were analyzed and two collective monographs prepared (Gabiani & Gachechiladze 1982, Gabiani et al. 1985).

It appeared that there were major contrasts in the level of conviction, mostly correlating with the level of crime. The highest level was found in larger cities and the coastal areas and the lowest in highland and purely rural areas. Thus, convictions for crime against personal property constituted 7.5–8.4 per 10 000 persons in the CRSs of Sokhumi and Zugdidi, where much wealth had been accumulated, and 1.2–1.4 in the eastern rural social regions. Classification of the social regions of Georgia by pattern of conviction permitted the distinction of the following types: "urban", in the larger cities and coastal social regions where crimes against personal property and those connected with corruption predominated; "rural", in the mountainous and other less urbanized social regions where crimes against the person and State property were more widespread; and "mixed", in the medium-size urban social regions and most of the rural social regions located in lowland areas, where the structure was more balanced, with neither type of crime predominating. As in the case of Western cities, the mapping of crime in Georgia gave a clear systematic character to the social problem. As Herbert says (1976: 89–90):

> When deviance data are mapped, the revealed patterns are rarely random or haphazard, but take the form of well defined clusters. Further, when these distributions are examined in closer detail, it is apparent that they show consistent associations with particular attributes of the sociospatial environment. These facts are important in themselves in that they indicate the validity of residential area as an indicator of societal groups. Evidence does exist, however, to suggest that spatial distributions of deviance are not merely those that could be predicted from a knowledge of the deviancy rates of various social groups and the spatial arrangements of those groups. Spatial qualities, of location, contiguity and environment, are themselves of relevance in the comprehension of the geographical distribution of deviance.

Spatial aspects of deviance

Mapping the data on crime by social regions of Georgia gave generalized patterns of this social pathology. Figure 7.1 demonstrates the number of registered criminal offences per 10 000 persons in the years 1988–9; the annual average for these years is the last, more or less reliable, information, as thereafter data were incomplete for all CRSs and districts of Georgia. The average figure for Georgia as a whole was 23.9 per 10 000, varying between 12.0 in West Kavkasioni and 71.3 in the city of Sokhumi. The crime rates were well above average in rural Abkhazia (45.7), and the cities of Tskhinvali (43.8) and Batumi (41.5). It was expected that the city of Zugdidi, high-ranking in material welfare, would also be in this group. However, because a single police force (militia) served both city and rural district, the data could not be calculated separately. The conviction rate, calculated on the basis of court data, given separately for the rural and urban population, supports the expectation. Coastal areas with high population mobility, many tourists and a relatively high level of welfare, produced fertile ground to engender crime. Most of the rural areas were at the average level or below.

An even clearer geographical pattern is revealed when serious crime is mapped. The pattern of serious crime per 10 000 persons (Fig. 7.2) has a close resemblance to that of public opinion of the distribution of material welfare: the higher the welfare level, the higher the serious crime rate. The highest indices of serious crime were obtained in the urban social regions of Sokhumi (9.4 per 10 000), Tskhinvali (6.0), Batumi (5.5), Tbilisi (5.5) and Kutaisi (5.3), the areas where the most wealth was concentrated. Among rural areas, the rather wealthy social region of Guria displayed a higher level of serious crime. Eastern Kavkasioni, through which the major route to the north Caucasus passes, also had an above average rate of serious crime. The other highland rural social regions had serious crime rates below the national average (3.5); that is, the poorest social regions according to public opinion and the "reversed rating scale" generally coincided with the areas of lowest serious crime rates.

The conviction rate (number of convictions for all criminal offences per 10 000 persons) in 1988–9 (Fig. 7.3) mostly repeated the crime rate pattern. The figure proves our suggestion that in the CRS of Zugdidi there was one of the highest levels of crime, exposed by the conviction rate. Among the social regions at the top of the list along with Zugdidi, are once again Rural Abkhazia, "Rural Tskhinvali", East Kavkasioni and Tbilisi.

Coastal social regions and the CRS of Zugdidi had the highest level of convictions for crimes against personal property; the CRSs of Tskhinvali and Gori, Eastern Kavkasioni and other rural areas in the eastern part of the country had worse conviction figures for crimes against public order and public security, meaning primarily serious traffic violations and hooliganism.

The lowest level of general conviction rate was in the southern social regions, especially that of Meskheti–Javakheti. An explanation of this phenomenon was that the local adult male (Armenian) population annually spent several months in the northern areas of Russia, engaged in more profitable construction jobs. The region does not lie on major traffic routes and is relatively isolated. Hence, the

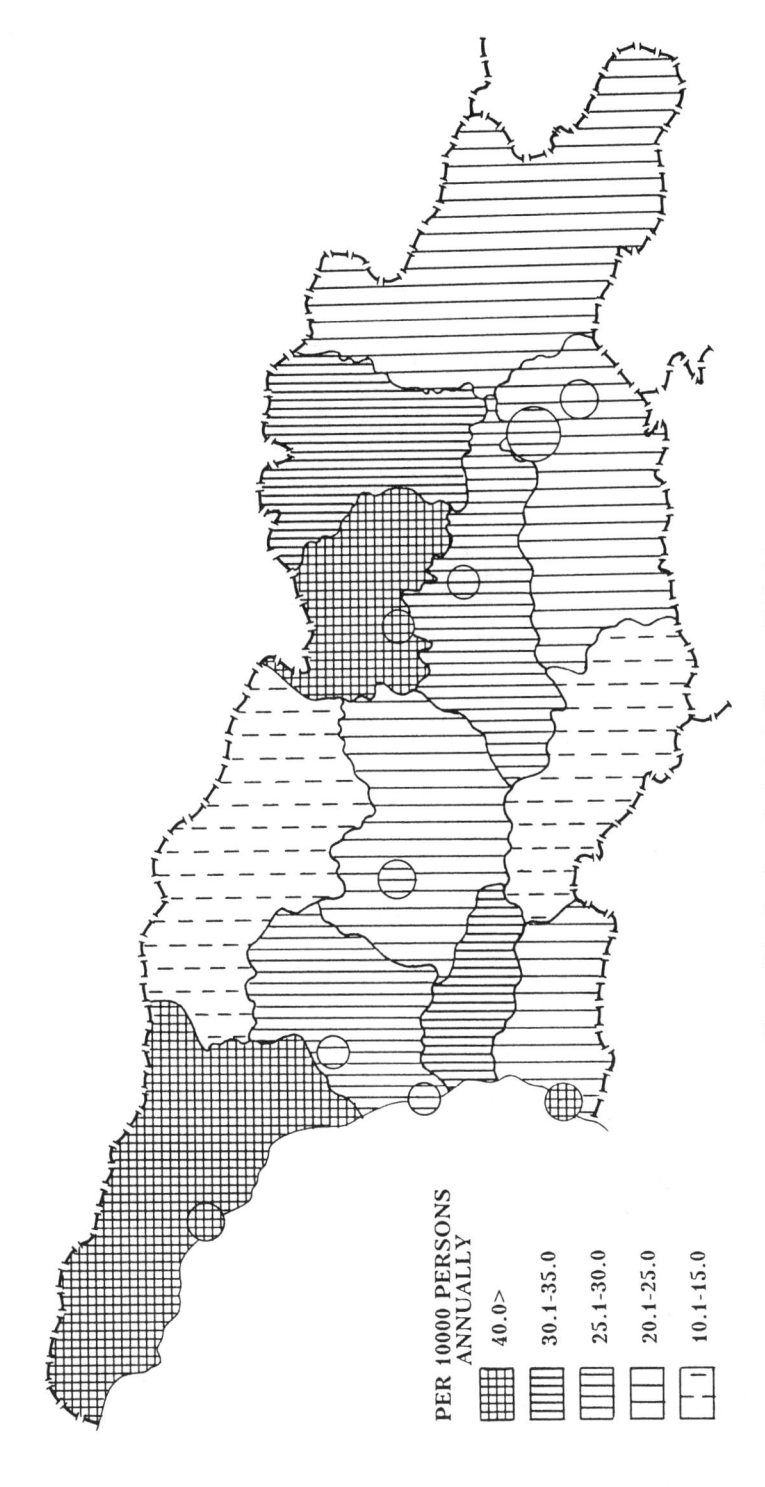

Figure 7.1 Registered criminal offences, 1988–9 (average).

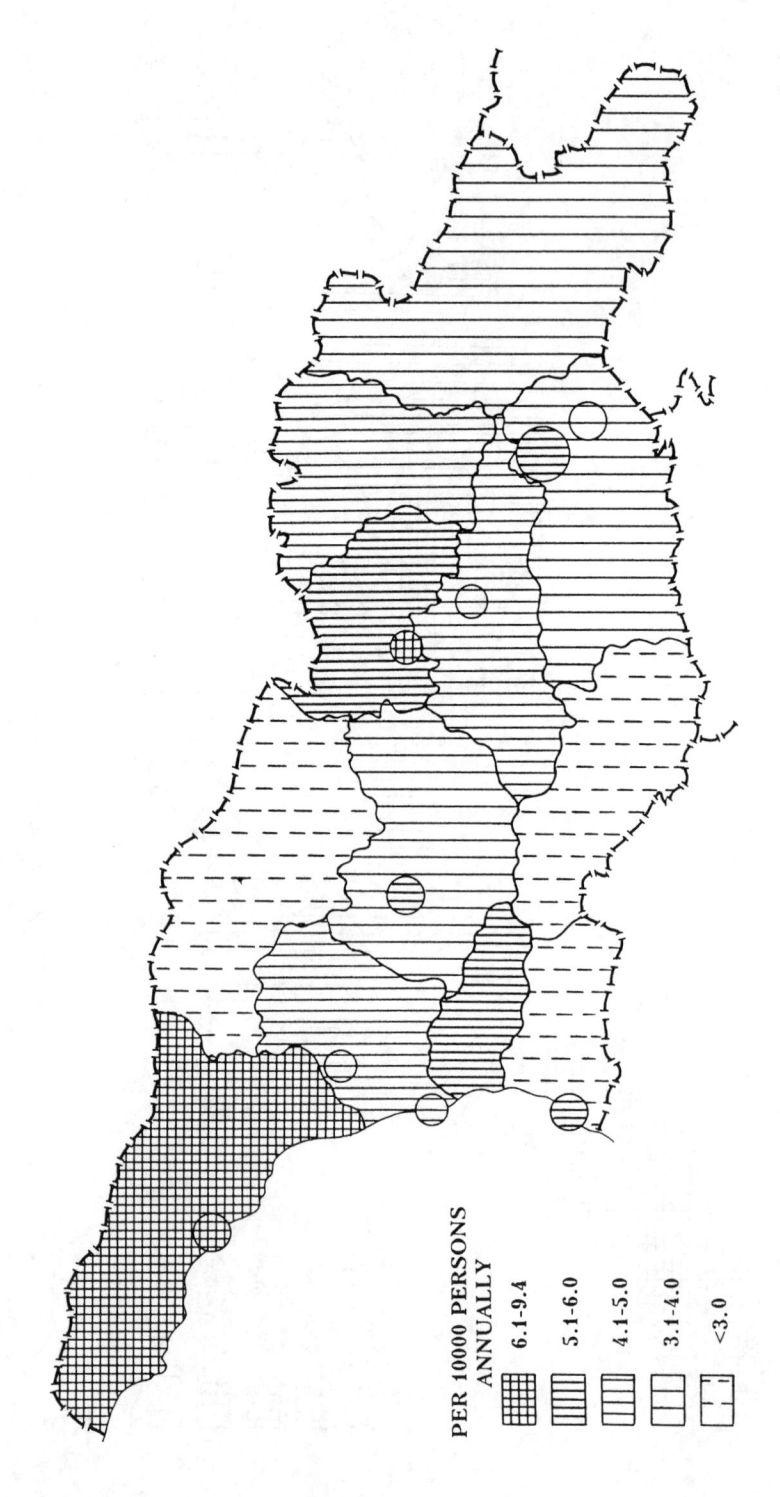

Figure 7.2 Serious crime, 1988–9 (average).

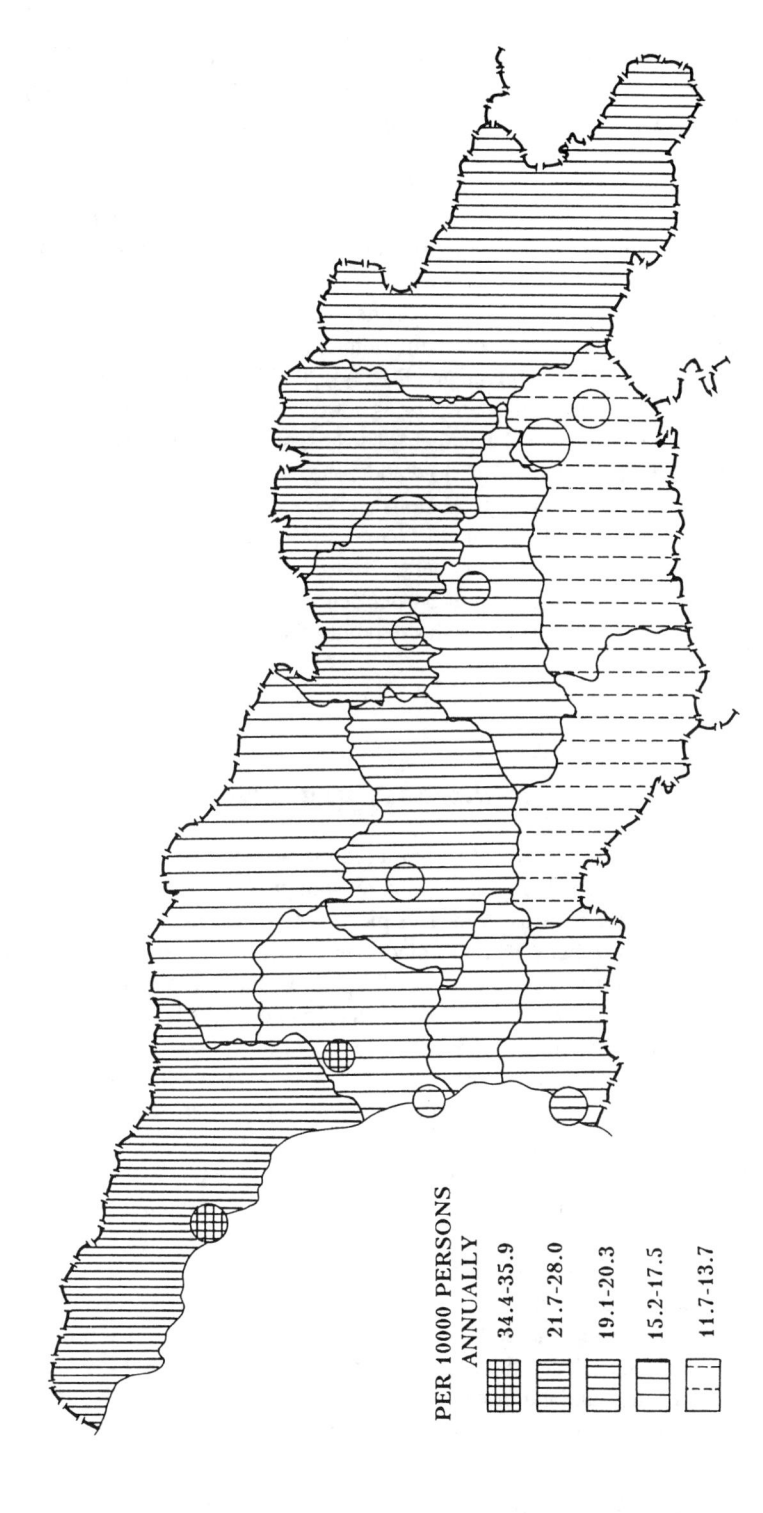

Figure 7.3 Convictions for criminal offences, 1988–9 (average).

PER 10000 PERSONS ANNUALLY
- 34.4–35.9
- 21.7–28.0
- 19.1–20.3
- 15.2–17.5
- 11.7–13.7

background in the area was less seriously conducive to crime.

Under-age convictions constituted 4 per cent of the total. The level was higher in the urban centres, where social control is generally weaker. Female convictions comprised 23–38 per cent in the coastal areas and the CRS of Kutaisi, 16–18 per cent in Samegrelo, "Rural Tskhinvali" and Tbilisi, but only 6–9 per cent in the less urbanized rural social regions of eastern Georgia. Most of the women convicted in the Soviet period were accused of economic crimes (*spekulyatsia*, defrauding consumers, etc.).

There is one further social aspect of crime; serious repeat offenders were concentrated in urban areas, especially in medium-size and coastal ones (Fig 7.4). In Batumi, Sokhumi, Gori, Tskhinvali and Rustavi, 20–24 per cent of all those found guilty had one or more previous convictions not yet cancelled. In Poti and Zugdidi such persons amounted to 17–19 per cent. The largest cities of Tbilisi and Kutaisi, along with most rural areas in the lowland zone, were on the average national level. In the peripheral rural social regions and especially in the mountains, most persons were first-time offenders. In "Rural Tskhinvali" social region, repeat offenders constituted a mere 3.8 per cent.

With the level of urbanization at 54 per cent, 68 per cent of all crimes were committed in urban areas. Thus, from the point of view of crime, the rural areas on the whole were safer to live in.

Spatial aspects of drug abuse

For quite a long time in the USSR Georgia led the way in studies of drug abuse, mostly because of the work of Anzor Gabiani, who published the first monograph in this field of study as early as 1976. This pioneering gave grounds to top officials of the USSR, and after them the mass-media, to consider drug abuse as an exotic deviance, peculiar only to Georgia. To be fair, it must be said that the acting leadership of those times, with Edouard Shevardnadze in office, tried to avoid paying attention to such an attitude of "the Centre" and continued to support the studies. Moreover, there was a real attempt to fight this deviance, with some success at least in containing it within limits. In the other republics, where the "problem was unknown" and rather swept under the carpet, its serious manifestations became apparent much later. At least it must be said to the credit of the then acting power in Soviet Georgia that the country did not become and presumably has not yet become, a producer of narcotic plants. The raw materials are still imported from the Russian Federation, Central Asian States or Azerbaijan.

Drug abuse, together with the activities of the narcotics mafia, was becoming an overwhelming problem already in the former Soviet Union. Now it is admitted as such in the Russian Federation, the major post-Soviet State where the drugs are produced, consumed and exported, not to mention the other Newly Independent States (Fyodorovskiy 1993). The problem for the Western world lay, and lies, not

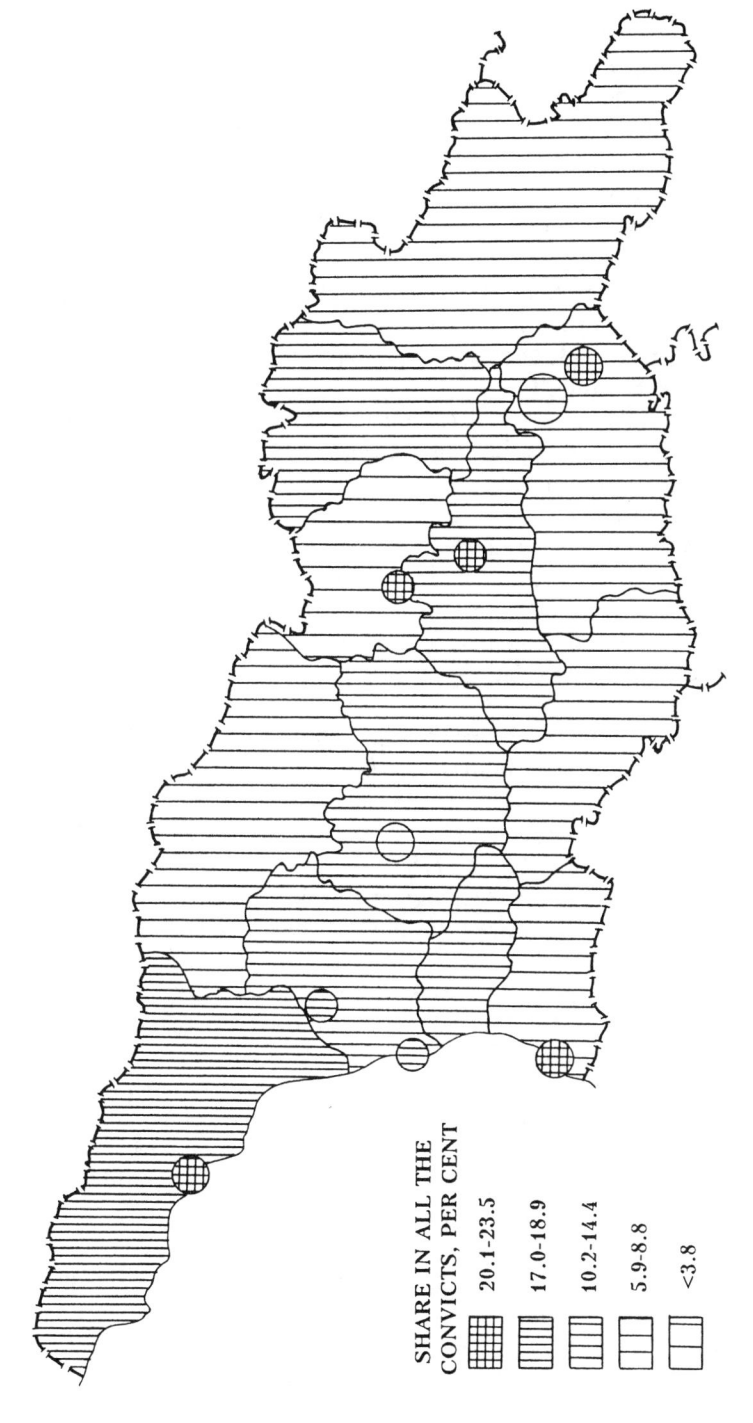

Figure 7.4 Serious repeat offenders, 1988–9 (average).

only in the use of the territory of the former USSR as a transit route for drug trafficking from Asia to Europe and on to North America, but also in the fostering and strengthening of the new mafia in this vast territory.

As long as hard currency use was strictly forbidden in the USSR, the international narcotics mafia had little interest in the country and mostly used its territory for the relatively less troublesome transit. However, once dollars appeared in the pockets and bank accounts of former Soviet persons, the "barons of drug supply" developed an acute interest in this potential market.

Georgia is no exception. Its location at a crossroads is already being used for illegal trafficking, highly profitable to the criminal world, presumably the international narcotics gangs. There are already reports of drugs trafficked through Turkey that were carried via Georgia. The country is not yet a major transit area, but it needs more support from the international community to avoid becoming such.

A public opinion poll carried out in Georgia by the USIA Office of Research in early 1993 demonstrated that the use of illicit drugs was considered a "very serious problem" by almost 80 per cent and a "somewhat serious problem" by additional 15.5 per cent of the respondents. Drug trafficking through Georgia appeared as a very serious problem to 64.3 per cent and a somewhat serious problem to additional 22.4 per cent. It is clear that the problem deserves attention and that public conscience in the country is really aware of it. Society definitely would support the passing of tougher laws against drug suppliers and the purchasers of illicit drugs for personal use. There were already strong appeals to introduce capital punishment for the illicit drug trade and even for drug use.

Until the mid-1970s the most widely used narcotic drug in Georgia was morphine; it was relatively cheap and easily obtainable in the pharmacists and hospitals, as long as the number of drug addicts was small. Later, this channel was largely closed and most of the "morfinists" had to change to cannabis, although morphine is restricted to the "elite group of drug abusers". Heroin and cocaine were practically unknown in the local drugs market, at least until recently (Gabiani 1988: 26–7).

Now hashish and marijuana, obtained from the cannabis plant, and some opiates, including poppy straw, are the most widespread narcotic drugs in Georgia. Smoking of hashish among "the morally unstable young people remains a fashionable amusement" (ibid.: 33). The opium poppy is not grown in Georgia, although there were recent reports that plantations of cannabis had been spotted by police. The local drug abusers have to rely upon imported narcotics, a supply more available were the country a transit route for illicit drug trafficking.

It might be supposed that such social pathologies as drug abuse, alcoholism, prostitution, suicides, and so on, are more common in the cities than in rural areas, just taking into account the sociospatial characteristics of the population. This, however, needs to be proved by concrete figures. In studying the geography of crime, it became apparent that twice as many of those convicted for drug related crime (producing, obtaining, storing, trafficking of illicit drugs) resided in urban areas, as in the villages (Gabiani et al. 1985). The explanation really lies in sociocultural factors. In the cities, social control is looser and the crisis of traditional morality, depersonalization, alienation are displayed much more strongly than in rural areas. To some extent drug abuse is spatially linked with higher incomes, especially when these are obtained through the "second economy" and ordinary crime. Public opinion attributes the consumption of illegal drugs to richer people 4.4 times more frequently than it does to poorer people.

This is linked to the high price of narcotic drugs, which not everyone can afford. The spatial aspect of the social problem is complicated by the empirically observed fact that drug abusers usually do not depend on their household incomes, but rather on their involvement with criminal activities and the ever wider spread of their habits among new addicts, who become consumers of drugs supplied by the old drug abusers, working for the narcotics mafia. This leads to the involvement of the new consumers. Unfortunately there are no official comparative figures; the rare publications expose just the tip of the iceberg of this deviance. Nevertheless, to some extent public opinion can serve as a barometer, sometimes good enough for spatial comparisons.

Several public opinion polls conducted under the direction of the present author were in fact designed to measure the comparative weight of different social problems (Gachechiladze 1990c). The responses demonstrated that drug abuse is of greatest concern to the younger generation, up to 25 years old, in the capital and other cities, notable among the leaders being the sea ports of Sokhumi and Poti, and also Zugdidi. Rural areas were less involved in this social pathology in the late 1980s. Drug abuse was mentioned among the leading social problems by 37 per cent of respondents in the CRS of Zugdidi, but only by 7 per cent of respondents in the rural district subordinate to the same city (Gachechiladze 1990a: 34).

But narcotics consumption has begun to penetrate the rural areas as well. Already by the mid-1980s, Gabiani observed the geographical expansion of drug abuse to the small towns of Georgia. Recently this process has been especially stimulated by the civil wars and economic crisis. Many of the young, rural, male population were called to the colours in poorly disciplined military units, where criminal elements with their drug abuse habits held sway. With the ending of the civil wars, but with the impossibility of obtaining jobs giving a subsistence minimum, not to mention the fall in the real value of money as a result of the total economic crisis, the young unemployed, many in rural areas, found refuge in drug addiction and, even worse, in the drug trade. This is a straight path to crime.

Another spatial problem connected with drug abuse is the existence of some sorts of "terminals" or "drug nodes" near the borders of Georgia, whence illicit drugs are imported, some of which are probably trafficked on farther to the west.

The major drug-trafficking route goes through the Roki tunnel leading to North Ossetia in the Russian Federation. Opened in 1988, from 1991 the tunnel has been under the control of the Ossetian separatists in Georgia. The rebellious city of Tskhinvali and the township of Java, both on this road and now out of reach of the State police, are major centres, where the Ossetian narcotics mafia imports drugs produced in the Russian Federation and the Georgian narcotics mafia and ordinary consumers obtain them (Shakarashvili 1994). No ethnic conflicts spoil relations between the criminals, who are much more internationalist than the proletariat was supposed to be. Until recently, no real control existed from either side of the Roki tunnel. The Russian side, although declaring the northern entrance to the tunnel a new State border, in fact did not care that it had become the "narcotics route" from the north and "the route of stolen cars" from the south. The Ossetian guerrillas who actually control the southern entrance of the tunnel do not care either. Stolen cars and jewellery are changed by the drug abusers for narcotics. In 1992 and 1993, 4867 cars were stolen in Georgia; only 1333, (27%), were returned to their owners, and estimated 1500–2000 were taken to the north Caucasian black market. The proximity of the towns of Oni, Sachkhere, Kareli and the CRS of Gori to this area, all controlled by the Georgian police and until recently rather tranquil in terms of criminal activity, made these urban centres and adjacent villages into a Mecca and Medina for Georgian drug abusers. From 1994 police control on the Georgian side of the "Northern drug route" became harsher and this immediately resulted in a relative decrease of car crime in this country, and caused a price rise for illicit drugs.

Another route of drug-trafficking runs from Azerbaijan, where there is a substantial market for opium. The area of Tsiteli Khidi, the bridge over the River Algeti, which divides Georgia and Azerbaijan, is a "drug node" of Transcaucasian importance. Armenia lies nearby, whence drug abusers arrive via Georgia; they cannot enter Azerbaijan directly, because of the Nagorno–Karabakh war. Stolen car export moves in this direction as well, although in that matter police control is normally stricter.

A third route of drugs from Russia goes through Abkhazia. At the moment it ends there, but before, and probably during, the civil war this drug route also existed and after normalization of the situation in the area, it will need additional attention not to allow the restoration of illegal drug-trafficking links. As the market for narcotic drugs in Georgia expands, there are reports of traders importing synthetic drugs, even by air from India. It would be no surprise if China should be mentioned as the next source of such imports. Thousands of so-called tourists from the FSU – called in Russian *chelnok*, "the Shuttle" – are in reality importers of goods for sale, if not smugglers (Khelashvili 1993). They are less likely to resist the temptation of drug trafficking, with huge incomes as the major incentive, and especially when legislation is inadequate, a sound and effective strategy for drug abuse prevention is not in place, legal practice is ineffective and international co-operation is practically absent.

CHAPTER 8

Tbilisi and its metropolitan region: social problems in space[1]

Tbilisi Metropolitan Region against the background of Georgia

The capital city and its immediate vicinity usually constitute the most important nodal region of any country. This is especially true for the post-Soviet States, which have developed under a centralized planning and management system over the past several decades. It is beyond the scope of this book to discuss the methodology of delimiting the boundaries of a metropolitan region, or as it is called in Russian and other "Post-Soviet" languages, including Georgian, "agglomeration". The Tbilisi Metropolitan Region (TMR) is regarded in this chapter as comprising the zone of enhanced gravitation around the capital city (Gachechiladze 1990b).

Actually Tbilisi and its metropolitan region have a special importance for the country, and the role of the capital in political and socio-economic processes on the all-Georgian scale is really outstanding. Even the following general geographical characteristics will be enough to illustrate this idea.

In 1989, the year of the last Soviet population census, 30 per cent of the total population and 48 per cent of the urban dwellers of Georgia were concentrated in the TMR. Population density reached 556 persons per km^2, that is eight times the average for the republic. In Tbilisi alone over 30 per cent of the total industrial output of Georgia and over 40 per cent in the TMR were concentrated. The capital city accounted for a disproportionate provision of welfare. Although 23 per cent of the national population lived there, the city had 27 per cent of private motor vehicles, 27 per cent of monetary income, 30 per cent of retail trade turnover, 33 per cent of the provision of everyday services, 33 per cent of deposits in saving accounts, 46 per cent of home telephones and 49 per cent of all the physicians of Georgia.

It is hardly necessary to continue the list, because even a superficial examination makes it obvious that the TMR is the key region of the State, with its own very specific social environment. It is the epicentre of many essential political and socio-economic processes and the focus of the majority of social achievements and problems. It is noteworthy that the turbulent events of the past five years

---

1. Written in co-operation with Joseph Salukvadze.

(Ch. 2), which affected many fields of human activity, did not undermine the leading position of the capital region on the scale of Georgia as a whole. Without doubt, the importance of Tbilisi for Georgia is much greater than that of London for Britain, Paris for France, or even of Moscow for Russia.

Therefore, it is absolutely impossible to get a reasonably full and accurate sociogeographical image of Georgia without concentrating attention on the TMR, especially on the capital, as the most representative model in the examination and analysis of the general features and major characteristics of the urban population, the character and trends of urbanization, social problems in urban areas and their reflection in the urban landscape, and so on.

The pre-eminence of Tbilisi over all other cities and the social regions of Georgia has its centuries-old traditions and objective historical and geographical background. Over the past 15 centuries, Tbilisi has performed metropolitan functions. It was the capital of the united Georgian kingdom and of several East Georgian kingdoms, from the fifth to nineteenth centuries. It was the centre of an emirate during the Arab conquest between the eighth and twelfth centuries, the centre of a *gubernia* and the residence of the viceroy of the Caucasus under the Russian Empire (1801–1917), the capital of an independent republic (1918–21, and since 1991), of the Transcaucasian Federation of Soviet republics (1922–36), and the capital of a Soviet republic (1921–91). Metropolitan functions are not new to Tbilisi.

The idea that no other city in the country could claim first place in the urban hierarchy of Georgia was promoted, even at times when the country was split into feudal kingdoms and principalities, by several factors. First, there were the convenient geographical situation in the centre of the Transcaucasus and favourable natural conditions, which were so important in medieval times, the rugged and mountainous relief for fortification, good soil and climatic resources for supplying the urban population with food from the vicinity. Then there were the city's economic prosperity, based on local handicraft and international trade, and its role as the real centre of the Georgian Orthodox Church.

Since the early nineteenth century after the annexation of Georgia by the Russian Empire, Tbilisi, at that time a typical Middle Eastern medieval city "locked up" in its city walls, gradually transformed into a bourgeois city. Already in the period of capitalist development from the late 1860s, Tbilisi (or Tiflis as it was known to Russians and Europeans) became an important centre of the Russian Empire, with a polyfunctional structure. For some time it was fourth in size after St Petersburg, Moscow and Odessa. The transformation of Tbilisi into the regional centre of Russian Transcaucasia was accompanied by perceptible growth of population and urban territory. The superiority of Tbilisi over the other Georgian towns became more evident in the beginning of the twentieth century. In 1926, 11 per cent of total population and 50 per cent of the urban population of Georgia lived in Tbilisi.

Especially rapid growth began after the establishment of Soviet power in Georgia. From the 1920s and 1930s, a substantial share of industry and an overwhelming share of the administrative and cultural functions of urban Georgia became

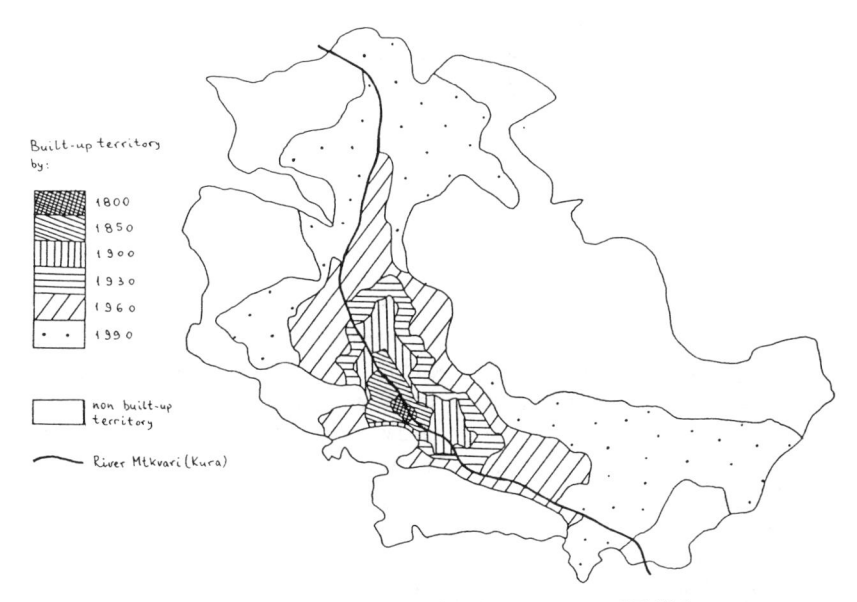

Figure 8.1 The extension of the built-up area of Tbilisi.

concentrated in Tbilisi. The highest rate of population growth, 4.6 per cent annually, occurred in the period 1926–39. Later the growth rate decreased to 2 per cent per year (1959–89). At the same time, the share of the capital in the total population of the republic has gradually increased, from 11 per cent in 1926 to 17 per cent in 1959 and 23 per cent in 1989, when the absolute figure attained 1264000.

The official area of Tbilisi also increased substantially, from 35 km^2 in the 1920s to 365 km^2 by the mid-1980s. The sprawl of Tbilisi was especially extensive over the past four decades (Fig. 8.1). From the end of the 1930s, Tbilisi Metropolitan Region has been intensively developed. At Rustavi, within 25 km of Tbilisi down stream on the River Mtkvari, on the site where a medieval town had existed until the thirteenth century, a huge steel plant was constructed in 1944. This had the greatest impact on the spatial expansion of the TMR. By 1950 its area had grown to 813 km^2 and its population to 600000. Subsequently, Rustavi became a large centre with diversified heavy industries, the fastest growing city in Georgia; in 1989 it was third in the urban hierarchy with 159000 inhabitants. In the extensive territorial growth of both Tbilisi and Rustavi, only 10 km of unbuilt space was left between the two cities, a space where any kind of construction is now prohibited in order to prevent the towns merging and thus supposedly worsening the already poor ecological situation in the area. The administrative centres of Mtskheta and Gardabani Districts, small towns with 9000 and 16000 inhabitants, have practically merged with Tbilisi and Rustavi, respectively.

In addition to these urban areas, many urban and rural settlements were gradually included in the TMR. The existence of regular transport links, at all events until the 1990s, promoted intensive industrial, labour and cultural ties among these settlements. The highest level in Georgia of urbanization of a rural area was achieved within the TMR. Commuting was a typical social phenomenon in the area. By 1989, the TMR embraced a total area of 2800 km^2, that is to say 3.8 per cent of national territory, with a population of about 1 700 000.

Development of the TMR under socialism

It follows from what has been said that, in spite of the long history of Tbilisi as the central city, the formation of the TMR occurred in Soviet times. Although Tbilisi still preserves some specific characteristics and originality, deriving from its micro-geographical location and historical development, such as the medieval and nineteenth-century planning systems of the town and some traditional elements of the urban way of life, nevertheless most of the urban environment, including social environment, in practice has been formed under the influence of the conditions of Soviet socialism.

Soviet power brought to Tbilisi the universal conditions of development, or rather rigid frameworks, which applied all over the USSR. Without emphasizing some of these universal conditions, the following analysis might be rather obscure. The management system was one of the most important universal conditions. It was characterized by extreme centralization. An administrative (political) centre became the major seat of decision-making on practically every issue concerning the territory under its jurisdiction. Moscow dominated in the USSR, Tbilisi in the Georgian SSR. At first sight this situation might have had some advantages for effective management and, theoretically, might have been equally pertinent to the whole area. However, in practice the very centralization stimulated territorial disparities in social justice, which were manifested in the creation of favourable opportunities for the development of the centre itself, not infrequently to the detriment of the rest of the territory. Metropolitan Regions had no administrative status in the USSR (nor do they now) and thus a capital city "produced advantages" in the first place for itself.

Another universal condition was the State ownership of land, the only form of land ownership since the 1920s and still preserving its dominance over other forms in most post-Soviet cities. It seemed to be an advantageous condition, since a collective managing body lacks a personal interest in land distribution and, in theory, the optimal form of land use could be found. But if such a situation might in part prevent large-scale speculation, it could not escape the problem of the misuse of land. Indeed, this condition gave rise to a disgraceful attitude towards urban land and the surrounding territory. In other words, the most valuable and expensive resource in Western cities was practically free in Soviet cities and land-use depended on bureaucratic decisions, with corruption sometimes "playing the role" of the market mechanism.

The most evident and significant result of these two conditions jointly was the hyper-urbanization of Metropolitan Regions, developing themselves into major social and spatial features. The best illustrations of this are the smaller post-Soviet republics, such as Latvia, Estonia, Armenia and Azerbaijan, where from a third to two-fifths of the total population are concentrated in the respective capitals. From 1970 to 1989, the population of the capitals of ten out of the fifteen Soviet Union republics grew much faster than the total population. The exceptions were the Central Asian republics and Azerbaijan, which had a very high birthrate among the rural Muslim population.

Hyper-urbanization of the metropolitan regions (MRs) was a logical result. It was also the price of the so-called "agglomeration effect", that is the gain of additional economic benefits from the concentration, or rather overconcentration, of decision-making, diversified employment opportunities and better infrastructure in the capital city and its neighbourhood, a process that had become a major principle of centrally planned economies. MRs were considered "nodes of growth", that is, relatively small developed areas in the setting of the huge, mostly underdeveloped, territory. The smaller capitals, such as those of the autonomous areas, with smaller MRs were lesser nodes of growth; most of the rest of the areas under their jurisdiction received substantially fewer benefits. This pattern was demonstrated in Chapter 6 in the context of the spatial distribution of material welfare. Metropolitan regions are still considered the most attractive place of residence by the active sector of the population, especially young people from small towns and the countryside, who prefer to move to an MR. For example, Tbilisi is by far the most attractive city for the people of Georgia.

Many "metropolitan problems" arose directly from these advantages of capital cities, which were passed on with a lesser degree of intensity to the immediate neighbourhood of the capitals. It is natural, therefore, that the population of the capitals and their MRs experienced, and continue to experience, most sharply the problems arising from hyper-urbanization. There is a further specific characteristic of the hyper-urbanization of Soviet MRs that has influenced spatial patterns. Centralized management created as a universal condition the designated financing of social programmes, housing among them. A city council received investments for housing construction within the city boundaries and tended to build on the sites closest to the already built-up areas. It was not very difficult to persuade the government of a Soviet republic to extend the boundaries of the capital at the expense of the countryside, since the land was State-owned and free of charge. Thus, a capital, in receipt of the most investment for housing, sprawled outwards, creating "dormitory areas" within its new boundaries. Although the inhabitants of the capital profited from practically free residence within the city, social problems arose from unlimited urban sprawl, manifested in large-scale commuter movements, an extra burden on generally weak communal services. Moreover, the opportunity to acquire a free apartment in the capital, with all the advantages accruing as its registered occupier, drew many people from the countryside and small towns. The same "cast-iron" link with the apartment, not officially private, stopped many families from leaving the capital or other large city, because it was almost impossible to return later to the same place.

This circumstance was closely connected with another universal sociopolitical characteristic of Soviet cities, which was to a large extent inherited by post-Soviet places, namely the administrative control of urban population growth through the system of internal passport registration – the *propiska* – in force since the early 1930s. The purpose of limiting the growth of large cities was to avoid squatter settlements, unemployment, an extra burden on housing, and so on, which might all follow a huge, unlimited inflow of rural migrants; an unofficial argument was the fear of a lack of manpower in the agricultural sector. All this was controlled by the passport registration system. In fact, a wide range of methods of evading these rules was invented. The "*limitchik*" system specially permitted the recruitment of labour from other areas for certain important jobs, with a guarantee of a free apartment in the "limited" city. Marriages, including fictitious ones, and downright corruption were among other methods of evasion.

Thus, the extensive territorial growth of Soviet MRs was encouraged by financing housing and certain other matters on the one hand, whereas on the other, purely administrative measures were implemented to regulate their limitless growth through internal migrations. All these "universal conditions" and their implications are entirely valid for Tbilisi and its MR. The rate and volume of Tbilisi's growth in the Soviet period were clearly predetermined by the all-Union interests. Thus, the first Master Plan of Tbilisi, worked out in 1933 in the period of "industrialization", stipulated the construction of several large enterprises of all-Union importance, hence the development of new areas for industrial land-use followed. From that period onwards, the city, then quite compact, began to sprawl along the course of the River Mtkvari. Today the built-up area extends for 40km in length (Fig. 8.2).

During the Second World War, unplanned industrial development added to the process. Military factories evacuated from the Ukraine and European Russia were installed in Tbilisi. Most of them have remained ever since at the new sites. In addition to all this there was substantial in-migration from the Slavic republics and rural Georgia, which in its turn required the implementation of a large-scale housing programme. This in fact became possible only in the 1950s. Subsequent expansion of the residential area was the major factor in the further sprawl of the TMR, which was reflected in the two successive Master Plans of 1953 and 1970. After the 1960s new industrial development in Tbilisi was restricted, but the military–industrial complex always found ways to evade such limitations and new "post boxes" (closed military factories) appeared in Tbilisi even in the 1980s. Moreover, in the other towns of the TMR and in the area just over the city boundaries, such limitations were invalid. Thus, a large area of valuable agricultural land was built over or in some way became derelict.

Analysis of the development of the TMR leads to a simple, but nevertheless important conclusion. Economic policy, which covered more than the economic sphere, was carried out from the point of view of the centrally planned system and

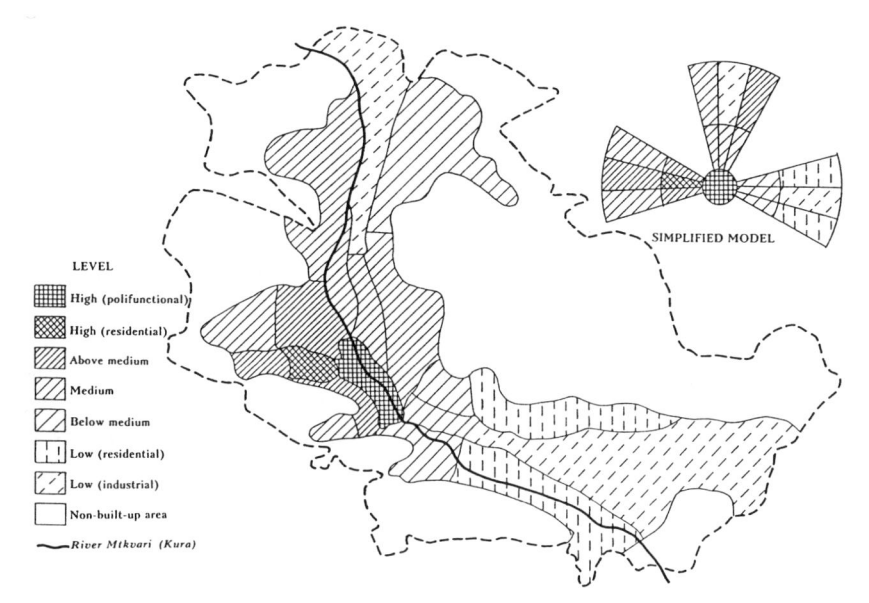

Figure 8.2 Environmental quality by town planning sectors (as perceived by public opinion).

considered Tbilisi, like any other city in any Union republic, as merely part of the all-Union economic space, and the scale of its development was pre-determined by the requirements and standards of that immense State. Possibilities and requirements on the republican scale were completely ignored.

The centralization and over-concentration described were remarkable only from the point of view of a small Union Republic; against the background of the USSR it was next to nothing. Thus, no optimal proportions of development were followed. The socio-economic potentials of the other areas (including other urban), which were losing not only financial and material resources but also labour and intellectual resources, were sacrificed to the growth of the capital cities and their MRs.

In practice, planning of Tbilisi's economic development was carried out in such a way that local manpower was never sufficient to fulfil the plan. Thus, workers (*limitchiki*) were recruited from the countryside, and free apartments were promised in return. This was one reason why half the city's growth was attributable to in-migration. The "other people" (that is, other than the *limitchik* workers) had to invent different methods of evading the strict passport registration system. In 1987, 46 per cent of newcomers who registered in the capital gave marriage with a local dweller as a reason for moving to the city. As the limitations grew stricter, the number of such marriages tended to grow. Many people simply lived and worked in the capital without registration and to a large extent were socially deprived.

This development was not the result of "the ill will of the Kremlin" alone. The local leadership, in effect the Party aristocracy, welcomed and even promoted such trends in development, because, under the State administrative system, the larger the capital city, the larger were the side benefits for the ruling bureaucracy. In any case, they could always use the excuse, "The population needs apartments! The population needs jobs!".

The process of hyper-urbanization of the TMR really requires a multifaceted evaluation. It might have been hardly possible to concentrate huge economic, social and cultural potential in Tbilisi and environs without centralized planning and the implementation of administrative methods, or to improve the municipal economy, to raise cultural and educational levels of the population, sometimes close to European standards. Rustavi, in the current period of crisis, with its huge factories capable of production for export, is probably the only hope of industrial revival in Georgia. But the paradox is that these achievements have led to the aggravation of social problems, which had already become acute in the 1980s. In the 1990s these and further new problems, which arose out of the disproportionate size of the capital and its TMR, became next to insoluble.

Social problems of the TMR in late 1980s

Human geographers of Tbilisi State University and the Institute of Geography of the Georgian Academy of Sciences contributed a great deal to the study of the spatial structure of Tbilisi and its MR, including population, land-use, social problems and the like (Gachechiladze & Gujabidze 1979, Gujabidze 1983, Jaoshvili 1989, Rondeli 1990, Salukvadze 1993, etc.). Public opinion polls, carried out by the CSS in 1988–9, revealed some specific problems of the TMR (Gachechiladze 1990c,d). It appeared that the major concerns of its population were the problems of improving the material quality of life, such as the supply of consumer goods and housing and municipal, transport, communications and other everyday services. These were followed by problems of improving the physical quality of life – medical care, social maintenance, ecological conditions, possibilities of recreation and leisure, the level of social pathologies (crime, drug and alcohol abuse) – and by the problems of improving the mental and spiritual quality of life – school and pre-school education, upbringing of the younger generation, care of the historical and cultural heritage, ethnic and neighbourhood relations.

Among the most serious reasons for people's dissatisfaction were retail trade shortages and the low level of service provision. The same problems were fundamental in the other regions and cities of the Georgian SSR, as indeed in the other Soviet republics, and they were connected with the overall mismanagement. The problem in the TMR included the extremely uneven and inefficient distribution of service units over its area. Tertiary functions, underdeveloped as a whole, were overconcentrated in the central parts of the city, in contrast to the outlying areas, which lacked not only traditional central place functions, but some of the important commercial and everyday services as well. The level of services in most of the other settlements of the TMR outside Tbilisi was even lower. In such circumstances, people tried independently to overcome the spatial injustice in the supply of goods and services by commuting in overloaded trains and buses to the more fortunate capital, giving rise to significant competition with the local customers and causing queues, for which Soviet cities were notorious throughout the world.

Housing was another very sensitive social problem in the TMR. Although 47 per cent of Georgia's urban population lived in Tbilisi and Rustavi, these cities possessed only 41 per cent of the total urban living space. The average city dweller in the TMR lived in poorer conditions than inhabitants of small and medium-size towns; dwelling space in Tbilisi and Rustavi consisted of one- to four-room apartments of limited size in municipal, departmental, or co-operative ownership. More than four rooms per apartment was rare. Some houses in the suburbs and almost all those in rural areas of the TMR were in private ownership. The average provision of useful living space in Tbilisi was $14.1 m^2$ per capita, which was slightly less than the all-Union urban level. Living-space was $10.7 m^2$; the distinction between living space and useful living space in official Soviet statistics is that the "useful" space figure includes kitchen, bathroom and corridors. To be registered on the waiting list for a new or larger apartment, there had to be less than $5 m^2$ of living space for each member of the family, and even in this case it might be up to 20 years on the waiting list before a free apartment was allocated. The increasing need for living space was the main reason for the spatial expansion of the rapidly growing capital, which sprawled especially fast from the 1960s as a result of the mass housing programmes outlined in second and third Master Plans of Tbilisi.

In spite of large-scale residential construction over the past three decades, with some newly built-up districts providing accommodation for 50 000–100 000 persons, the housing problem did not become less acute for Tbilisi. At the beginning of 1988, 151 000 families and single persons were registered for improvement of their housing conditions in Georgia, 51 per cent of whom were already residing in Tbilisi and 9 per cent in Rustavi. In the capital alone, every fifth family was on the waiting list.

The housing problem was aggravated by the uneven distribution of living space. Larger families with children waited for an apartment, while retired, childless persons enjoyed considerable living space. Theoretically, the latter might have preferred to move to the countryside farther away from the noisy and polluted cities, but they had to stay because of the uncertainty of getting an apartment in another place on their low pensions, and because of the chronic deficiency of practically all types of goods and services outside the capital.

Thus, the provision of free living space from the city council made the population quite immobile. This is true even for residents of the central districts of Tbilisi, who live predominantly in rather inconvenient three- to five-storey city houses with inner yards, common balconies, common toilets, and quite often without bathrooms. Such houses were typical of Tbilisi in the nineteenth and first half of the twentieth centuries.

The absence of an urban land price and equal rent in every part of the city allowed the citizens to keep their lots and apartments, in spite of existing competition with other large land-users. This was the main reason why, in Tbilisi as in other Soviet cities, no central business district or downtown centres (in the Western sense) were developed, and why the population density in the centre was one of the highest among the city districts.

It is to be expected that the living environment in the old-fashioned houses of the central city is not of the highest level. Notwithstanding the romantic tales of "when people lived in harsher conditions but more openly", where the houses described are concerned, a survey of 1083 persons in Tbilisi and Rustavi, carried out under direction of R. Gachechiladze in March 1989, showed that merely 5 per cent preferred such old city houses "with common balconies". Only 26 per cent liked the apartments in high-rise houses, where the majority actually lived. Fifty-one per cent would have liked to live, if they had a free choice, in an individual, one- or two-storey house with, or even without, a small yard. The romanticism referred to has a real sociological explanation; people living in isolated flats in new apartment houses and having no opportunity to choose their neighbours lead a more secluded way of life and are more alienated.

A problem of urban morphology and city aesthetics is also worthy of note. In spite of relatively poor living conditions, only the central areas of Tbilisi display the real image of the city, retaining a unique architectural and planning environment and still remaining the most attractive part. It is remarkable that almost 90 per cent of the buildings, or urban complexes, of undoubted architectural and aesthetic value are located inside a 3 km radius from the city core, that is to say mostly in the areas of pre-socialist development.

In the districts built up in the 1930s–1950s, one can find monumental, ponderous buildings in the so-called "Stalinist style", with a particular planning layout. But if those parts of the city still display some unique features, the areas of mass housing construction, put up since the mid-1950s, are epitomized by ugly standard "boxes" and high-rise houses, usually lacking any architectural and planning concept. These new districts of Tbilisi are deprived of originality. Rustavi never had any. One should once again stress the Soviet city-planning practice of extensive territorial growth, which encouraged allocation of housing construction on vacant land, as it required relatively low inputs and thus gave high immediate productivity. The relatively low quality of new housing construction and infrastructure in most such districts was the result of unrealistic financing.

Ecological problems can be considered as metropolitan, since they troubled people more in the TMR than in other areas. A poll revealed that most people in Georgia were ecologically careless, owing to the low level of ecological education (Gachechiladze 1989b). It was a social problem, especially when rendered more serious by weak environmental control. Although Georgia had a State Committee on Environment, the first Union republic to do so, its role in the centralized management system was insignificant. For example, fines for pollution were paid by factories owned by the State itself. Air pollution and noise were serious problems in Tbilisi, where more than one-third of the motor vehicles in the republic were concentrated and where over 17 per cent of built-up land was occupied by industrial enterprises. The main source of air pollution in Tbilisi was heavy traffic, for which the street network was not prepared. In Rustavi, industrial plants, namely the steel works and cement factory, are the main sources of air pollution; there, 95 per cent of the city population complained of poor air quality, the highest index among the cities of Georgia. The TMR remained one of the major polluted areas. Mostly raw sewage was, and still is, emptied into the River Mtkvari; refuse dumps occupied large areas.

Problems of social pathology were also aggravated in the TMR, even if its crime rates were not the highest among the regions of the republic. Among the types of crime in the cities of the TMR, those against public order (delinquency, etc.) led, followed by economic crimes and crimes against personal property. This is understandable, as the higher the concentration of economic activity and welfare, the greater the stimuli for particular crimes (Ch. 7). Drug abuse, heavy drinking and prostitution were more characteristic of the TMR than of rural areas. But it must be added that these kinds of social pathologies were actually invisible to the majority of the population and could not be considered very burdensome social problems in those days.

Particular interest is aroused by the fact that, in spite of the concept of social equality advocated by Soviet ideology, there are evident spatial differences in equality and welfare, not only on the level of the urban and rural social regions of Georgia, but on the intra-urban level as well. Tbilisi is a wholly representative example of significant differences in environmental quality (Fig. 8.1). The "prestigiousness" of particular districts serves as a basis for a degree of social segregation of the population (Salukvadze 1993). Such segregation, perhaps, was not as deep as in some Western cities, but it clearly existed and was influenced by the "black market" prices of apartments and land lots. Officially, of course, there was no land market. The actual differences in prices between districts were quite significant. The highest, according to polls, were in the Vake area in western Tbilisi, followed by the Vera and Saburtalo areas. Thus, until recently, in addition to some very "Soviet" features, Tbilisi also bore certain non-Soviet characteristics, in spite of developing within the socialist legal and socio-economic environment.

New trends in the social problems of the TMR

A new stage in the development of Tbilisi and its MR began in the 1990s. The sociopolitical processes that affected Georgia and the FSU as a whole considerably changed the "universal conditions" that determined the creation, the very existence and the functioning of the TMR under socialism. The social environment, which not long before had been dominant in the capital, started to change rapidly, giving rise to new social problems, or aggravating older ones. Some problems switched places on the "scale of urgency". The dismantling of the system of socialist economic management looked more like destruction than reconstruction and very soon exposed the artificiality of Tbilisi's scale of development – and no doubt the artificial scale of most huge capital cities in the smaller ex-Soviet republics. The hypertrophic character of the functions fulfilled by the capital, regardless of the potentials of local resources, became more apparent. After the abrupt halting of centralized financing from Moscow and the cutting of economic links with enterprises in other republics, the municipal economy of Tbilisi was in effect knocked out, as indeed were other branches of the economy and other regions of Georgia. This might easily have been envisaged, but it was entirely ignored by the first national governments of independent Georgia. Factories stopped; so did most urban transport; electricity failed; central heating radiators became useless decorations in the apartments and new generations of children have to have explained to them why they had been installed in ancient times. The city emerged as unprepared for the new situation, unable to purchase raw materials, fuel or machinery at market prices and in the quantities required for an urban settlement of such a size.

Public transport and municipal services came to the fore as the major urban problems. At present they are far more important to the population than retail trade, other than staple food supply, because the shortage of consumer goods in the State shops can be covered by the many commercial enterprises. A situation where (small) supply exceeds (even smaller) demand, absolutely impossible to conceive under socialism, is becoming characteristic of Tbilisi. However, it is evident that such a situation is attributable entirely to lack of cash on the part of the majority, who are still wearing out old acquisitions.

Against this background, problems of unemployment and social defence have become more prominent, especially when account is taken of the many displaced persons from Abkhazia, who found refuge in the TMR and other areas of inner Georgia. Among the social problems, increased deviance has become more serious, especially crimes against the person and personal property (Ch. 7). The economic problems, aggravated by increasing crime, are the major factors promoting emigration of urban population from the TMR. The scale of emigration from Tbilisi has been increasing since 1990. The majority of emigrants are non-Georgians, but they have recently been joined by increasing numbers of ethnic Georgians, who in 1989–93 composed more than a quarter of all emigrants abroad (Gachechiladze & Bradshaw 1994). Most of the latter, businessmen and freelance workers, leave their homeland because of the economic instability and lack of legal support for the market economy.

Most emigrants are white-collar workers; some are representatives of the numerically few middle or even upper middle classes, all of them urbanized. The "substitute" population in Tbilisi is represented by in-migrants from small provincial towns or rural areas of Georgia and the TMR in particular. They are predominantly young, less educated people, who use Tbilisi as the arena of their commercial, and sometimes criminal, activities. Some of the IDP also attempt to settle in the capital.

This substitution of the urban population may lead to certain changes in the social structure and social environment as a whole, especially when one recalls that earlier in-migrants to Tbilisi were former peasants, bearers of a rural psychology and subculture and more used to the rural way of life. The recent in-migrants are substantial in number, because the limitations are not observed very strictly, if at all. They cannot adapt very rapidly to the urban way of life, because "urban activities" are restricted by the economic crisis. Before their full assimilation can happen, the presence of newcomers will give the capital a certain "touch of provincialization". In this way, the phenomenon of degradation of the urban sociocultural environment can be observed in the TMR. It must be hoped that this trend will not last too long.

Housing remains a constantly urgent social problem, but it is acquiring new features. It is noteworthy that it is precisely in house-ownership and house-construction, together with the retail trade, that the most prominent changes to the market economy are displayed. These changes meant taking housing out of State control through privatization and demolishing the State monopoly in house construction. The total privatization of urban dwellings in 1992–3 activated the housing market, which became completely legal once the sale and purchase of dwellings were legitimized.

The turnover of the housing market increased through the emigration of quite large numbers. For the first time in the past seven decades, there was housing available for purchase. Obviously this phenomenon will by no means solve the housing problem inherited from the communist era. The prices of apartments, although not very high by European standards, are absolutely unapproachable for the majority of the local population. Figure 8.3 demonstrates the cost of a square metre of living space in Tbilisi at the beginning of 1994. The cheapest dwellings are situated on the periphery of the city, at less than US$150 per square metre. In Didi Digomi, previously one of the favourite new districts, because it has the worst transport accessibility, the cost of living space nowadays has fallen to $60 per square metre. The most expensive, from $450 to $600, are the apartments in the core areas of the city, Vake, Vera and part of Saburtalo. For comparison, the monthly wages of the highest paid State servants at the same time were equivalent to $1–1.5 (sic!). It is obvious that such an anomaly cannot last long. Meanwhile, it is equally obvious that purchase of the apartments could be afforded only either very successful businessmen or actual criminals, who had acquired wealth illegally through corruption, narcotic drug trade, looting, and so on. Rarely, there might be members of the elite intelligentsia, working abroad. This leads to even greater social differentiation and aggravates social injustice.

The problem is rendered more serious because neither the impoverished State nor the city municipality are able to construct new and sufficiently cheap housing. In previous decades, as previously described, the major source for new housing construction was centralized financing, using very cheap construction materials, free land and practically free (State subsidized) equipment and fuel. Today all these have become extinct.

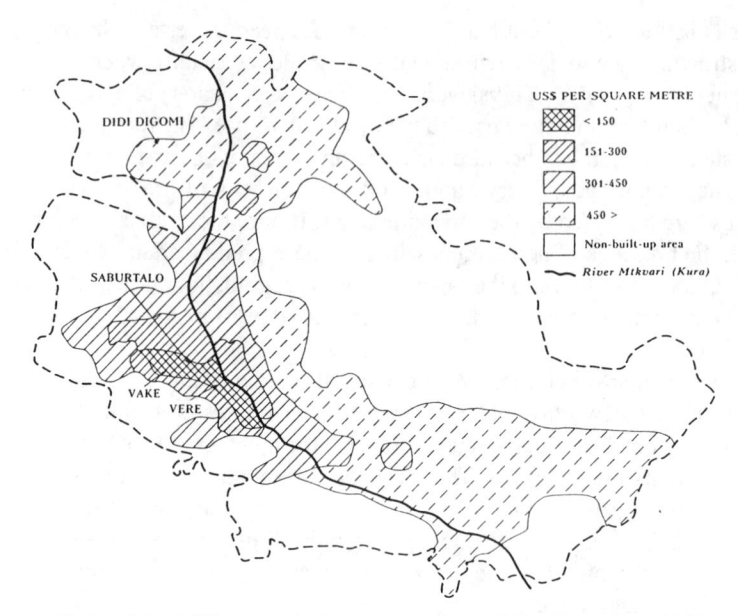

Tbilisi and its metropolitan region: social problems in space

Figure 8.3 Differences in the average value of dwelling space, 1994.

A new geographical trend has appeared. The only construction firms operating in the TMR are private ones, that construct very expensive houses and sell them to rich customers. The cost of construction of a square metre of living space was US$300–350 at the beginning of 1994. This means that the only area where this kind of business is profitable is the central part of the capital. This area is limited in space and already densely populated. Demolition of the older houses and compensation for the previous residents increase the costs of construction. Moreover, residential land use in central parts of Tbilisi has to compete with no less profitable land-users, commerce, banking and insurance. Nevertheless, housing construction nowadays goes on in the zones of reconstruction in the central parts of the city, and not on the vacant peripheral sites, as had been the practice in the Soviet period.

One of the most important factors in the cost of urban land, together with its prestige, is its accessibility. The sprawl of Tbilisi in its phase of hyper-urbanization resulted in several peripheral parts of the city becoming in effect isolated from the centre, because of the high cost of transportation. The only cheap, in fact State subsidized, urban transport remains the underground railway; opened in 1966, it is overexploited and working at the limits of its capacity. Areas not accessible by underground, such as Didi Digomi, are losing attractiveness and many residents of central areas do not perceive them as integral parts of Tbilisi.

The situation candidly described above may lead to frustration and hopelessness on the part of a friendly reader – and no other will afford the time to read this book through!. But it must be stressed that this chapter is dedicated to the social problems of a city that is loved by the authors of this chapter. The more exact the diagnosis, the more efficacious the treatment may be. The logic of the historical process leads to a sociogeographical understanding that Tbilisi will not be that which it was for a long period of the twentieth century. The city will not grow in size in the foreseeable future and perhaps this is no bad thing. More social differentiation and the aggravation of social inequalities and their spatial manifestations are to be expected. Tbilisi is fast becoming the most expensive city in Georgia and that part of its present population which is not directly connected with metropolitan or wholly urban functions will inevitably move to other areas in Georgia; some will prefer to go abroad. But it is clear that the other cities and regions of Georgia will benefit from utilizing the human potential, which was limited in availability to them when everything was strictly centralized.

At the same time, some of the problems, especially crime, delinquency and inadequate transport and municipal services, will lose their gravity as soon as political stabilization is achieved and economic revival begins. And these processes are inevitable. Certainly the spatial patterns of Tbilisi in the opening decades of the twenty-first century will resemble more closely those of Western cities.

As a prominent Russian geographer wrote:

During its fifteen-century history, Tbilisi was looted and destroyed by the Byzantines, Arabs, Khazars, Khoresmians, Mongols, Turks, Persians. Rustavi, a close neighbour, could not rise from its ruins after multiple destructions by the Mongols and ceased to exist as a town from 1265. Tbilisi, however, held out and did not forfeit its role as the major economic and cultural centre of Georgia. The invaders were not able to pull out the roots that gave life to this outstanding city. (Lappo 1976: 29).

There is no doubt that Tbilisi will hold out once again this time. The city, which will not lose its multi-ethnic, even cosmopolitan, flavour, will revive once again as one of the most attractive cultural and financial centres in this part of the world.

CHAPTER 9
Ethnic tensions in geographical context

Background for ethnic tensions

It has already been mentioned (Chs 2 and 4) that multi-ethnicity, although not inevitably leading to conflict on an ethnic base, is a serious obstacle to nation-State building in the post-Soviet era.

Gleason (1990) argued that in formulating principles of ethnicity and nationality in fundamentally spatial terms and not in terms of citizenship, Leninist nationality policy laid out the fundamental logic of today's conflicts and fragmentation, a logic that is strengthened when processed through an inherently territorial-based Soviet bureaucracy.

Everything was done in the USSR to make the Union republics as heterogenic as possible. This policy was especially effective in the Transcaucasus and Central Asia until the end of the 1950s, and lasted in the Baltic republics up to the end of the 1980s. Apart from its economic objectives, it had a strong political significance, by helping to avoid any serious strengthening of the "titular nationalities" of the Union republics. As a result, none of the NIS are now ethnically homogeneous; the only exception is Armenia, especially after 1988 when the substantial Azeri minority was compelled to leave that country. The borders of the republics constituting the USSR were delimited, mostly in the 1920s, in such a manner that national minorities were left in all of them. But once established it became impossible to change these borders, even in the name of obtaining greater justice.

Ethnic suspicions were an inherent feature of "The Fraternal Family of Soviet Peoples". The Soviet nationality policy was in essence directed towards the "merging of nationalities" into one, presumably "Soviet", nation that would be Russian speaking. What it actually did, at the same time, was to encourage the division of the population on an ethnic basis. The Soviet system established a "*matrioshka* (nesting doll) type" of State-administrative hierarchy with decreasing rights, from Union republic down through autonomous republic and autonomous oblast to national okrug. Claims for territory were made even more complex because people were divided into the "titular", or "indigenous", nationalities and "non-indigenous" nationalities and it was tacitly understood that the "titular nationalities" should have greater rights than "the non-indigenous" in obtaining local governmental and administrative positions – a very important advantage in the bureaucratic State.

Soviet power never gave the people of the Union republics, which were all "sovereign States" according to the Soviet Constitution, their own citizenship, but only "nationality". A very important, and still persisting, social institution was the system of internal passports, which specified nationality. Its indication in the document usually meant more than an actual feeling of self-identity, and a prolonged procedure was required to "change nationality". Under these conditions, a civic society could not develop effectively, either in the USSR as a whole or in the Union republics.

One of the leading Russian experts in the field of ethnic relations makes this comment on the consequences of the lack of citizenship:

> ... the nations are not considered to be Kazakhstanians, the citizens of the State, nor the citizens of Latvia, Georgia and Azerbaijan, but only ethnic Kazakhs, Latvians and Azeris, although Kazakhstan along with the other States of the CIS entered the UN, an organization that unites nation-States. Only the Georgians had recently to make a small concession and to announce officially that "Georgia is the nation-State of the Georgians and the Abkhaz". This concession was dictated by the strong political status of the Abkhaz autonomous area. As far as the other groups are concerned, such as the Ossetians, Armenians and Meskhetian Turks, they are considered as "non-indigenous population". (Tishkov 1993: 6)

This quotation demonstrates a particular approach to the internal factors of ethnic tensions. The only comment required here is that the "Law of Citizenship of the Republic of Georgia", which was adopted in March, 1993 (in all fairness, after the article just cited was written), declared all the actual residents of the State were citizens of Georgia, irrespective of ethnic origin, unless they themselves renounce it; it does not require any knowledge of the State language. Only in the case of foreigners applying for citizenship of the republic, is one of the prerequisites a minimal knowledge of either Georgian or Abkhaz (sic) languages (Law 1993). Thus, formally there is no "non-indigenous population" in Georgia. Unfortunately, however, ethnic tensions in this country did not end after this "concession made by the Georgians".

It is evident that a mere change in legal attitudes to minorities in the Newly Independent States will not help to end the ethnic tensions. The malaise has been too long neglected and its treatment does not depend on the good will of only one side. It is hard to say whether a declaration giving the non-Latvians, non-Georgians and so on, full rights as citizens of the respective States would solve the problem. The Armenians of Karabakh, the Ossetians of Shida Kartli, the Abkhaz of northwestern Georgia would hardly accept such a "concession" as a full guarantee of their autonomy. After all, "autonomous status" did not satisfy them earlier under Soviet power.

To continue the earlier quotation:

> ... the ground for Georgian–Ossetian and later for Georgian–Abkhaz conflicts was laid by the claims of the leaders of the South Ossetian and Abkhaz autonomous areas to create "nation-States" of their own. This was despite the fact that even more ethnic Ossetians resided outside South Ossetia in other areas of Georgia, and in Abkhazia the "indigenous nation" of the Abkhaz amounted to less than a fifth. (Tishkov 1993: 7)

As soon as it became clear that the "Pax Sovietica" was going to crash, old taboos over the re-carving of the political map were removed. A fierce struggle followed for control of the greater part of the Soviet legacy and naturally the principal wealth was territory. This led to full-scale wars, as over Nagorno–Karabakh. As there was no private property in land, the territory was supposed to belong to a nationality, ethnic group or community. Ethnicity was the strongest factor to use to consolidate support by the acting elite structures or by those pretending so to become, quite often disguised in the clothes of national liberation movements. Georgian patriotism was exploited by the new Georgian political parties and even to a certain extent by the Communist Party of Georgia. Abkhaz, Ossetian and other patriotisms were exploited by the local elites, in fact groups of local Communist Party leaders. Thus, political struggle for power and wealth was transformed into what is called "ethnic tension".

No less important for the comprehensive explanation of ethnic tensions within the former Union republics, other than Russia proper, are external factors. It seems that some leaders of the USSR decided that the best way to save the Empire was to stir up ethnic conflicts within those Union republics, where the major "titular nationality" was striving for full independence. Thus, the Supreme Soviet of the USSR passed in 1990 the "Law of Secession", which called for referenda, not to be held by the Union republics, but by their constituent autonomous units and even by certain areas (e.g. villages) settled by ethnic minorities. It is no surprise that the "Law of Secession" has been called the "Law of Non-secession" in the Union republics.

An expert in Soviet history argues:

> ... the "Novo–Ogariovo process" [1990–1, *R.G.*], when Gorbachev in his struggle with Yeltsin brought into the negotiations over the future of the USSR, representatives of all the autonomous units; this *de facto* meant that national-territorial units were equal to the Union republics and considered as "States". This policy of the Kremlin led to the "Parade of Sovereignty by the Autonomous Areas" all over the USSR, including Georgia where Abkhazia declared itself a Sovereign Republic and the South Ossetian Autonomous Region a Republic. But such a policy of Gorbachev's team only accelerated the fall of the USSR. (Menteshashvili 1993)

The factor of national minorities in the Union republics was exploited by the Kremlin especially in the years of the crisis of power. The national feelings and understandable aspirations of smaller peoples to achieve real equality were used as an instrument of political pressure on the obstinate Union republics. For example, in 1988–91, the Polish minority in Lithuania became the object of Moscow's "special care", but the Russian newspapers forgot about them as soon as Lithuanian independence was recognized by the USSR. Similar incitements were given to the Gagauz and "Transdnestrovians" in Moldova, to the "Russian speakers" in Estonia and Latvia, and to the Abkhaz and Ossetians in Georgia.

This does not mean that these and other minorities had no problems at all and that their human rights were entirely secure, but instead of solving the problems by mutual consent, the steps undertaken by Moscow, such as the "Law of Secession", had aroused strong suspicions that these problems were to be solved at the expense of the major ethnic group in each Union republic. In the Georgian case, suppositions "both on the national sentiments of small peoples striving for the assertion of their own dignity and also on the mistakes of Georgian ideologists, sometimes displaying unpardonable deafness to the pain, hopes and interests of 'other' peoples of Georgia" (Chervonnaya 1993) were strong instruments in the hands of those who were preparing the Abkhaz war from the outside.

After the USSR was dissolved, the former "Elder Brother" spoke out about its "obligations" to secure the rights of the Russian-speaking population, not just ethnic Russians, in the new States. A high-ranking Russian official, who claimed that his ideas did not differ from those of the Ministry of Foreign Affairs, announced that:

> ... many of the [Newly Independent] States are doomed either to become our satellites or to die ... Our special relations [with these States] must cover first of all the economy and the problem of ethnic minorities living in these States. Russia must take under protection the Russians residing in the Near Abroad. And if ethnic minorities live compactly, they must be granted autonomy; the States have to become federative. The special status of regions settled by ethnic minorities must be confirmed by the guarantees of Moscow ... In Georgia these areas are Abkhazia and South Ossetia. In Moldova, Transdnestrovia and Gagauzia. In Kazakhstan, the northern part of the Republic. In the Ukraine, the eastern regions and the Crimea. (Rotar 1994)

There is an even more significant matter:

> Russia's political leaders, by default, ceded an important part of initiative in constructing policy towards the "near abroad" to the Russian armed forces – a conservative establishment that is both skeptical of Russia's integration into the Western community and still smarting from Russia's loss of both Eastern Europe and its "internal empire". (Lough 1993: 23)

Russia itself, of course, is not an "evil force"; it has its own interests, which do not always coincide with the interests of the other nations. It is inevitable that imperialistic attitudes in the huge country will not die out with a declaration of adherence to democracy (Afanasyev 1994). Thus, for all the other NIS, Russia is a constant external factor, which must be taken into account.

A geographical approach to ethnic tensions in Georgia

The interest of the geographer in ethnic conflicts is aroused by their spatial character. The most important motive of such conflicts is the possession of territory; disputes between different ethnic groups over dominance in holding the land always lead to conflict. The location of the area in dispute in its geographical context can quite often help to explain the degree of gravity of the conflict. There are other motives for conflict, usually less profound but nevertheless of some importance, which also have social space and locational implications. These motives may be socio-economic, such as competition for profitable spheres of employment between the representatives of the different ethnic groups, notably management in a bureaucratic State; this is particularly characteristic of areas where parochialism is present. Or the motives may be sociopolitical, for example, real or alleged political or social inequality on an ethnic basis.

These motives for ethnic tensions may exist for quite a long period without open expression and so an illusion of "inter-ethnic peace" may be created. As soon as the established balance is disturbed, these and other motives become possible factors for ethnic tensions that very soon tend to turn into conflicts, if State power is not strong and especially if it is weakened from outside.

A geographical approach to the conflicts implies examining the interlocation of the active and potential subjects of conflict (ethnic groups) in the area, as well as in the broader spatial context. Thus, during the quite lengthy presence of the Russian community in Georgia, there were no ethnic conflicts between them and any other group. In spite of serious efforts on Moscow's part, it had no success in creating an "Interfront" in Georgia in the late 1980s; this was an organization of Russians and Russian-speakers, aimed at opposing national liberation movements in the Union republics and which was rather effective in the Baltic republics. One reason, apart from a real absence of discrimination against Russians in Georgia, was the dispersed character of their settlement.

Tsalka District, settled by Greeks who migrated to Georgia in the nineteenth century and constituted an absolute majority in the district, has never been mentioned as a potential area of ethnic conflict, even though there too quarrels may occur between representatives of the different ethnic groups. Such an attitude can be explained, first of all by a geographical factor: Greece is far away. The local Greek population never considered the land where they live to be a separate part of Georgia. The Greeks did not "Georgianize" at all. On the contrary, they have shown a stronger inclination towards learning the Russian language, although most in the area are Turkish-speakers. Yet because they do not reside on the periphery of the country adjoining a motherland, they are loyal to Georgian statehood.

The same can be said about the Jews, who are highly respected by the Georgians, or about the Kurds, gradually becoming one of the "major minorities" in the capital city, or about the Kistis (Chechens), who constitute a substantial community in Akhmeta District (Kakheti province) and who have no tensions with the Georgians. Even the Ossetians, two-thirds of whom resided in Georgia outside the South Ossetian Autonomous Region, were not involved in any ethnic tensions after the 1920s. Until 1988, the mass consciousness of ethnic Georgians considered the Ossetians mostly as good neighbours and they were quite frequently relatives, and never as potential adversaries in an ethnic conflict; hardly anyone in Georgia could have predicted the heavy bloodshed and mutual atrocities in the core area of the country.

A certain contrast is demonstrated in Javakheti province, which was settled by Armenians, who arrived here at the same time as the Greeks in Tsalka District. Javakheti borders Armenia and this fact alone explains almost everything. In addition, however, Armenian historians have shown great zeal in search of arguments such as "whereas the area belonged to Armenia in the second century BC, it fell to the Georgians in the fourth century AD", as if the actual existence of an Armenian population in the area is not an argument strong enough for respecting their legal rights within Georgia. Potential irredentism is nourished among ordinary people by such mythology and it is no less characteristic of other peoples of the post-Soviet realm, including the Georgians. Such irredentism is capable of creating certain ethnic tensions between peoples who for millennia and up to the present have been mutually friendly and helpful to each other. In this, the geographical factor seems to be very important.

There is some similarity with this example in the geographical location of the area settled by Azeris in Kvemo Kartli region. In essence there are no real grounds for ethnic conflict between the Georgians and Azeris, both ethnic groups having their own economic niches in the area. The Azeris are engaged in agriculture, are very industrious and peaceful in character and had no real tensions with any other ethnic group, not even with the local Armenians, despite the war in Karabakh. The Georgians are more engaged in industry and tertiary activities. Rare irredentist activities in the area were not supported by Azerbaijan proper. Some ethnic-type social tensions at the beginning of the 1990s were caused by the criminal actions of gangsters, predominantly of Georgian origin. But crime has no ethnic boundaries. Nevertheless, the geographical factor of contiguity with the country whence irredentism may theoretically derive always makes public opinion suspicious. A geographer cannot avoid mapping such an "area of potential ethnic tension" (Fig. 9.1).

The same geographical feature – the direct contiguity of the areas settled by the Abkhaz and Ossetians with areas of the Russian Federation settled by the same or related ethnic groups – continues to play a dramatic role in the contemporary history of Georgia. Figure 9.1 depicts the major areas of conflict in Georgia, where ethnically grounded tensions already exist, as in Abkhazia, and "Tskhinvali

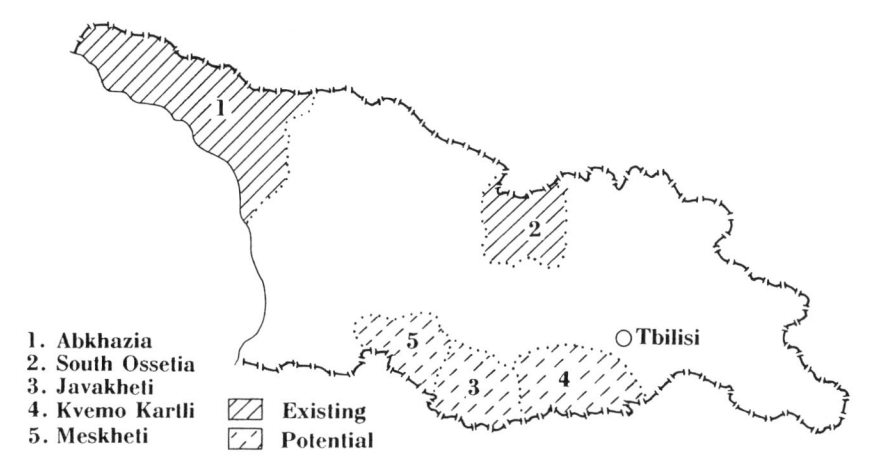

1. Abkhazia
2. South Ossetia
3. Javakheti
4. Kvemo Kartli
5. Meskheti

▨ Existing
▨ Potential

Figure 9.1 Areas of ethnic tension in Georgia.

Region" (former South Ossetia), and where there is a theoretically possible potential (Javakheti, Kvemo Kartli, Meskheti). It can be easily seen that all existing or potential ethnic tension areas are situated along the borders. This is particularly alarming for the ethnic Georgians and it affects their attitudes towards minorities.

A survey carried out by the USIA in Georgia in 1993 showed that towards minorities ethnic Georgians demonstrated more tolerance than intolerance. Between 51 and 67 per cent of respondents agreed with the ideas that national minorities should have the right to establish organizations to preserve their traditions and cultures, to publish books and other printed material, to conduct classes or religious services in their own language, to have their representatives in Parliament. However, there were 22–36 per cent of Georgian respondents who denied these rights for minorities. The only explanation of such an attitude are the lessons taught by a separatism that aims at the dismemberment of the country. True and stable statehood will undoubtedly increase the level of tolerance, as long as there is no threat from the minorities towards the territorial integrity of Georgia.

The geopolitical context of the conflict in Abkhazia

Some of the conflict areas are now considered in greater detail. Abkhazia, the gravest tension area in contemporary Georgia, has been given the greatest attention. In discussing the so-called "ethnic conflict" between Georgians and Abkhaz, the broader geopolitical context is sometimes left without proper attention. From one point of view, the conflict in Abkhazia is not "ethnic", but rather a struggle for the control of an important area between several factions. Nor are the two peoples mentioned the only actors in the real drama, although they became the major victims of it. The direct political interests of at least four sides are involved in the

Abkhaz conflict – Georgians, Abkhaz, the north Caucasus (represented by the "Confederation of Peoples of the Caucasus") and Russia. Turkey and Armenia are not directly involved, but are interested parties.

Turkey theoretically might prefer to be kept at a distance from a still dangerous Russia by the double buffer of Georgia and a putative "north Caucasian State". The responsible leaders of Turkey however understand the unreality of such a development and prefer Georgia to maintain sovereignty over its territory, because the dismemberment of Georgia could lead to the aggravation of instability in the region and might create a bad precedent for the victory of separatism. Moreover, Turkish authorities have never allowed tensions to arise among their own Georgian and Abkhaz- or Circassian-speaking citizens.

Armenia, on the other hand, might theoretically be interested in achieving a precedent for the official break-up of a neighbouring UN member country, because this could be an excuse for recognition of the independence of the Armenian-settled Nagorno–Karabakh within Azerbaijan. Fortunately, official statements of such a nature have never been made by Armenian officials. On the contrary, they stress that the problems of Abkhazia and Karabakh are not at all parallel. Nevertheless, it is likely that the actual existence of such a popular concept and aspirations led some Armenian organizations in Abkhazia to support the Abkhaz cause. During the recent war, Armenian voluntary forces were formed who fought against the Georgians.

Among the direct actors in the conflict, the Georgian interests are the most straightforward. Their desire is to restore the status quo, which is formally supported by the international community. Top politicians in Georgia have very often declared that in the democratic State that is likely to emerge as Georgia becomes politically more mature, the political and cultural rights of all ethnic groups will be guaranteed. The new Law of Citizenship of Georgia passed by Parliament in March 1993 is a good example of such attitudes. The "argument", as an excuse for separatism, that Georgia is an "eternally chauvinistic country, which aims to assimilate all its minorities" is absolutely groundless. The Abkhaz language and culture (as well as those of the Ossetians, Armenians, Russians, Azeris and so on) had and will have full guarantees in Georgia. However, some irresponsible declarations and condemnable actions of individual Georgian political and military leaders past and present could have caused serious distrust. Thus, cast iron constitutional guarantees are required for the minorities. The Georgian leaders have declared that the Republic of Georgia is ready to guarantee Abkhaz statehood within Georgia and the legal rights of the Abkhaz. It is clear that without meddling from outside this internal problem of Georgia could have been solved peacefully, or even never have arisen.

The essential desire of the Abkhaz leadership, representing a minority of the population (Ch. 4), is to secede the province from Georgia and to form an independent State, subject to international law. The major obstacle to this was supposed to be the will of the majority of the population – the Georgians – who do not want to become a minority in another State. Until recently, the idea of merging with Russia was also quite widespread (Achba 1992). On 23 March 1993 the Abkhaz-dominated "rump" of the Supreme Council of the Autonomous Republic officially addressed such an appeal to the Congress of People's Deputies and Supreme Soviet of the Russian Federation (Congress 1993). At the end of 1993, after the success of the Abkhaz side in the civil war (Ch. 2), it looked as if the Abkhaz leadership had given up a third option, which had earlier been declared as the principal option, that of entering Georgia on a loose federative basis, with special rights more resembling confederation. It was easy to predict the intention to make secession a legal act, which was the major reason why the Georgian side opposed it. However, it still looks as if the final solution of the problem will be in the formation of the federal system in Georgia.

The Abkhaz are very small in number, with 1.8 per cent of the population of Georgia, although they control 12.5 per cent of its territory and over half its coastline; they are a minority of 18 per cent even in their autonomous area, where the local Georgians outnumber them by 2.5 times. The question arises why they were so insistent on an enhancement of their political status, and why they were so successful (at least for the time being) in their struggle, whereas other much larger minorities of the former USSR are less successful?

In answering this question, one must turn again to the geographical factor, apart from the actual weakness of Georgia's statehood in the early stage of its development. Abkhazia neighbours the Russian Federation. Moreover, Abkhazia possesses the best resort area in the former USSR. "For decades, retainer clans grew up in the elite ministerial and government recreation zones, among whom is the very large social category of the militarized guard, traditionally linked with the services of USSR law-enforcement ministries" (Chervonnaya 1993). In no other autonomous republic were its leaders so close to the governing Politburo members of the CPSU and Soviet (Russian) generals as in Abkhazia. Russia encouraged, at least indirectly, Abkhaz separatism within Georgia, whereas most of the other minorities having their autonomous areas within the Russian Federation had no "strong patron" to support their own aspirations.

The military success of the Abkhaz can again be explained in geographical terms; it was backed up by the human resources of the adjacent areas of the north Caucasus and it received official aid of various kinds – moral support through the mass media, economic "humanitarian" aid – and unofficial but very substantial military aid from Russia proper (Chervonnaya 1993, Laber 1993, Yakov 1993). Aid came predominantly from non-governmental organizations, presumably close to the military–industrial complex.

The Abkhaz turned for support not only to Russia. In some Middle Eastern countries there are small but increasingly active groups of the Abkhaz diaspora and so a "Muslim card" was played. Since the north Caucasian "Confederates" became involved in the conflict with their own interests in mind (see below), this "card" was intended for them as well. But the "imperial card" still remains the most important. It involves promises to allocate land to the Russian Cossacks, no doubt the land where the Georgians used to live (Chernishova 1993), to extend the resort zones for the Russian military and to give Russia greater access to the Black Sea. The Abkhaz ethnic leadership, although not representing the majority of the population, hopes to maintain their leading role in the supposed independent State or in a republic within Russia. The major competitors for leadership, who in their opinion could only be the ethnic Georgians, had to be eliminated.

A leading problem in the Abkhaz conflict was demography. The Abkhaz resented being actually the minority in the autonomous republic, whereas the Georgians were presumptuously confident of their majority. In fact there was no hatred on an individual level. Even during the recent civil war, many of the Georgians in Abkhazia, for example most of those from Gali District, did not participate in the fighting, although this did not save them from banishment after the separatists were victorious. With reference to the demographic situation, a leading Abkhaz official announced to a reporter on a Russian newspaper that "the Abkhaz will not permit themselves to be again a minority in their own country" (Rotar 1993a). This obviously cannot be achieved by the heavy return migration of the Abkhaz diaspora from the Middle East, as it is rather small in number. More likely policy is to attract north Caucasians, mostly Abazins and Circassians (Adiges), who will be ready to "Abkhazianize", in practice by formally changing the nationality in their internal passports. The goal could be achieved by forcing out most of the non-Abkhaz. According to the latest (1989) population census, even without a single Georgian the Abkhaz did not make up more than 32.7 per cent of the population of the autonomous republic. Obviously, the demographic potential of the Abkhaz is restricted and the "vacant places" will once again be occupied by the non-Abkhaz, who might be Russians, Armenians, or particular north Caucasians; the territory is a titbit for newcomers to relish.

In the event, after the unsuccessful conclusion by the end of 1993 of the civil war for the Georgians, most of them had to flee to avoid extermination. The Abkhaz also suffered heavy losses in the conflict. In addition, many mixed Abkhaz–Georgian families emigrated in the early stages of the conflict to avoid participation in the fratricidal warfare. The demographic changes will scarcely proceed exactly along the lines predicted by the advocates of secession. The local Georgians insist on returning and this desire is considered as legitimate by the international community.

One of the active participants in the conflict over Abkhazia was the "Confederation of Peoples of the Caucasus", proclaimed in 1991 by the radical political leaders of 16 different nationalities of the area. In fact the leadership of the "Confederation" was never formally elected by democratic vote and from this point of view does not represent any of the "founder peoples". However, in the main the "Confederation" expresses popular sentiment, "the national idea" of the peoples of the Caucasus, although there are always other, influential, local leaders in the area, who do not support the methods of action or even the ideas of the "Confederation". Nevertheless, there was a temporary unity of the interests of more than a dozen different peoples, most of whom belonged to the world of Islam; there was popular sympathy towards the "Confederation" in the north Caucasus. This was engendered by its participation in the war in Abkhazia, on the side of the potential underdog. Also they were "kindred people"; the Abkhaz and their close relatives the Abazins are linguistically akin to the Adigheans, the Circassian super-ethnos comprising the Kabardians, Cherkess, Adige and Shapsugs. All of these, apart from the Abkhaz, reside in the north Caucasus.

The leaders of the "Confederation" are obviously interested in the break-up of Georgia and the creation of an independent Abkhaz State. That would give coveted access to the sea to the putative "Confederative State" (Savichev 1992). The city of Sokhumi has already been declared its "capital" (Soslambekov 1990). At the present time, the incorporation of Abkhazia into the Russian Federation might also seem desirable for the "Confederation". As citizens of a single State, it would be easier for members of the "Confederation" to settle in the coastal area and develop the "demographic weapon" to use against Russia in the interests of the future self-determination of the "Circassian State". The interests of the "Confederation" are rather arbitrarily considered as unitary. Ignatenko & Salmin (1993) argued that there are inevitable controversies between the interests of the 16 founding members of the "Confederation", for example between the Ossetians and the Ingush, the Balkars and the Kabardians, the ethnic north Caucasians and the Russian Cossacks. Equally, there would be conflicts of interest between the "Confederation" as a whole and the Russian Centre. The rhetoric of "mutual friendship of the Caucasians and Cossacks" (Minasian 1993) is intended as a mere populist veil. These controversies will constrain the interference of the "Confederation" in the internal affairs of Georgia, once the latter has come to terms with its own minorities.

Russian authorities chose not to interfere in the aggression directed from their territory against the "not-friendly enough" neighbour, that is to say the Georgia of 1991–3. This acquiescence may cost Russia proper dearly. Military traditions have been established and unofficial armed units created in the south of Russia, and it is possible that this military potential might be used against Russia itself. The Chechen crisis of 1994–5 proves this. "Confederate" forces were needed to help the Abkhaz side during the war and it still needs "demographic aid". Some individuals, mostly of Circassian and Chechen origin, have already been allocated the land and houses previously belonging to Georgians. But the pronounced anti-Russian attitudes of the "Confederation" might be embarrassing for the Abkhaz, who still have to rely upon the help of Russian generals.

For the understanding of Russia's geopolitical interests in Georgia and Abkhazia in particular, one must take into account the Russian military need for access to warm water. Moreover, the Black Sea resorts of Georgia, especially those situated to the northwest of Sokhumi, were intensively exploited by the Soviet political elite. For example, Gorbachev was building his villa in Miussera (Gudauta District), where in an earlier period Stalin also had a summer house; Khrushchev had a holiday home in Bichvinta (Pitsunda). High-ranking Russian military officials possessed in this area up to 30 large sanatoria and holiday homes, belonging to the Soviet Ministries of Defence and Interior Affairs and the KGB.

Although the Communist Party leaders eventually lost their game, for the Russian generals who until recently were wearing Soviet uniform and stars, it might be rather difficult to give up all these earthly blessings.

The involvement of the Russian Federation in the conflict is more than clear (Skachko 1992, Laber 1993, Shevardnadze 1993b, Yakov 1993). All the three cease-fires were reached with Russia's brokerage and all of them were broken by the Abkhaz side with Russian acquiescence (Medvedev 1993). It is obvious that a solution to the conflict would depend not only on the good will of the ostensibly conflicting sides, but on the entire Caucasian policy of Russia, which has to deal with its own troublesome subjects in the south. Meanwhile, as experts of International Alert wrote in late 1992, "Russia's approach to the north Caucasian Confederation of Peoples has been ambiguous and does not appear to serve Russia's own interests. The same appears true of Russian moral (and presumably, unofficial material) support for Abkhaz self-determination" (Es-Saïeed et al. 1993).

Sometimes it has been suggested in Georgia that there are "two Russias" – one "reactionary" and the other "democratic", the first stirring up conflict and the other trying in vain to bring it to an end. There is, however, a consistent logic in the behaviour of Russia as a whole; it wants to protect its own strategic interests in the Caucasus. All the other participants in the conflict are looked upon as mere pawns that may be sacrificed at the right moment. As an American observer wrote recently, "[Georgia's] ultimate vulnerability lies in its strategic importance to Russia. Of all the former Soviet republics that the Russian Army calls "the Near Abroad", Georgia is regarded as the most vital . . . Russia's policy towards Georgia has been the same whether the Tsar was Peter the Great, Stalin or Yeltsin: create chaos so that Russian troops are called in to 'keep the peace'" (Montefiore 1993: 18).

Obviously, Russia does not need a State called the "Confederation of Peoples of the Caucasus" on its southern border. The Confederation's leading body is not even officially registered as a political organization and formally still remains illegal. However, for the time being, Russia has tolerated the "Confederation", as its military activities were directed abroad. In any case, Russia was not entirely able to stop the activities of the Confederation, especially in the turmoil that has become characteristic of Russian political life. Serious measures against the "Confederates" might have blown apart the fragile peace in southern Russia. The genie let out of the bottle with the intention of damaging an obstinate "Near Abroad", is likely to bring harm to his releaser. The true interest of Russia, paradoxically enough, must lie in the territorial integrity of Georgia, albeit preferably a Georgia dependent on Russia. In the negotiations held during the Tbilisi Summit on February 3, 1994, Russia insisted on the 'increased degree of statehood for Abkhazia and South Ossetia within 'a territorially integral Georgia'".

Conflict in Tskhinvali region, formerly South Ossetia

The history of the designation of the South Ossetian Autonomous Region, described in Chapter 2, shows that there were seeds of conflict sown in this part of Georgia as early as the 1920s. Even so, the existence of the autonomous region within Soviet Georgia in practice never gave rise to any special tensions. The Ossetians, with close and generally friendly relations with ethnic Georgians for decades (Ch. 4), were not even suspected of separatism. Georgian public opinion was in fact ignorant of the processes that were going on in South Ossetia, and with some surprise discovered in late 1988 that another area of ethnic tension existed in the central part of the country. The reaction to this fact of some influential leaders of the Georgian national movement was not always adequate, was lacking in patience and foresight, and thus in its turn helped to aggravate the conflict. To some extent Georgian nationalism "helped" Ossetian nationalism to gain more support.

In reality, however, conflict in the area was long nourished and prepared. The geographical contiguity of the Ossetian settlements on both slopes of the Great Caucasus Range was the major argument for the secessionists. This argument was given even greater weight after an automobile tunnel was opened under the Roki pass in September 1988. Its construction took almost two decades and was of course financed by the all-Union government; its precise location was chosen at the insistence of military circles in Moscow. This "technological achievement of Soviet power" made it possible in the fullness of time to use the Ossetians against the Georgian national movement.

Two Ossetian scholars (one now the President of Northern Ossetia) wrote, with reference to the nineteenth-century change in the Ossetian alphabet from Georgian script to Cyrillic, "the issue was not the quality or merits of the alphabet . . . Tsarism did not want the South Ossetians to vanish completely among the Georgians. South Ossetia was to be preserved as a secure bridgehead from which it would be possible, if necessary, to put pressure on the occasionally obstinate Georgian rulers" (Galazov & Isayev 1987: 74–5). At the end of the twentieth century, the construction of a similar bridgehead cost the now Soviet Empire much more in finance, but it proved to be more effective than the cultural pressure of the Tsarist government.

The South Ossetian leaders were more nationalistic than their northern brethren in their yearning for the unification of the two autonomous areas existing within different Soviet republics. It was assumed that it would be easier to achieve at the expense of the weaker republic, that is Georgia, and to do so while the Soviet Union still existed. It was clear that an independent Georgia would never give up a substantial part (5%) of its historical territory and would never yield to the establishment of a new State border in the heart of the country. When in the autumn of 1990 the (South) Ossetian ethnic leadership unilaterally declared a new "Soviet republic" within the USSR, an act that inevitably would have led to conflict, they did not take into account the interests of the 60 per cent majority of Ossetians who lived outside the autonomous region. These were often members of mixed families, almost always some kind of relatives of the Georgians. These Ossetians became one of the major victims of a confrontation they never desired (Bloodshed 1992). Even less did the secessionists care about the ethnic Georgian population of the CRS of Tskhinvali and adjoining villages, who were made refugees in their own country.

The geopolitical context of this conflict is less complicated than in the case of Abkhazia. Tskhinvali Region, or South Ossetia, sometimes rather arbitrarily called "Samachablo" in the Georgian media, has only one all-year round traffic connection with north Caucasia: the Roki Tunnel. The other mountain passes are passable only on foot in summer time. The region is completely surrounded by areas settled by Georgians and in the event of a military conflict, without foreign interference, would be doomed to defeat. It could maintain itself only if Georgia were too weak and there were a constant Russian military presence in the area.

North Ossetia itself has rather tense relations with its neighbouring peoples, notably with the Ingush, who claim the territory east of Vladikavkaz, the capital of North Ossetia, and even part of the capital city itself, areas that in fact belonged to the Ingush before 1944. Ingush–Ossetian conflict has already been smouldering since the early 1990s, with periodical serious outbreaks. There is a potential conflict between the Ossetians and Kabardians, who also claim some areas now under North Ossetian jurisdiction. The "Confederation of Peoples of the Caucasus", of which the Ossetians also are members, does not support them in their conflicts. In consequence, North Ossetia is not itself interested in alienating Georgia, with which there has always existed mutually fruitful economic, cultural and simply human relations.

In these circumstances the Ossetians have to rely entirely on the support of the Russian centre and are seen by some Russian nationalist forces as "the major ally of Russia against the Caucasian Muslims and the Georgians" (Savostyanov 1992). The Georgian–Ossetian conflict that began in 1989, was seriously aggravated in 1990 and subsequently developed into a prolonged civil war, which ended in a cease-fire in mid-1992. Since then the Tbilisi government has been seeking a peaceful solution to suit both sides. This is very difficult to achieve, as popular sentiment in Georgia opposes the restoration of autonomy in the area, especially under the name of "South Ossetia" as that would imply once again the "unification of the two Ossetias". On the other side, the de facto government in Tskhinvali still insists on merging with Northern Ossetia, which would imply the annexation of a part of Georgia by Russia. It is less likely that the leaders of Russia would undertake such a step and even North Ossetian leaders do not support this idea. It is clear that the "maximalism" of the Tskhinvali government is a part of a bargaining plan to achieve better terms for a restored autonomy within Georgia. A compromise solution of the Georgian–Ossetian tension is very likely to be achieved, if both sides are willing to make some concessions to each other.

The problem of the return of the Meskhetian Muslims

The return of the Meskhetian Muslims to their original place of residence is one more factor capable of creating an area of ethnic tension (Fig. 9.1). Some of these people are Islamized Georgians, others are ethnic Turks, Kurds and Hemshins; partly bilingual (Turkish–Georgian), they are frequently erroneously referred to as Turk-Meskhetians.

At the end of 1944, according to the decision of the State Committee for Defence of the USSR, about 70 000 of these people (Natmeladze 1993: 34) were deported to Central Asia from Turkish border areas of the USSR in Georgia and to some extent Armenia. In fact, this inhuman action was carried out in order to prepare for the Soviet invasion of Turkey. Active intervention of the Western powers prevented this adventure. Subsequently, the Soviet authorities equally forcibly resettled the area with Georgians and Armenians, who built houses and gradually adapted to the rather harsh environment.

Although rehabilitated under Khrushchev in 1956, by the decision of the rulers in the Kremlin the Meskhetian Muslims were not allowed to return to the restricted border area; the defence of State borders was not a matter for Union-republics. In June 1989 yet another inhuman action was carried out against this people, who by then had settled down in Uzbekistan and had become more or less integrated. The social environment was linguistically and confessionally more acceptable, since the Uzbeks like the Meskhetian Muslims are Turkic-speaking and Sunni Muslim. A "spontaneous" quarrel in a market turned into well organized violence against the entire ethnic group in various settlements. They were compelled to leave Uzbekistan within a couple of days and had to insist on their return to Georgia.

The Soviet power of that time, still one-party governed and in full control of the army, police and secret police, did nothing to prevent the banishment of the entire ethnic group. The Communist Party leader of Uzbekistan was promoted to Moscow shortly afterwards. In Georgia, this "operation" was suspected by many people to be aimed against Georgia, where by then the national liberation movement had acquired strength and was becoming dangerous to the Soviet Empire. It was probably assumed in Moscow that the fear of one more potential ethnic conflict in the republic would have sobered the "stubborn Georgian nationalists".

The return of the deported people, who now numbered between 150 000 and 200 000 according to different estimates, was recognized by some intellectuals in Georgia as their full right (e.g. Gelashvili 1993), but it might have been much easier to achieve before the end of the 1980s, when Soviet power was strong enough. But when some leaders of the Meskhetian Muslims declared their desire to form an autonomous unit along the southern border of Georgia (Natmeladze 1993: 48), this aroused strong suspicions in every successive government of Georgia, including the communist administrations before the end of 1990. Even more concern was felt by the local population, who have been living in the area for two generations already, and who have strong fears of ethnic conflict, with the possible loss of property and even the lives of themselves and their children.

The proposals of the Soviet Georgian government to resettle the descendants of deported Meskhetian Muslims in inner areas of Georgia was accepted by some of them, who have already taken the opportunity. They returned some decades ago and are successfully integrating into Georgian society. However, the leaders of the majority of the Meskhetian Muslims, who in fact are residing in the north Caucasus and Azerbaijan, have not yet accepted this proposal and insist on forming a genuinely autonomous territorial community in the borderland of Georgia. More objective observers consider that the return of the Meskhetian Muslims is inevitable. It is hard to say when exactly this may occur, but if this can be done when the country has returned to a normal pace of economic and political development, the step may have less grave results.

CHAPTER 10
Conclusion

The geographical realities described in the present book may give a certain picture of a Newly Independent State – the Republic of Georgia. This background text was aimed mostly to show the relative place of Georgia as a social entity in the World and to reveal some social aspects of development of Georgia as they are located in space.

The relative place of any post-Soviet State cannot be understood without realities of the former superpower. It might have been unnatural if the break-up of such a centralized State as the USSR was to happen peacefully, to the pleasure of all its constituent parts and the division of the extended family property by the divorcing sides had been just and fair. The biggest and strongest "Elder Brother" got more inheritance (and a lot of obligations and problems as well), the lesser brothers got less wealth, while the share of some of them in the legacy of unsolved problems appeared to be larger.

Most of the new States were born in torment. The economic problems of Georgia that developed so gravely affect social life and its spatial manifestations. The internal spatial structure will by no means remain stable in the future as the change to a market economy becomes more salient.

Political problems of the country are no less important. The major effort of the emerging Republic of Georgia is to maintain its recent geographical configuration. As Edouard Shevardnadze said in his speech at a dinner at the US Department of State (7 March, 1994): "... Georgia is in trouble – because it's fighting, struggling for freedom. It's not yet free, because freedom is to be gained. I once said that freedom is a very very expensive kind of happiness. Now we are paying this price". The paying for this kind of happiness has already cost the country a lot and not everything is paid as yet. But it is evident that the State will persist. While impartially describing a lot of objective and subjective obstacles to State-building in Georgia – an analysis containing the harsh truth that most negative factors are internal – a thorough young American scholar nevertheless came to a conclusion that: "there is no intrinsic reason why the process [of State-building] cannot be successful in Georgia. The Georgians are a fully conscious nation which has formed several political entities in the past. They have persevered throughout history to preserve their language and culture despite centuries of foreign occupation. They live in a country which has numerous economic opportunities due mostly to its geographical location . . ." (O'Halloran, 1993: 28). I tried to show in the present book a spatial background of social life in Georgia. Obviously this involved regarding the most recent (and sometimes not so recent) past. The present spatial patterns have been examined as well. I didn't dare look at the future development, which in a country under total crisis is quite obscure, completely covered with clouds. But still some kind of general deduction is on the tip of my pen.

The long-term prospects for the social development of this country do not seem to be as dark as it appears from quite a few pages of this book. After political stability is restored and if the trends of democratic development become clearer, the existence of highly qualified intellectuals, quite skilled workers, industrious farmers, the emerging class of businessmen (not all of them will emigrate, and many will return with capital if the situation improves), along with some other geographical and geopolitical factors (natural resources, the balance of the strategic and economic interests of the World powers) may give a chance to Georgia to follow the narrow path of State-building and to create a dynamic, democratic society. Naturally this cannot happen in months or even in several years after independence.

The existence of Georgia within an Empire for almost two centuries changed the social structure and even the mentality of the population that got used to the conditions of a huge country. It is a rather painful process adjusting to new circumstances, when part of a State is becoming a State itself. Serious social change is going on in the post-Soviet space. And it will take a long time and a lot of sweat and also, unfortunately, blood and tears, to rearrange this space in a new mode.

And despite everything, I believe, Georgia will come closer to the way of development that all progressive countries of the West have already followed. After some time a new social geography will have to be written of Georgia as an integral part of Europe.

REFERENCES

Abayev, V. 1992. The tragedy of South Ossetia: the way to agreement [in Russian]. *Nezavisimaya Gazeta* (22 February).

Abuladze, T. 1989. *15th–18th century Ottoman documents and narrative sources for the history of Georgia* [in Russian]. Tbilisi: Institute of History, Archaeology and Ethnography, Academy of Sciences of the Georgian SSR.

Achba, Z. 1992. It's time to understand that Abkhazia is Russia [in Russian]. *Den* (29 November to 5 December).

Afanasyev Y. 1994. A new Russian Imperialism. *Perspective*. Publication IV(3), pp. 1–7, Institute for the Study of Conflict, Ideology & Policy, Boston University.

All-Union Population Census of 1926. Georgian SSR, Part I: *Nationality–vernacular–age–literacy*. 1929 [in Georgian and Russian]. Tbilisi: Central Statistical Board of the Transcaucasian Federation.

Analysis of the activity of the aAutomobile service enterprises in 1984 [in Russian]. 1985. Togliatti: Scientific Information Institute of the Ministry of Automobile Industry of the USSR.

Anchabadze, Z. 1976. *An essay on the ethnic history of the Abkhaz People* [in Russian]. Sokhumi: Alashara.

—— 1959. *From the history of medieval Abkhazia (VI-XVII centuries)* [in Russian]. Sokhumi: Alashara.

Anin, A. 1994. Once more about the Russian–Georgian Treaty [in Russian]. *Nezavisimaya Gazeta* (24 February).

Antadze, K. 1973. *The population of Georgia in the 19th century* [in Georgian]. Tbilisi: Metsniereba.

Appeal of the Presidium of the Supreme Council of the USSR to the Supreme Council of the Georgian SSR and the Regional Council of the South Ossetian Autonomous Region [in Russian] 1990. *Izvestiya* (16 December).

Appeal to the General Secretary of the Central Committee of CPSU, The Chairman of the Supreme Council of the USSR Comrade M. S. Gorbachev [in Russian] 1989. *Sovetskaya Abkhazia* (24 March).

Arutyunov S. 1992. War in the mountains of the Caucasus [in Russian]. *Rodina* 1, 68–72.

Aves, J. 1991. *Paths to national independence in Georgia, 1987–90*. London: SSEES, University of London.

Basic law (constitution) of the Union of the Soviet Socialist Republics [in Russian] 1931. Moscow: All-Union Central Executive Committee.

Bater, J. H. 1989. *The Soviet scene: a geographical perspective*. London: Edward Arnold.

Batiashvili, I. 1994. Vicious circle [in Georgian]. *Iveria-Expressi* (5 February).

Bgazhba, Kh. 1974. *Studies and essays* [in Russian]. Sokhumi: Alashara.

Blankoff-Scarr, G. & J. Blankoff 1993. Open letter to Georgian friends [in Georgian, translated from French]. *Sakartvelos respublika* (18 October).

Bloodshed in the Caucasus. Violations of humanitarian law and human rights in the Georgia–South Ossetia Conflict. 1992. New York & Washington: Helsinki Watch [a division of Human Rights Watch].

Bosanquet, B. 1899. *The philosophical theory of the State*. London: Macmillan.

Bromley, Y. (ed.) 1988. *Peoples of the world: an historical–ethnographical handbook* [in Russian]. Moscow: Sovetskaya Entsiklopedia.

Butenko, A. 1988. On the revolutionary restructuring of State-administrative socialism [in Russian]. In *Inogo ne dano*, Yu. N. Afanasyev (ed.), 551–68. Moscow: Progress.

References

Chervonnaya, S. 1993. The technology of the Abkhazian war. *Moscow News* (17 October), 42.
— 1994. *Conflict in the Caucasus: Georgia, Abkhazia and the Russian shadow*. Glastonbury, England: Gothic Image Publications.
Chelnokov, A. 1993. The Abkhazian apocalypse: a bloodthirsty feast of the triumphant in Sokhumi [in Russian]. *Izvestiya* (12 October).
Chernishova, N. 1993. We were promised the houses of the Georgians . . . [in Russian]. *Svobodnaya Gruziya* (26 March).
Chkhetia, Sh. 1942. *Tbilisi in the 19th century (1865–1869)* [in Russian]. Tbilisi: Academy of Sciences of the Georgian SSR Publishing House.
Coates, B. E., R. J. Johnston, P. L. Knox 1977. *Geography and inequality*. Oxford: Oxford University Press.
The concise Oxford dictionary of quotations. 1964. Oxford: Oxford University Press.
Code of statistical data of the population of the Transcaucasian Region, calculated from the household lists of 1886. 1893. [In Russian]. Tiflis: Martirosiants Printing House.
Congress of the People's Deputies of Russia charged the Supreme Council to consider the request of the Supreme Council of Abkhazia on admittance as a member of the Russian Federation [in Russian]. *1993. Svobodnaya Gruziya* (31 March).
Consumption and household budget in 1992. 1993. *Sakartvelos Respublika* (3 February).

Daines, V. 1993. Thank God, Russia didn't disintegrate in those times! [in Russian]. *Argumenty i Fakti*, 25.
Dennis, R. & H. Clout. 1980. *A social geography of England & Wales*. Oxford: Pergamon Press.
Djaparidze, G. 1993. The Arabic designations of the Georgians and Georgia [in Georgian]. In *Foreign and Georgian terminology designating Georgia and the Georgians*, G. Paichadze (ed.), 121–45. Tbilisi: Metsniereba.
Dragadze, T. 1994. Conflict in Transcaucasus and the value of inventory control. *Jane's Intelligence Review* (February), 71–3.
Dyatlov, A. 1989. First time and forever? Briefing in the Ministry of Interior of the USSR: criminal statistics opened [in Russian]. *Komsomolskaya Pravda* (15 February).

The Economist 1994. Crime in Russia: the high price of freeing markets. (9 February).
Emelyanenko, V. 1993. Georgia: where is the edge of the friendly bayonets [in Russian]. *Moskovskiye Novosti* (31 October), 44.
Essaïed, A., P. Henze, S. E. Wimbush 1993. *Georgia on the path to democracy and the Abkhaz Issue: a report of an International Alert Mission. 22 November to 4 December, 1992*. London.

Fyodorovskiy, V. 1993. The country of cheap hashish [in Russian]. *Moskovskiye Novosti* (14 February).
Fernandez-Armesto, F. (ed.) 1994. *Guide to the peoples of Europe*. London: Times Books.
Filippov, F. 1988. The social structure of Soviet society: trends and contradictions of development [in Russian]. *Obshchestvennyye Nauki* 1, 21–35.
From the history of interrelations of the Georgian and Ossetian peoples (Findings of the Committee on the Status of the South Ossetian Autonomous Region) 1991. Tbilisi: Tsodna.

Gabashvili, V, (ed.) 1957. *Studies in the history of the Near East (period of feudalism)* [in Georgian]. Tbilisi: Tbilisi University Press.
Gabiani, A. 1988. *Narcotism yesterday and today* [in Russian]. Tbilisi: Sabchota Sakartvelo.
Gabiani, A. & R. Gachechiladze 1982. *Some problems of the geography of crime (according to the materials of the Georgian SSR)* [in Russian]. Tbilisi: Tbilisi University Press.
Gabiani, A., R. Gachechiladze, M. Didebulidze 1985. *Crime in the cities and rural areas* [in Russian]. Tbilisi: Sabchota Sakartvelo.
Gachechiladze, R. 1972. Kartvelian-speaking population in Turkey [in Georgian]. *Mimomkhilveli (Tbilisi)*, 6–9, 172–6.

References

— 1982. Geography and the social consumption funds [in Russian]. *Izvestiya Akademii Nauk SSSR, Seriya Geograficheskaya* **3**, 42–7 [translated in *Soviet Geography*, 1985, XXVI(1), 19–26].

— 1987. Analysis of regional differences in material welfare of the population: the Georgian SSR [in Russian]. *Izvestiya Akademii Nauk SSSR, Seriya Geograficheskaya*, 6, 90–94 [translated in *Soviet Geography*, 1988, XXIX(4), 413–19).

— 1989a. *A social atlas of Georgia* [in Georgian and Russian]. Tbilisi: Georgian Institute of the Scientific and Technical Information, Registration No. G-640.

— 1989b. On the ecological culture of the population [in Georgian]. *Sakartvelos Komunisti* **2**, 72–6.

— 1990a. *The social geography of a Union republic. The case study of the Georgian SSR* [in Russian]. Tbilisi: Institute of Geography, Academy of Sciences of Georgia.

— 1990b. An approach to social regionalization: the case study of the Georgian SSR [in Russian]. *Izvestiya Akademii Nauk SSSR, Seriya Geograficheskaya* **4**, 111–15.

— 1990c. Social–geographical problems of a metropolitan region within a Soviet republic (a case study of the Tbilisi Metropolitan Region, Georgia, USSR). *Geoforum* **21**(4), 475–482.

— 1990d. Public opinion study and social geography (according to materials of the Georgian SSR) [in Russian]. In *Geografiya, Politika i Kultura*. V. S. Yagya, (ed.), 135–37. Leningrad: Nauka.

— 1990e. What the public anticipates [in Georgian]. *Komunisti* (26 August).

— 1991. Multi-party elections in Georgia [in Russian]. *Sotsiologicheskiye Issledovaniya* (Moscow) **5**, 53–63.

— 1992a. Besonderheiten der sozialpolitischen Transformation in der ehemaligen Sowjetrepublik Georgien. In *Soziologen-Tag Leipzig 1991. Sociologie in Deutschland und die Transformation Großer gesellschaftlicher Systeme*, H. Meyer (ed.), 1443–9. Berlin: Akademie.

— 1992b. The truth about the Georgian winter [in Russian]. *Sotsiologicheskie Issledovaniya* (Moscow) **8**, 3–12.

— 1993. Public opinion in Georgia on relations with Russia [in Russian]. *Svobodnaya Mysl* (Moscow) **12**, 105–10.

— 1994a. The problems that disturbed the population of Georgia in 1992 and 1993 [in Russian]. *Svobodnaya Gruziya* (1 January).

— 1994b. War in Abkhazia: one more view on the problem. *The Georgian Times* (18 February).

— 1994c. Geopolitics of the Georgian state. *Jane's Intelligence Review* **VI**(12), 574–5.

Gachechiladze, R. & M. J. Bradshaw 1994. Changes in the ethnic structure of Tbilisi's population. *Post-Soviet Geography* **XXXV**(1), 56–9.

Gachechiladze, R. & V. Gujabidze 1979. The study of the quality of the urban environment (the case of Tbilisi Metropolitan Region) [in Russian]. In *Geography of population in the system of complex economic and social planning*, N. P. Agafonov & O. P. Litovka (eds), 90–96. Leningrad: Geographical Society of the USSR.

Gachechiladze, R., M. Najafaliyev, A. Rondeli 1984. Regional problems of development of Transcaucasia. *Geoforum* **15**(1), 65–73.

Galazov, A. & M. Isaev 1987. *People–brothers, tongues–brothers (Russian–Ossetian linguistic–cultural contacts)* [in Russian]. Ordzhonikidze: Ir.

Gamkrelidze, T. & V. Ivanov 1984. *The Indo–Europeans and Indo–European language* [in Russian], vol. II. Tbilisi: Tbilisi University Press.

Gelashvili, N. 1993. Muslim Meskhetians – the painful problem still unsolved [in Georgian]. *7 dge* (7–13 May).

Georgia in Figures in 1990 1991. Tbilisi: Committee for Social–Economic Information of the Supreme Council of the Republic of Georgia.

Georgia-2000-Regions: A complex program of economic and social development of the regions of the Georgian SSR until 2000, vol. VII: *population, labour resources, settlement* [in Russian]. 1987. Tbilisi: State Planning Committee of the Georgian SSR.

Georgian SSR. Encyclopaedic Handbook [in Georgian] 1981. Tbilisi: Kartuli sabchota entsiklopedia.

Giddens, A. 1989. *Sociology*. Cambridge: Polity.

Gleason, G. 1990. In *Soviet nationality policies: ruling ethnic groups in the USSR*, H. R. Huttenbach (ed.). London: Mansell.

References

Gogebashvili, J. 1912. *An introduction to natural sciences* [in Georgian]. Tbilisi: Losaberidze Press.
Gokadze, G. 1992. *Monoethnic and biethnic marriage* [in Georgian]. Tbilisi: Centre of Ethnic Relations Studies.
Goldthorpe, J. 1980. *Social mobility and class structure in modern Britain*. Oxford: Oxford University Press.
Gordeziani, R. 1993. *The problem of the formation of Georgian self-identity* [in Georgian]. Tbilisi: Tbilisi University Press.
Gujabidze, V. 1983a. Urbanization and ethnic processes (the case of Transcaucasian Soviet Republics) [in Russian]. In *Problems of the geography of population and spatial organization*, R. Gachechiladze (ed.), 10–30. Tbilisi: Tbilisi University Press.
— 1983b. Urban agglomerations of the Georgian SSR (the problem of delimiting large urban agglomerations) [in Russian]. In *Problems of the geography of population and spatial organization*, R. Gachechiladze (ed.), 132–74. Tbilisi: Tbilisi University Press.
Gvelesiani, G. 1965. *The development and location of socialist production in the Georgian SSR* [in Russian]. Tbilisi: Metsniereba.

Harvey, D. 1973. *Social justice and the city*. London: Edward Arnold.
Herbert, D. T. 1976. Social deviance in the city: a spatial perspective. In *Social areas in cities*, vol. I: *spatial processes and form*, D. T. Herbert & R. J. Johnson (eds), 89–121. Chichester: John Wiley.
Herbert, D. T. & D. M. Smith (eds) 1979. *Social problems and the city: geographical perspectives*. Oxford: Oxford University Press.
— 1989. *Social problems and the city: new perspectives*. Oxford: Oxford University Press.
Hewitt, G. 1993a. The North West Caucasus (an ignoble tradition continued or the unknown diaspora). Paper submitted to the Conference on the North Caucasus at SOAS, April 1993.
— 1993b. Clouds over the Caucasus. *The Guardian* (24 September).
Households of Georgia (according to the 1989 all-Union Population Census) [in Georgian]. 1991. Tbilisi: Committee for Social–Economic Information of the Republic of Georgia.
Human Development Report 1994. Published for the United Nations Development Program. New York: Oxford University Press.

Ignatenko, A. & A. Salmin 1993. Confederation of the Peoples of Caucasus in the political context of the Caucasian Region. *Mirovayia Ekonomika i Mezhdunarodniye Otnosheniya* **9**, 96–107.
Inal-ipa, Sh. 1990. *The foreign Abkhaz (historical–ethnographical studies)* [in Russian]. Sokhumi: Alashara.
— 1976. *The problems of ethno-cultural history of the Abkhaz* [in Russian]. Sokhumi: Alashara.

Jaoshvili, V. Sh. 1968. *The population of Georgia* [in Russian]. Tbilisi: Metsniereba.
— 1978. *The urbanization of Georgia* [in Russian]. Tbilisi: Metsniereba.
— 1984. *The population of Georgia in the 18th–20th centuries: a demographical–geographical study* [in Georgian]. Tbilisi: Metsniereba.
— (ed.) 1989. *Tbilisi: an economic–geographical study* [in Georgian]. Tbilisi: Sabchota Sakartvelo.
— 1993. *An economic and social geography of Georgia* [in Georgian]. Tbilisi: Engineering–Economic Institute of Georgia.
Javakhishvili, I. 1979. *A history of the Georgian nation: collected works*, vol. I [in Georgian]. Tbilisi: Tbilisi University Press.
Jones, S. 1993a. The unbearable freedom. Georgia on the precipice. *Armenian International Magazine* **4**(8), 16–21.
— 1993b. Georgia: a failed democratic transition. In *Nation and politics in the Soviet successor States*, I. Bremmer & R. Taras (eds), 288–310. New York: Cambridge University Press.
— 1994. Populism in Georgia: The Gamsaxurdia phenomenon. In *Nationalism and history: the politics of nation-building in post-Soviet Armenia, Azerbaijan and Georgia*, Donald V. Schwartz & Razmik Panassian (eds), 127–49. Toronto: Centre of Russian and East European Studies, University of Toronto.

References

Johnston, R. J., D. Gregory, D. M. Smith (eds) 1994. *The dictionary of human geography*, 3rd edn. Oxford: Basil Blackwell.

Kaiser, R. J. 1991. Nationalism: the challenge to Soviet federalism. In *The Soviet Union: a new regional geography?*, M. J. Bradshaw (ed.), 39–66. London: Pinter (Belhaven).
Kakabadze, S. 1920. *Research on problems of the history of Georgia* [in Georgian]. Tbilisi.
Kakuria, Sh. 1979. *Population of the city of Tbilisi, 1803–1970* [in Georgian]. Tbilisi: Metsniereba.
Kampfner, J. 1993. Russia adopts its own "Monroe Doctrine". *Moscow News* (6 August).
Kashia, J. 1992. A technology for the restructuring of totalitarianism [in Georgian]. *Mamuli* (6), 1.
Kavkazskiy kalendar (Caucasian Calendar). 1902. [In Russian]. LVII. Tiflis.
Kekelia, N. 1988. The peculiarities of land use on personal plots in the Georgian SSR [in Russian]. *Contemporary problems of geology and geography*, 53–8. Tbilisi: Tbilisi University Press.
Khelashvili, J. 1993. Tourism from Georgia. Paper submitted to the First British–Georgian Geographical Seminar, Tbilisi, September, 1993.
Khutsishvili, G. 1994. Intervention in Transcaucasus. *Perspective*. Publication IV(3), pp. 2–6, Institute for the Study of Conflict, Ideology & Policy, Boston University.
Kobyakov, D. 1880. Tiflis according to the one-day census of 25 March of 1876 [in Russian]. In *Sbornik Statisticheskikh Svedenii o Kavkaziye* (vol. 6), 1–187. Tiflis: Caucasian Viceroy's Major Board Printing House.
Khorev, B. (ed.) 1986. *The location of population in the USSR: regional aspects of the dynamics and policy of population* [in Russian]. Moscow: Mysl.
Konstantinov, O. A. 1985. A new trend in social geography [in Russian]. *Izvestiya Akademii Nauk SSSR, Seriya Geograficheskaya* 6, 139–40.
Kuper, A. & J. Kuper (eds) 1989. *The social science encyclopedia*. London: Routledge.
Kvirikashvili, D. 1994. Two at the crossroads: comparative figures of accidents [in Georgian]. *Tbilisi* (1 March).

Labakhua, Z. 1993. Georgian–Abkhazian Reconciliation [in Russian]. *Nezavisimaya Gazeta* (24 November).
Laber, J. 1993. Helsinki Watch – to the Russian authorities: Russia exceeded the limits of the goodwill mission [in Russian]. *Nezavisimaya Gazeta* (11 November).
Lang, D. M. 1966. *The Georgians*. London: Thames & Hudson.
Lappo, G. M. 1976. *Stories of cities* [in Russian]. Moscow: Mysl.
Lavrov, S. B., A. A. Anokhin, N. T. Agafonov 1984. Social geography: problems of establishing a scientific trend [in Russian]. In *Sotsialnaya geografia SSSR (problemy metodologii i teorii)*, S. B. Lavrov (ed.), 3–13. Leningrad: Geographical Society of the USSR.
Lavrov S. B. & O. P. Litovka 1984. Review of A. A. Gabiani and R. G. Gachechiladze: "Some problems of the geography of crime (according to the materials of the Georgian SSR)" [in Russian]. *Izvestiya Vsesoyuznogo Geograficheskogo Obshchestva* 116(1), 86–7.
Law of the Abkhazian ASSR 1991. On the amendment of the law of the Abkhazian ASSR on Elections to the Supreme Council of the Abkhazian ASSR [in Georgian]. *Abkhazetis Khma* (30 August).
Law of the Republic of Georgia 1993. On the citizenship of Georgia [in Russian]. *Svobodnaya Gruziya* (31 March).
Lebanidze, Sh. & L. Toklikishvili 1993. Bearing [in Georgian]. *7 dge* (14–20 April).
Lenin, V. 1905 (1947). *Collected works* [in Russian], vol. 8. Moscow: OGIZ.
—1922 (1968). *Last letters and articles* [in Russian]. Moscow: Politizdat.
Lomouri, N. 1993. The designation of Georgia in Byzantine sources [in Georgian]. In *Foreign and Georgian terminology designating Georgia and the Georgians*, G. Paichadze (ed.), 73–91. Tbilisi: Metsniereba.
Lomsadze, T. 1993. General Grachev: "What concerns our military units in Georgia – Batumi, Gudauta and other places. They are strategically important to Russia. Otherwise we will lose the Black Sea" [in Russian]. *Svobodnaya Gruziya* (24 February).
Lordkipanidze, M. 1987. *Georgia in the 11th–12th centuries*. Tbilisi: Ganatleba.

References

Lordkipanidze, O. 1990. Georgian civilization: when did its history begin? [in Georgian]. *Literaturuli Sakartvelo* (14 September).

Lough, J. 1993. The place of the "Near Abroad" in Russian foreign policy. *International Relations* 2(11), 21–9.

Mackie, J. D. 1969. *A history of Scotland*. Harmondsworth: Penguin.

Mars, G. & Y. Altman 1983. The cultural bases of Soviet Georgia's second economy. *Soviet Studies* 35, 546–60.

Maier, J., R. Paesler, K. Ruppert, F. Schaffer 1977. *Sozial-geographie*. Braunschweig: Westermann.

Medvedev, O. 1993. Pressure over Abkhazia has so far given no results [in Russian]. *Commersant Daily* (22 September).

Melikishvili, G. (ed.) 1989. *Essays on the history of Georgia*, vol. I [in Russian]. Tbilisi: Metsniereba.

Melkadze, V. 1978. *Regional structure of the national product and national income of the Georgian SSR* [in Georgian]. Tbilisi: Sabchota Sakartvelo.

Menteshashvili, A. 1990. *From the history of interrelations of the Georgian, Abkhaz and Ossetian peoples (1918–21)* [in Russian]. Tbilisi: Tsodna.

— 1993. Lessons that history teaches us: consensus between the Georgians and the Abkhaz is possible [in Russian]. *Politika* I(9), 16–24.

— 1994. *The troubles in Caucasus*. New York: Nova Science.

Metreveli, R. 1990. *David IV rebuilder: a survey of contemporary social–economic and political–cultural history* [in Georgian]. Tbilisi: Sabchota Sakartvelo.

Minasyan, L. 1993. The end of the Russian–Caucasian War: the Mountaineers and Cossacks have come to terms 200 years after [in Russian]. *Nezavisimaya Gazeta* (30 April).

Mikadze, A. & M. Shevelyov 1993. From the political bloc "Soyuz" [in Russian]. *Moskovskiye Novosti* (1 August).

Montefiore, S. S. 1993. Edouard Shevardnadze. *New York Times Magazine* (26 December), 16–19.

Morozov, E. 1992. Russia and the south: a geostrategic problem [in Russian]. *Nash Sovremennik* 11, 146–9.

Muskhelishvili, D. 1980. *Principal problems of the historical geography of Georgia* [in Georgian]. Tbilisi: Metsniereba.

— 1993. A contribution to the history of the self-designation of the Georgians [in Georgian]. In *Foreign and Georgian terminology designating Georgia and the Georgians*, G. Paichadze (ed.), 337–76. Tbilisi: Metsniereba.

National Economy of the Georgian SSR in 1985. Statistical yearbook [in Russian]. 1986. Tbilisi: Central Statistical Board of the Georgian SSR.

National Economy of the USSR in 1990. Statistical yearbook [in Russian]. 1991. Moscow: Finansy i Statistika.

Nationality structure of the population of Georgia (according to the 1989 all-Union population census) [in Georgian]. 1991. Tbilisi: Committee for Social–Economic Information of the Supreme Council of the Republic of Georgia.

Natmeladze, M. 1993. *Demographic processes in Georgia in the 1940s (deportations of Turks and other groups of population from Georgia in 1941–51)* [in Georgian]. Tbilisi: Metsniereba.

Nizharadze, G. 1994. Business and national character [in Russian]. *Svobodnaya Gruziya* (2 March).

Noin, D. & R. Woods (eds) 1993. *The changing population of Europe*. Oxford: Basil Blackwell.

Number, sex and age structure, marriage and divorce in Georgia according to the 1989 all-Union population census [in Georgian]. 1990. Tbilisi: State Committee of Statistics of the Republic of Georgia.

O'Halloran, B. 1993. *The bumpy road to democracy: State-building in the republic of Georgia*. Government honours thesis, Colby College, USA.

On the events in the Abkhaz Autonomous Republic. 1992. *Utskebani* (21 August).

Pachkoria, T. 1993. Lorik Marshania: the salvation of the Abkhaz and the Georgians is in mutual

References

understanding and unity [in Russian]. *Svobodnaya Gruziya* (17 January).

Paichadze, G. (ed.) 1993. *Foreign and Georgian terminology designating Georgia and the Georgians* [in Georgian]. Tbilisi: Metsniereba.

Polyakov, Yu. A., V. B. Zhiromskaya, I. N. Kiselyov. 1990. A half-century of silence (the all-Union Population Census of 1937) [in Russian]. *Sotsiologicheskiye Issledovaniya* 7, 50–70.

Population of Tbilisi according to the 1989 all-Union population census [in Georgian] 1991. Tbilisi: Tbilisi City Board of State Statistics.

Population of the Republic of Georgia. Statistical handbook [in Georgian] 1991. Tbilisi: Committee for Social–Economic Information of the Supreme Council of the Republic of Georgia.

Preobrazhenskii, V. S. 1991. The first social atlas of Georgia [in Russian]. *Izvestiya Akademii Nauk SSSR, Seriya Geograficheskaya* 6, 130–33.

Project for the division of Georgia into new administrative units. Memorandum – statistical tables [in Georgian] 1920. Tbilisi: State Printing House.

Report on the social–economic situation of Georgia in 1992 [in Georgian] 1993. Tbilisi: Committee for Social–Economic Information of the Republic of Georgia.

Report on the social–economic situation of Georgia in 1993 [in Georgian] 1994. Tbilisi: Committee for Social–Economic Information of the Republic of Georgia.

Republic of Turkey 1963. *23 October, 1960 General Population Census* [in Turkish]. Ankara: State Institute of Statistics.

Resorts and resort resources of the Georgian SSR. Atlas 1989 [in Georgian, Russian and English]. Moscow: Main Administration of Geodesy and Cartography of the Council of Ministers of the USSR.

Rondeli, A. 1990. *Urban geography* [in Georgian]. Tbilisi: Tbilisi UniversityPress.

Rosen, R. 1992. *The Georgian republic: an independent tradition.* Lincolnwood: Passport Books.

Rotar, I. 1993a. "Even regular forces sometimes maraud" (interview with V. Ardzinba) [in Russian]. *Nezavisimiya Gazeta* (15 October).

—— 1993b. Green cloth on the door – here live the Abkhaz [in Russian]. *Nezavisimaya Gazeta* (12 October).

—— 1994. To become our satellites or to die: such is the opinion of the Near Abroad of Konstantin Zatulin, the Chairman of the Committee on CIS Affairs and the links with compatriots of the State Duma. *Nezavisimaya Gazeta* (5 May).

Rowell, A. 1993a. Georgia: tricked and abandoned. *The Economist* (2 October).

—— 1993b. Shevardnadze in hiding as Sokhumi falls to rebels. *The Guardian* (28 September).

Russell, J. C. 1948. *British medieval population.* Albuquerque: University of New Mexico Press.

Salukvadze, J. 1993. The post-Soviet cities: spatial and social structure in the time of transition (the case study of Tbilisi, Georgia). Paper submitted to the First British–Georgian Geographical Seminar, Tbilisi, September 1993.

Savichev, V. 1992. Cossack's land, fiery land [in Russian]. *Argumenty i Fakti* **37**, 2.

Savostyanov, S. 1992. Alania: Russia's strategic key to the Caucasus [in Russian]. *Golos Rossii* (Reprinted in *Iberia-Spektr* 16–22 April, 1992).

Settlements and population of Georgia. Statistical handbook [in Georgian] 1990. Tbilisi: State Committee for Statistics of the Georgian SSR.

Scruton, R. 1990. *The philosopher on Dover Beach: essays.* Manchester: Carcanet.

Segal, I. 1880. Review of accidental deaths, suicides and crimes in the Caucasian Region in 1877 [in Russian]. In *Sbornik Svidenii o Kavkaziye*, vol. VII, N. Zeidlitz (ed.), 277–326. Tiflis: Caucasian Viceroy's Major Board Printing House.

Shakarashvili, V. 1994. It's time for the bells to ring [in Russian]. *Svobodnaya Gruziya* (5 February).

Shevardnadze, E. 1993a. Appeal to all the friends of my country [in Russian]. *Svobodnaya Gruziya* (21 September).

—— 1993b. 26 May – the great national festival of freedom and independence [in Russian]. *Svobodnaya Gruziya* (25 May).

Sitin, P. 1921 (1993). Report to the Government of RSFSR, 22–30 April 1921. Material from the Geor-

References

gian Central State Archives: Fund 1874, Inv. I, file 4 [in Russian]. *Iveria Expressi* (nos 127–35), 15–24 August.

Skachko, V. 1992. The Yalta Agreement in jeopardy: Ukraine accuses Russia of one-sided use of the Black Sea Navy [in Russian]. *Nezavisimiya Gazeta* (1 October).

Slider, D. 1985a. Crisis and response in Soviet nationality policy: the case of Abkhazia. *Central Asian Survey* 4(4), 51–68.

— 1985b. Party-sponsored public opinion research in the Soviet Union. *Journal of Politics* 47(1), 209–27.

Smith, D. M. 1977. *Human geography: a welfare approach*. London: Edward Arnold.

— 1973. *The geography of social well-being in the United States*. New York: McGraw-Hill.

— 1989. *Urban inequality under socialism: case studies from eastern Europe and the Soviet Union*. Cambridge: Cambridge University Press.

— 1992. Geography and social justice: some reflections on social change in eastern Europe. *Geography Research Forum* 12, 128–42.

— 1993. Social justice after socialism: the relevance of Western experience. Paper prepared for the First British–Georgian Geographical Seminar, Tbilisi, September, 1993.

— 1994. *Geography and social justice*. Oxford: Basil Blackwell.

Social–economic development of the USSR in 1989. 1990 [in Russian]. *Pravda* (28 January).

Soslambekov, Yu. 1990. Long drawn-out walk on the verge of a precipice [in Russian]. *Kavkaz* (1 October; newspaper of the Assembly of the Mountainous Peoples of the Caucasus).

Statistical Handbook 1993. *States of the former USSR*. Studies of Economies in Transformation, Paper 8, The World Bank, Washington DC.

Statistical tables of the population of the Caucasian Region.[in Russian] 1880. In *Sbornik Svedenii o Kavkaziye*, vol. VII, N. Zeidlitz (ed.), i-lxxv. Tiflis: Caucasian Viceroy's Major Board Printing House.

Suni, R. G. 1988. *The making of the Georgian nation*. Bloomington: Indiana University Press, in Association with Hoover Institution Press, Stanford.

Surguladze, A. & P. Surguladze 1991. *A history of Georgia 1783–1990* [in Georgian]. Tbilisi: David Agmashenebeli Society Press.

Susokolov, A. A. 1987. *Interethnic marriages in the USSR* [in Russian]. Moscow: Mysl.

Svobodnaya Gruziya (10 December)1993.

Tashan, S. 1993. Caucasus and Central Asia: strategic implications. [Paper submitted to the First International Conference, George Marshal European Centre for Security Studies, Garmisch, Tbilisi 5 July 1988][in Georgian].

Tishkov, V. 1991. The Soviet Empire before and after perestroika. In *Nationalism and empire: the Habsburg Empire and the Soviet Union*, R. L. Rudolph & D. F. Good (eds), 199–224. New York: St Martin's Press, in association with the Center for Austrian Studies, University of Manitoba.

— 1992. Inventions and manifestations of ethnos – nationalism in and after the Soviet Union. In *Ethnicity and conflict in a post-communist world: the Soviet Union, eastern Europe and China*, K. Rupesinghe, P. King, O. Vorkunova (eds), 41–64. New York: St Martin's Press.

— 1993. On the nature of ethnic conflict [in Russian]. *Svobodnaya Mysl* 4, 4–15.

To the question of ethnic composition of the population of the Republic of Georgia [in Russian] 1993. Tbilisi.

Togoshvili, G. 1981. Historical outline of South Ossetian Autonomous Region [in Russian]. *Gruzinskaya SSR Entsiklopedicheskiy Spravochnik*. Tbilisi: Kartuli Sabchota Entsiklopedia, 353–5.

Toidze L. 1994. To the question of the political status of Abkhazia (pages of history of 1921–1931) [in Russian]. *Svobodnaya Gruziya* (20–21 April).

Tokmazishvili, M. 1990. Anatomy of the shadow economy [in Georgian]. *Sakartvelos Komunisti* 10, 28–33.

Topchishvili, R. 1993. *Problems of the ethnic history of the mountainous population of Georgia* [in Georgian and Russian]. Tbilisi: Institute of History, Archaeology and Ethnography, Academy of Sciences of Georgia.

References

— 1990. Again on the restoration of nationality [in Georgian]. *Literaturuli Sakartvelo* (18 May).
Totadze, A. 1993. *A demographic portrait of Georgia* [in Georgian]. Tbilisi: Samshoblo.
Townsend, P. 1993. *The international analysis of poverty*. London: Harvester Wheatsheaf.
Trade and paid services in Georgia 1990 [in Georgian]. Tbilisi: State Committee of Statistics of the Georgian SSR.
Troinitskiy, N. A. (ed.) 1905. *First general census of population of the Russian Empire*, vol. II [in Russian]. St Petersburg.

Velichko, V. L. 1904. *Full collection of publications*, vol I: *Caucasus: the Russian cause and inter-ethnic questions* [in Russian]. St Petersburg: Muretova.
Vinogradov, B. 1933. *Constitutions of the USSR and Union Republics* [in Russian]. Moscow: Vlast Sovietov Publishing House.
Vostrikov S. 1994. Foreign policy priorities of Russia in Asia [in Russian]. *Nezavisimaya Gazeta* (22 March).

Weber, M. 1923. *General economic history* (translated by F. H. Knight). London: Allen & Unwin.

Yakov V. 1993. "Wild Geese" of Russia, or an evening with a mercenary [in Russian]. *Izvestiya* (24 March).

Zhidkov, S. 1993. Mingrelia (Samegrelo) – the second Abkhazia? *Pravda* (22 September).
Zhorzholiani, G., S. Lekishvili, L. Mataradze, L. Toidze, E. Khoshtaria-Brosset 1992. Such is the truth. To the Chairman of the Helsinki Group Heino Rantala [in Russian]. *Svobodnaya Gruziya* (23 June).

INDEX

Abasha 5, 42, 63
Abastumani 59
Abaza 81
Abazg 20
Abazgia 20
Abazins 9, 83, 178, 179
Abkhaz xx, 2, 3, 9, 36, 41, 54, 75, 78, 79, 81–6, 96, 98–9, 103–4, 170–1, 175–80
    Autonomous Soviet Socialist Republic (ASSR)/Autonomous Republic 5, 7, 33, 37, 41, 43, 56
    constituencies 41
    dynasty 20
    ethnocracy 37
    insurgents xii
    language 30, 37, 56
    leaders 42
    nobility 30
    population 24, 28, 37, 43
    separatists 42
    State University 37, 85
Abkhazia (Abkhazeti)
    principality of 24, 27, 28
    province/Social Region 2, 4, 8, 10–11, 16, 21, 24, 32, 40, 42, 44, 53, 63, 70, 79, 112–14, 121, 126, 130, 144, 152, 164, 174–5, 177–80, 182
Abkhazian autonomy 30
Abkhazian Kingdom (*Abkhazta samepo*) 20–21
Abkhazianization 82, 182
Abzhu Abkhaz 85
Adigheans 9, 179
Adjara
    Autonomous Soviet Socialist Republic (ASSR)/Autonomous Republic of 5, 7, 34, 98
province/Social Region 8, 10–11, 16, 25, 28, 32, 47, 50, 56, 61, 70, 130, 135
Adjarans (a Georgian ethnic subgroup) 3, 98
Afghanistan 40, 96
Africa xi
Akhalgori 7
Akhalkalaki 27, 89, 124
Akhaltsikhe 27, 49, 121

Akhaltsikhe *pashalik* 25
Akhmeta 64, 98, 174
Alans 9
Albania 45
Albania (Caucasian) 20
Albanians (Caucasian) 19, 20
Alexander i, the Tzar 27
Algeti, River 152
Alma-Ata 38
Ambrolauri 50
American
    films xii
    expert 35
    gerontologists 53
Anatolia 4, 93, 94
Anatolian shore 93
Ancient Slavic 17
Anglo-Saxon 17
apparat 60
Ankara 3, 34
Apsua (self-name of the Abkhaz) 24
Arab
    countries 81
    Khaliphate 10
    occupation 21, 154
Arabic
    language 20
    alphabet 86
Arabs 19–20, 81, 154, 167
Aragvi 9
Argentina 32
Argonauts, legend of 18
Armenia 1, 2, 4, 12, 23, 26, 32, 37, 45, 47, 49, 68, 89, 95, 96, 111, 124, 140, 152, 157, 169, 174, 176, 183
Armenian
    merchants and craftsmen 28
    creditors 29
    language 35
Armenians 4, 17, 19, 28, 29, 43, 54, 56, 68, 73, 75, 77, 79, 81, 83, 85, 89, 90, 96, 99, 103, 170, 174, 176, 178, 183
Armenian Republic 89, 90
Asia 5, 8
Australia xi

Index

Austria xi
Autonomous Republic 5, 34
Autonomous Region 5, 34
Avarians 79, 98
Azerbaijan 2, 4, 12, 20, 23, 26, 29, 33, 45, 49, 61, 66, 75, 92, 111, 121, 126, 140, 148, 152, 157, 170, 174, 176
Azerbaijani railways 4
Azeris (Azerbaijanis) 4, 15, 35, 50, 53–4, 56, 73, 75, 78–9, 92, 98, 103, 124, 130, 169, 170, 174, 176

Babylonian Captivity 73
Bagrationi
  House of 19, 21, 22, 24
  Kakhetian branch of 26
Baku xiv, 32, 92, 140
Balakan 75
Balkars 2, 179
Baltic Republics 37, 44, 49, 68, 124, 128, 169, 179
Baptists 98
"Barrack socialism" xiii
Batumskiy okrug (Batumi region) 28
Batalpashiskiy uezd (Batalpashinsk district) 83
Batumi 4, 5, 7, 16, 25, 28, 32, 47, 56, 59, 60, 67, 69, 75, 114, 130, 148
Belgians 1
Belgium 8, 32
Berlin 27
Bichvinta (Pitsunda) 179
Black Sea 1–4, 8, 10, 23, 25, 93, 178
Bolnisi 50, 92
Bolsheviks 31–5, 60
Borchalu 92
Borchalo 27
Borjomi xii, 12, 128
Brest–Litovsk, Treaty of 31
Britain xiii, 20, 137, 154
British xi, xii, xviii, 88, 137
Buffer State 1
Bukhara People's Socialist Republic 33
Bulgarians 81
Byelorussia 137
Byelorussians 35, 79, 90–1, 96
Byzantines 167
Byzantium 10, 19, 20, 22–3, 93
Bzyb Abkhaz 85

Calvinism 108
Capitalist Spirit 108–9
"Capitulations" 25

Catholicos-Patriarch of the Georgian Orthodox Church 96
Catholicism 25, 90, 108
Catholics 25, 96, 98, 108
Caucasia 28
Caucasian
  policy of Russia 27
  viceroy 30
Caucasians xii
Caucasus xi, xii, xxi, 1, 3, 8, 9, 23, 26, 28, 29, 40, 61, 86, 87, 90, 122, 154, 176, 178, 180, 182
Central Asia xix, 4, 49, 61, 86, 121, 148, 157, 169, 183
Central powers 31
Centre of Sociological Studies (CSS) 110, 111, 133
Chalcedonian faith 19
Chechens xi, 179
Cherkess 9, 179
Chiatura 5, 28, 49, 63
China 152
Chinese xv
Choloki, River 50
Christianity
  Orthodox xvi, 50, 83, 85–6, 96, 98
  religion of 19, 20, 25, 108
  world of xx, 8
Christian(s) 19, 20, 24, 25–6, 28, 34, 93
Cimmerians 19
Circassian 3, 81, 178–9
City of Republican Subordination (CRS) 5, 7, 16, 110, 121, 124, 128, 130, 133, 135
Colchis 18
Commonwealth of Independent States (CIS) 39, 42–4, 170
Communist 31
  era 66
Communist Party xiii, xvii, xviii, 13, 35, 36, 53, 60, 64–6, 107, 114, 133, 171, 179, 183
  of Georgia 38, 171
  of the Soviet Union (CPSU) 36, 73, 177
Confederation of the People's of Caucasus 2, 41, 176–80, 182
Confucius xv
Congress of the People's Deputies of the Russian Federation 177
Constitution
  of SSR Abkhazia (1925) 41
  of Democratic Republic of Georgia (1921) 32, 40
  of Georgian SSR (1978) 37, 38
  of Republic of Georgia 5, 16

198

Index

of USSR (1924, 1936, 1977)   33, 35, 38
Cossacks   177, 179
Crimea   172
Crimean SSR   33
Croatia   8
Cyprus   68
Cyrillic   17, 85, 181

Dadiani, Princes of Samegrelo   24
Dagestan   9, 122
Dagestani highlanders   26
Dar-i-Alan   9
Dar-ul-Islam   98
Daryal gorge   9, 87
David IV *agmashenebeli* (the Builder), King of Georgia   19, 21
Declaration of Independence of Georgia   32
Dedoplistskaro   92, 124
Denmark   8, 45
Developing country   xvii
Diamond, Derek   xi
Didi Digomi   165, 166
Dioskuria   93
Dmanisi   121, 130
Don Soviet Republic   33
Dubliners   xi
Dukhobortsy   89, 98
Dushanbe   xiv
Dusheti   27, 122
Dyelets   65
Dyhamo xii

economic regions of Georgia   14
Egri   18
Egrisi   18
England   xiii, 22
England and Wales   22
English   xi, xii, 137
    Parliament   23
Entente   32
Erekle II, King of Kartli–Kakheti   26, 27, 93
Erzurum   89, 93
Estonia   45, 121, 128, 137, 157, 172
Estonian(s)   28, 81
Ethnic Russians   68, 172
Eurasia   xiii
Europe   xix, 5, 8, 22–3, 77, 98
    continental   xiii
    Eastern   xx, 40, 172
    Medieval   23
    Southern   56
    Western   xi, xvi, 20, 21, 23, 26, 68

European
    commerce   28
    countries   52
    Eastern   109
    model of development   xix, 23
    nations   45
    powers   32
    Russia   158
    -style democratic socialism   31
    Union   107
    universities   30
Europeans   23, 25
Europeanization   26, 29

Far Eastern Republic   33
Fereidan District   77
Feudalism   xi, xiii, xiv, 22–3
Finland   45
First World War   32, 83, 89
France   32, 77, 154
Frangi   25
Former Soviet Union (FSU)   3, 4, 68, 152

Gagauz   172
Gagauzia   172
Gagra   5, 7, 85, 124, 128
Gali   42, 82, 84–5, 121, 126, 178
Galidzga, River   24, 82
Gamsahkurdia, Zviad   39, 41, 42, 78
Gardabani   64, 155
Gelashvili, Naira   73
Georgia   xii–xxi, 1–14, 16–45, 47, 49–54, 56, 57, 59–61, 63–71, 73, 75, 77, 78, 81, 84–96, 98–9, 103, 106–22, 124, 126, 128, 130, 133, 135, 138, 140–4, 148–56, 161–4, 167, 170–78, 180–82
    Democratic Republic of   31
    East   xix, 9, 10, 11, 19, 20, 25–7, 29, 64, 75, 86, 98, 148
    Medieval   22
    Republic of   xix, 1, 2, 5, 16, 50, 75, 170, 176
    Russian   29
    Soviet   32, 99, 114, 116, 121, 122, 135, 137, 148
    West   xix, 8, 10, 11, 12, 18, 20, 23, 27, 28, 31, 47, 70, 71, 75, 124
Georgian Kingdom   21, 82, 154
Georgian Military Highway   9
Georgian Muslims   33, 75, 89
Georgian Orthodox Church   154
Georgian(s)   xi, xii, xv–xvii, xx, 3, 8, 9, 10, 17–43, 45, 49, 53, 54, 60, 61, 64–6, 68, 73, 75, 77,

Index

78, 83–94, 96, 98–9, 103–4, 106, 108, 109, 111, 114, 140, 170, 172, 174–9, 181, 182
Georgian SSR   5, 34, 37, 65, 85, 88, 99, 106, 110, 120, 122
Georgianization   90, 99, 103
Georgievsk, Treaty of   26, 30, 32
German   98
Germans   28, 81
Germany   31, 32
Giorgi (George)   xii
   King of Kartli-Kakheti   19, 27
Glaswegians   xi
Gogebashvili, Jacob   78
Gorbachev, Michail   xiii, 37, 141, 171, 179
Gori   5, 7, 16, 27, 47, 49, 56, 59, 67, 114, 124, 130, 135, 144, 152
Great Britain   32
Great Caucasus Range   1, 2, 8, 181
Great Terror   xiii
Greece   xvii, 68, 94, 173
Greeks   54, 79, 81, 83, 93, 94, 96, 103, 173–4
   Anatolian   28
   Ancient   17, 18
   Milesian   19
   Pontic   93
Greek
   Orthodoxy   19, 26, 103
   language   20, 21
   schools   94
   state   23
Gregorian faith   103
Gruziny (Slavic name of the Georgians)   xii, 17
Gudauta   43, 85–6, 98, 179
Gulripshi   85, 90
Gumushane   93
Guria
   principality of   24–5, 27
   province/Social Region   8, 10, 16, 31, 42, 49, 50, 61, 70, 122, 130, 144
Gurjaani   128
Gurji (Middle Eastern name of the Georgians)   17, 77
Gvelesiani, Giorgi   14
Gyanja   92, 140
Gyenos   93

Hellenistic period   23
Hemshins   183
Henry II, King of England   21

Iberia/Iveria   10, 11, 18
Iberians (Iverians, *Iveroi*)   17, 29

Ibero–Caucasian linguistic family   17
Imereti
   Kingdom of   24, 27
   province/Social Region   8, 10, 16, 23, 42, 47, 70, 78, 128, 130
"Imperial Card"   177
Imperial Government   89
India   xiv, 23, 152
Indo–European(s)   86
Inguri, River   12, 24, 41, 44, 82
Ingush-Ossetian conflict   182
Ingushs   2, 179, 182
Intelligentsia   65
"Interfront"   173
Intermontane Lowland   8, 10, 11
International Alert   75
Iran   4, 10, 19, 47, 77
Iranian   23, 86
Irish   xi
Ireland, Republic of   8, 45
Iriston   86
Iron (self-name of the Ossetians)   86
Isfahan   77
Islam
   religion of   20, 25, 50, 77, 98
   world of   8, 23, 178
Islamic   85, 96
Islamization   98
Israel   8, 68, 79, 94
Italy   32

Japan   32
Japanese   53
Java   7, 87, 151
Javakheti   4, 8, 11, 24, 27–8, 61, 79, 89, 96, 174–5
Jewish   22, 94, 96
Jews   68, 73, 79, 174
   European   94, 103
   Georgian   33, 103
Jordan   81
Judaists   98
Jugashvili, Joseph   31
Jvari Pass   9

Kabardians   2, 9, 179, 182
Kakheti
   Kingdom of   24, 26
   province/social region   7, 8, 10–12, 16, 47, 49, 77, 79, 98, 124, 128, 130, 174
Kalaki ("the Town")   29
Kareli   152

Index

Karti tribes 18
Kartli
   Kingdom of 18, 19, 24, 26
   province of 7–11, 16, 29
   Kvemo (Lower) 8, 16, 47, 49, 92, 121, 124, 130, 174, 175
   Shida (Inner) 8, 16, 49, 170
Kartli–Kakheti, Kingdom of 27
kartlis tskhovreba (Georgian Chronicle) 26
kartveli (self-name of the Georgians) 17, 25
kartvelta samepo (Georgian Kingdom) 21
kartuli (Georgian proper) 17, 18, 20, 87
Kartvelian
   element 20, 82
   group 29
   language(s) 30, 82, 83, 84, 104
   linguistic family 17
   people(s) 82, 103
   population 23
   tribes 18
Kaspi 63
Kaspian Sea 7, 10
Kavkasioni 5, 8, 9, 11, 16, 47, 49, 50, 122, 128, 130, 133, 135, 144
Kazakhs 170
Kazakhstan 170, 172
Kazakhstanians 170
Kazbegi 5, 50, 122
Kazreti 12
Kenneth MacAlpin, King of Scots 20
KGB 179
Kharagauli 128, 130
Khashuri 49, 61
Khazars 167
Khevi Province 7, 9, 16
Khelvachauri 47, 122
Khevsureti Province 7, 10, 16
Khobi 42
Khoni 42
Khorezm People's Socialist Republic 33
Khorezmians 167
Khrushchev 179, 183
Khulo 122
Kiev xiv
Kishinev xiv
Kistis (Chechens) 79, 98
Kobuleti 25, 50, 122, 130, 135
Kodori, River 24, 82
Kolkheti 10, 11, 49
Kolkhoz xii, 13, 64, 92, 109, 112, 122, 126
Kolkhozniki 64
Komsomol 60, 65

Kornisi 7
Kremlin 33, 34, 37, 96, 159, 171, 183
Krishnaites 96
Kuban Oblast 83
Kulashi 94
Kurdish 53
Kurds/Yezid-Kurds 79, 92, 94, 95, 98, 103, 174, 183
Kutaisi 5, 16, 20, 21, 23, 26, 29, 32, 47, 56, 59, 61, 67, 69, 75, 94, 130, 133, 135, 136, 140, 144
Kutaisskaia gubernia (Kutaisi province) 27
Kuwait 8
Kvaisa 12
Kvareli 98

Lang, David xii
Latin alphabet 17, 86
Latvia 45, 128, 157, 170, 172
Latvians 170
Lazi 10, 18, 77
Lazika 18
lazuri (a Kartvelian language) 17, 18, 77
Lechkumi Province 8, 10, 16
Lenin xiii, 31, 32, 33, 35, 37
Leninist xiii
Leninist Nationality Policy 169
Leningrad xii
Liakhvi, River 7
Likhi Range 10, 25
limitchik 158, 159
lingua franca 91, 99
Lithuania 45, 128, 137, 172
London 154

Mahajirs (Abkhaz emigrants to the Ottoman Empire) 81
Maistre, Joseph de xvii
market economy xi, 3, 13, 141
Marneuli 49, 50, 79, 92, 93, 124
Marxist xii, xiii, xiv
Mecca 152
Medina 152
Mediterranean 23
Megrelians (a Georgian ethnic subgroup) 82, 83
Megruli/Megrelian (a Kartvelian language) 17, 18, 30, 77, 82, 84
Menji 12
Mensheviks 31
Merchule, Giorgi 20
Meskheti Province 8, 24, 25, 27, 28, 175
Meskheti–Javakheti, a social region 16, 133,

201

Index

144
Meskhetian Muslims (Turks) 92, 170, 183
Meskhi (a Georgian ethnic subgroup) 25
Mestia 5, 47, 128
Middle Ages xvi, 7, 9, 10, 11, 17, 19, 23, 26, 28, 73, 86, 89, 108
Military Council of Georgia (1992) 39, 40
Ministry of Labour and Social Affairs 63
Mirian, King of Kartli 19
Miussera 179
Moldova 37, 45, 172
Molokane 98
Mongol(s) 11, 22, 23, 167
Monophysitism, faith of 19
Monophysites 19, 103
Monroe Doctrine xi, 2
Moscow xii, xiv, 1, 2, 32–4, 35–6, 38, 64, 66, 85–6, 112, 154, 156, 164, 172–3, 181, 183
Moscow Treaty (1920) 32
Mtiuleti Province 7, 9, 16
Mtkvari (Kura), River 7, 11, 18, 155, 158
Mtskheta 61, 94, 126, 155
Muscovites xii
"Muslim Card" 177
Muslim
    countries xvii
    enclave 21
    feudal lord 25
    fundamentalism 96
    khanates 26
    peoples 23
    population 28, 157
    rulers 22
Muslims 86, 98, 182
Mussulman 92

Nagorny (mountainous) Karabakh 2, 4, 12, 73, 89, 170, 171, 174, 176
Nakhichevan, Autonomous Republic of/SSR 33
Nana, Queen of Kartli 19
nation-State xiii, 171
national okrug 169
Natsional-uklonisty (nationalist-deviators) 35
Natsmeny (non-Russian national minorities) 36
Nazis 45, 90
Netherlands 8
New York 137
Newly Independent States (NIS) xi, xv, xix, xx, 2, 106, 112, 137, 169
New World 23
Nino, (the baptiser of Georgia) 19

Ninotsminda 124
nomenklatura 65
Non-Slavic Union Republics 35
North America xiii, 98, 150
North Atlantic Treaty Organization (NATO) xix, 1
North Caucasian 81
    autonomous republics 61
    volunteers 43
    languages 17, 19
    homeland 34
"North Caucasian State" 176
North Caucasus 61, 83, 86, 152, 177–80
North Ossetia 34, 88, 122, 151, 182
Norway 45
Novo-Ogariovo 171
Novorosiisk 1

Ochamchire 42, 82, 85, 126
Odessa 33, 154
Odessa Soviet Republic 33
Odishi 24
Oguz Turks 20
Old Believers 98
Oni 50, 94, 124, 152
Orwell, George xiii
Ossetian(s) 2, 9, 16, 31, 33–4, 54, 56, 75, 78, 86–8, 96, 99, 103, 170–72, 174, 176, 179, 181, 182
Ottoman Empire 1, 4, 10, 23, 25–8
O (v) seti (Ossetia) 86
O (v) si (the Ossetian) 86
Ovsta kari 9
Ozurgeti 49, 50
Paris 137, 154
Parnassus xii
perestroyka xiii, xviii, 37, 61, 108
Persia 10, 23, 25–7, 92
Persian language 20
Persians 11, 17, 19, 167
Peter the Great, the Tsar 180
Phasis 93
Pictish 20
Picts 20
Pitius 93
Poles 28, 90, 103
Polish 90, 98, 172
Politburo 177
Post-socialist States xi
Post-Soviet
    era 169
    space 117, 174

Index

States xiii, xiv, 1, 3, 12, 60, 66, 69, 107, 138
Poti 4, 5, 16, 42, 49, 59, 63, 121, 128, 130, 148, 151
Protestant Churches 96, 98
Protestants 96, 98
Pshavi Province 7, 16, 19

Qakh 75

Racha Province 8–10, 16, 67
Red Army 32
Red Terror 34
Regional Soviet/Council 5, 7
Restoration of Independence Act 38
Roki Pass 9, 181
Roki Tunnel 151, 182
Romanov Empire 84
Romans 17–18
Rome 10, 19, 93
Round Table-Free Georgia 38
Russia xi, xii, xiv, xix, xxi, 1, 2, 3, 4, 12, 26–32, 34, 36, 39, 40, 42, 43, 89, 90–1, 94, 98, 99, 104, 114, 122, 124, 126, 135, 138
Russian
   arms, armed forces 28, 39, 42, 43, 44
   cities 88
   Empire xiv, 12, 26–32, 35–6, 40, 45, 60, 63–4, 96, 103, 154
   Federation 2, 3, 41–5, 88, 122, 148, 151, 174, 177, 179, 180
   generals 40
   geographers xviii
   government 30, 33, 43
   language 21, 30, 37, 61, 89, 99, 103–4, 120, 173
   linguist 85
   military intelligence 42
   military–industrial complex 42
   Minister of Defence 1
   nationalists 77
   nationality 96
   peace-keeping forces 41
   peasants 29
   Raskol'niki (Russian heretics) 28, 98
   rule 29
   schools 93, 103
   Soviet Federal Socialist Republic (RSFSR) 33, 37, 142
   speakers xi, 68, 172, 173
   state 36
   statistics 82
   Tzars 26, 36
   universities 30
Russians xi, xii, 1, 9, 17, 28, 35–6, 39, 43, 54, 56, 68, 75, 79, 81, 85, 88, 90, 91, 93–4, 169, 170, 172–3, 176, 178, 182
Russification 27, 29, 30, 37, 88, 90
Russo–Turkish war 25
Russophobia 29
Rustavi xx, 5, 16, 47, 59, 67, 75, 95, 130, 148, 155, 160–63, 167

Sabediano 24
Sachkhere 94, 122, 128, 130, 152
Safavid Persia, Safavids 23, 25
Sagarejo 92
Saingilo 32, 75
Sairme 12
Sakartvelo 17, 20, 21
Sakurapalato 21
Samachablo 182
Samegrelo
   principality of 24, 27
   Province of/Social Region 8, 10, 16, 42, 49, 70, 81, 82, 122, 124, 130, 148
Samtredia 42, 49, 61, 63, 128
Samtskhe–Saatabago, Principality of 24, 25
Samurzakano Province 24, 81–4
Samurzakanian(s) 82–4
Sarpi 3
Sassanid Iran 19
Scone 20
Scotia 20
Scotland 45
Scots 20
Scottish xi
Scythians 19
Second World War 45, 52, 70, 90, 96
Senaki 42, 63
Shapsugs 9, 179
Shervashidze
   Murzakan 82
   princes of Abkhazia 24
Shevardnadze, Edouard 39, 40, 149
Shi'a Muslim 23, 77, 92, 98
Shorapani 27
Shuakhevi 122
Signagi 27, 124, 128, 130
Sincretic faiths 98
Slavic
   households 53
   republics 49, 158
Slavs, Slavic peoples 17, 35, 60, 77, 79, 90, 91, 103

Index

Slovakia 45
Slovenia 45
socialist
  countries 59, 65
  system xi
  State 60
social democracy 31
Social Democratic Party of Georgia 31
social regions 14, 16, 124, 130, 133, 143, 148
somekhi (the Armenian, monophysite) 31
sosloviye 63
"South Ossetia" 7, 40, 86, 88, 119, 122, 133, 172, 181, 182
South Ossetian Autonomous Oblast (Region) 5, 9, 16, 38, 135
Southern Upland 8, 11, 128
Soviet
  administration 69
  Army 38, 40, 43, 60
  book xiv
  censuses 73
  cities 88, 113, 156, 161, 162
  criminal code 138
  geographers 143
  ideology xvi
  leaders, leadership 38, 84
  legacy xix
  management system 59, 60
  market xii
  military–industrial complex 43
  moral statistics xx
  nations xiii, xvi
  nationalities 106
  nationality policy 169
  peoples xviii
  period/times 66, 67, 69, 73, 108, 110, 140, 148
  political elite 179
  power xv, 30, 35, 96, 117, 154, 156, 170, 183
  press 137
  regime 115
  Republics xvi, 35, 41, 45, 63, 65, 68, 94, 106, 118, 128, 135, 142, 154, 157, 180–1
  roubles 121
  rule 34, 90
  Russia 31–2, 34
  science xii
  social geography xviii
  State 36, 73
  statistics 82, 120
  "titular nations" 75

Sovietization xix, 33, 108
Sovkhoz 13, 64, 109
spekulyanti 112, 126
Sri-Lanka 8
SSR of Abkhazia 33, 41
St Petersburg xii, 154
Stalin xii, xiii, 33, 35–7, 179, 180
Stalinism 84
State Council of Georgia 39
State-administrative socialism xii, 169
Stavropol Soviet Republic 33
Sokhumi 5, 7, 16, 20, 30, 32, 43, 47, 54, 56, 59, 60, 67, 69, 75, 82, 85, 90, 121, 124, 130, 133, 135, 143, 148, 151, 179
Sohkumskiy okrug (Sokhumi region) 27, 30, 32, 82
Sunni Islam 23
Sunni Muslim 77, 92, 95, 183
Supreme Soviet (Supreme Council)
  of Abkhazia 41
  of Georgia 7, 38, 53
  of the Russian Federation 42, 177
  of the USSR 171
Surami 94
Svans (a Georgian subethnos) 30
Svaneti
  principality 27
  province of 8, 16, 67
  Kvemo (Lower) 8, 10
  Zemo (Upper) 8–9, 71
svanuri (a Kartvelian language) 17, 77, 82
Sweden xi
Switzerland xi, 8
Syn otechestva 28
Syria 81

Tajikistan xi
Tallinn xiv
Tatar 25, 92
Tbilisi xii, xiv, xx, 5, 7, 11, 12, 16, 20–2, 26–9, 32–3, 35, 37, 39, 40–2, 47, 54, 56, 57, 60, 64, 67–9, 78–9, 87–91, 94–6, 98–9, 117, 121, 126, 128, 130, 133, 135, 137, 140–1, 148, 153–6, 158, 160–7, 180, 182
Tbilisi Emirate 21
Tbilisi Metropolitan Region (TMR) xx, 47, 61, 118, 122, 128, 153–66
Tbilisi State University 56, 126
"Tbilisi War" 111, 113
Teheran 47, 77
Telavi 27, 49, 56, 95
Terek, River 9

204

Index

Terek Soviet Republic 33
Third World xi
Tianeti 27
Tiflisskaia gubernia (Tbilisi Province) 27
Tkibuli 5, 12, 49
Tkvarcheli 5, 7, 12, 49, 85
Toliatti 128
totalitarianism xiii
Towns of District Subordination 7
Transcaucasia 29
Transcaucasian 152
    Federation (Socialist Federative Soviet Republic) 35, 41, 154
    Republics 2, 35, 49, 141–2
Transcaucasus 3, 4, 8, 9, 18, 20–1, 23, 25, 28–9, 31–2, 36, 90, 92, 135, 140, 169
Transdnestrovia 172
Trapezund Empire 23
Tsageri 50, 128
Tsaishi 12
Tsalka 79, 93, 124, 173–4
Tsarist Russia 2, 77
Tseva 78
Tskaltubo 5, 12
Tskhinvali 5, 7, 16, 33–4, 49, 56, 59–60, 67, 79, 87–8, 94, 112, 114, 122, 124, 130, 133, 135, 143, 148, 151, 182
"Tskhinvali Region" (former South Ossetia) 16, 49, 112–14, 182
Tsiteli Khidi 152
Tskhumi 82
Turkey xix, 1, 3, 4, 10, 17, 25, 28, 45, 68, 77, 81, 93, 150, 176
Turkic
    Khans 23
    languages xii, 35
    peoples 25, 92
    speaking 183
    States 4, 23
    tribes 73
Turkish
    authorities 176
    language 25, 92, 93
    speakers 173
Turks 19, 92, 167
Turk-Meskhetians/Meskhetian Turks 170, 183
Tusheti Province 10

Ubykhs 81
Uezd (district) 27
United Kingdom (UK) 20, 21, 59
Ukraine i, 1, 37, 90, 124, 158, 172

Ukrainians xi, 35, 79, 90, 91, 96
United Nations (UN) 39, 44, 113, 170, 176
Union Republics xiii, xiv, xvii, 33, 36, 38, 43, 54, 60, 106, 117, 159, 162, 169, 170–73, 183
Union Treaty 38, 41
Urum 93
USA 32, 77, 107, 112, 121
USIA 94, 114, 175
Uslar, Karl 85
USSR (Union of Soviet Socialist Republics, Soviet Union) xii, xiii, xiv, xvi, xviii, xix, 5, 7, 10, 12–13, 32–3, 35–9, 41, 45, 49, 54, 59–61, 65, 67, 73, 77, 94, 99, 103, 106, 108, 112, 121–2, 124, 126, 128, 135, 137–8, 141–2, 150, 156–7, 159, 169, 171–2, 177, 181, 183
Uzbekistan 66, 183
Uzbeks xi, 183

Vakhtang vi, King of Kartli 25
Vakhushti 26
Vani 121
"Versailles Syndrome" 1
Village Council 7
vir 17
Virk 17
Vladikavkaz 87, 182
Volga 128

Weidenbaum 30
Welsh xi
William II, King of England 21
World Revolution 31
Wyrshn 17
Westernization 108

Yakuts xi
Yejmiadzin 92
Yeltsin, Boris 171, 180
Yerevan 47, 89
    province 140
Yezidism 95
Yiddish 94
Yugoslavia xi
Young Communist League (Komsomol) 65

Zanuri (a kartvelian language) 17, 18
Zaqatala 27, 32, 75, 140
Zestafoni 49, 61, 69
Zoroastrianism 19
Zugdidi 5, 7, 16, 49, 59, 63, 67, 128, 130, 133, 135, 143, 148, 151
Zviadists 42